WHAT THE LIVING DO

Maggie Dwyer

 FriesenPress

Suite 300 - 990 Fort St
Victoria, BC, V8V 3K2
Canada

www.friesenpress.com

ISBN
978-1-5255-2868-2 (Hardcover)
978-1-5255-2869-9 (Paperback)
978-1-5255-2870-5 (eBook)

1. FICTION, CRIME

Distributed to the trade by The Ingram Book Company

Dedication

For Anna and Sylvia
and for CMDR 1945-2009

Murder is a contaminating crime which changes all who come in touch with it.

P. D. James –Time in Earnest

April 5/97

Hey Waylon.
Catch this: CIVILIZATIONS RISE AND FALL
Professor Reimer printed that sentence on the board at our first Anthro class. He said when we look at history we see this clearly. Then he wrote out a list of like the ancient Egyptians, the Incas, the Aztecs and the Mayans, and he talked about a lot of other ones whose names I never heard of. He said civilizations, whole cultures and languages were disappearing even while he was talking. All that's left is like maybe they invented mummies and embalming or the zero or something and they end up being a question on Jeopardy. Sacred to no one. Only geeks remember them.

The Cree people, my mother's people, our people I guess, that's one more civilization that's fallen. Our Cree ancestors are going, going, gone. No monuments, no pyramids, no petroglyphs. They are shrinking fast, like Granny Edna. Don't know what my other half is but I'm not full blood Cree. Too pale to be a FBI, full blooded like you. I don't really know any of my Cree family. Only Granny Spence and you. I see Granny more now since she moved down to the city for her health. That's good.

No one knows who my father was. I bet not even my birth mother, Ruby McKay. I've never seen a picture of her. I never knew her. You didn't either. You were just a little guy when I was born. They say she came to Winnipeg to go beauty school. She wanted to be a hair-dresser. She dropped out.

She left the space for my father's name blank on my birth cer-tificate. Why? I think he must have been a white man. A paler face.

1

French? If he was, I'd be able to talk to him. Mon Français, c'est bon. Been in Immersion since kindergarten. Am I a Métis? Another tribe that's suffering. The world is not all white. That's false information.

It's weird. I thought we were the same – Rona, Ben and I – Mom, Dad and I. That we all were Jews. Now it's like forget about being a Jew. Now I can feel like an Indian. So what? People are racist against both. Big fucking wow.

You know Rona. She's a real phase person. Uncle Markie is right about that. He says she ran a very successful catering business before I was born and she decided to be a full time mother. Ben and I have lived through weaving and quilting and photography, and tango lessons and contact bridge and jogging and stained glass and papermaking and hot yoga and raku pottery. Every one is like a new religion. She gets born again and believes that this might be the one that really might work. She works and works at it, and then when she gets really good, she quits and finds something else.

I think I started out as one of Rona's phases but I've lasted way longer than most. She's not a mother hen like Auntie Beryl. I had babysitters when I was a month old so she could go to her studio at the potters' co-op on Corydon.

I should e-mail her. They're in Costa Rica now, I think. It's better when we're apart. No screaming. I almost miss her. She'll be wondering what I'm doing 'cause she wants to know ALL ABOUT ME. She wanted a sweet daughter who likes what she likes and thinks like her. And guess what. I don't want her dreams. I am a branch that was grafted on to their family tree. More like a twig. A brittle twig that could be snapped off.

I have questions but they don't have the answers. I'm living in a half explained world. Ben and Rona are good people. I'm not trying to write them out of my life. I do love them. Like Uncle Markie said, it's not a crime; all they've ever wanted to do was love me. You can't change things back. You can only change yourself. Sometimes we do.

Which is better? Native or white? Why does one have to be better? Whatever you chose, you lose. It puts a mark on you, on your face. That's what people do, give you a category and try to keep you in that box for life. I did apply for a status card. Do I want to have a treaty number? Ben says that Jews are really against being numbered since the Nazis gave them all number tattoos. Nasties!

When I look in the mirror I think I could be French or Spanish. Way easy. My skin has an olive tone but I haven't got the real dark eyes, I freckle every summer. I don't sound Native. Sometimes I say I'm Spanish or Mexican. When I was waiting tables at Aristos, I had people believing I was Greek. I like disguising myself. I think I want to change my major to theatre arts. There's magic in acting that lets me be me in a different way. I love it. What if I became a famous actor? Awesome. Maybe that would make Rona happy for once.

Everybody's got an agenda. I don't want to be part of their program to find lost kids. And Cousin Bernice, she wants me to say that I want to be Cree. Full time. She took me to find our granny so I could hear about the old ways.

I am not; repeat I am not an Aboriginal woman with a capital on the A. Not like the ones on campus that asked me to join their group. Those people are so stoked about everything.

I don't want to be in a visible minority or a victim of cultural genocide. I am just not that into it. That's what I told them: I'm not the Indian you had in mind.

I'm going to make my life what I want it to be. I'll decide if I am a McKay or a Kay-Stern. So people, delete all the ideas you have about me.

The best thing about 1997 is that I changed my name. Everybody calls me Georgie now. I always hated being Georgia Lee especially when people called it out loud and the Lee part came out all high and squealy. That's so not me. Neither is Rosie, my Indian name. I cut my hair and dyed it black. I really do look more French. You'll see.

The other best thing is having my apartment. I thought I'd be lonely but I'm not. Ben helped me convince Rona it was a good idea. I love having my own place. I don't even want to be over at my friends now, especially if they smoke. I've got my books and everything is the way I want it here. And I have Nikolai Gadol for company.

Remember our little bird? When I come in late at night, he sings to me and I let him out to fly around for a while. I love looking down over the Assiniboine and the Legislature and seeing the Golden Boy holding his lamp high over all of us. Granny told me that Winnipeg has four rivers in its centre. There's the muddy Red, the Assiniboine plus two wide magnetic rivers that run deep underground parallel to them and they hold us here in place. Supernatural, eh?

Waylon – where are you? Waylon, I'm writing this down because I can't talk to you. I miss you. I need to talk to somebody. That's why I labelled this file TALKING TO WAYLON. It's hidden under unused desk icons. MAYBE I'll let you read it when you get back from Japan. Get e-mail, OK.

Only those who go too far know how far there is to go. Who said that? It's my new motto. Anyway I want to try everything. Even taste the dark that's inside me. I only let them see the light. It's what they want. Thanks to Ben for giving me the computer so I can write this letter, this journal, my autobiography, the history of who I am now at the beginning of it all and one day when I'm a rich and famous actress...HA HA HA !

The weather report says more snow later today and that will make the flooding worse. Worse than the big one in 1950 when Rona says their piano went floating around the living room. This year they say it could flood out the Forks, and swamp Louis Riel's grave.

Granny says the river is the river. It will flood if it needs to. It is so beautiful outside right now I am going to grab a coffee and bus it out to the Ruins. It's where they do Shakespeare's plays in summer. To the old monastery where I heard Ophelia's speech. It was so wonderful. I am going to practice for my theatre school audition. I will always remember seeing Hamlet there. It's awesome – it looks like an old castle.

I can stand in exactly the same place Ophelia did and say – There's rosemary, that's for remembrance. Pray you love, remember. And there is pansies, that's for thoughts.

I know the whole speech and I will do it. Perfectly. **I am happy** :)

Winnipeg   April 6, 1997

The first flakes of snow drifted down about 4 p.m. on Saturday, April 5th. Wet snow. The kind that made snowballs icy and shovelling tough work. The kind that unnerved the meteorologists because they knew the earth remained super-saturated from the fall rains. It made flood watchers shudder at the task of predicting rising river levels. The Red River, like the Nile, floods every spring.

Grey flannel snow clouds curtained the heavens. Beyond them, the stars shone as ever. The wind picked up, and the snow continued to fall all through the evening and the night. It fell all over the Red River Valley. It fell on every part of the city and countryside, on the still frozen ground that was the flat bed of the ancient inland lake called Agassiz. It fell on the ruins of the old Trappist monastery, on the dark, fertile, untilled fields, on the riverside statue of Louis Riel. It covered the houses of the living and the bones of the dead.

The sun began to limn the eastern sky with scarlet as Frank MacDonald neared the end of his circle of the Forks Park. Yes, this was the best part of the morning jog. No one in sight. No traffic. Air temperature 18 below zero and virtually no wind. No new snow since the blizzard five days ago. His breath hung like fog in the chilly air and froze his moustache in thick clumps. "I am the walrus," he sang as he listened to the music playing in his head. In another fifteen minutes, he'd be stripping down to step into a hot shower, feeling righteous and pleased that the only thing on his agenda was a slack professional development day. Even if you were a teacher in a hard-nosed, core area school, there were rewards.

That morning on the early news, he had heard that the weatherman had predicted an end to the cold snap. Said the Colorado low that had dumped 37 inches of wet snow over the city during the first weekend in April had moved on. Winter's back was finally broken. Daylight saving time had begun before the storm, and the weather bureau had moved on to predict that the flood of the century was bearing down on the province and the city. It could be as big as the one in 1826 that had wiped out the entire Red River settlement. There were worrisome predictions of a lake of floodwater measuring 24 by 90 kilometres and stretching from the city to the U.S. border.

Flood news was the first and often the only topic of interest. Call-in radio shows were drawing a higher than usual number of nutcases. The whole city was buzzing with talk of flood forecasts, of daily assessments of water levels, of how livestock and people were being evacuated in rural areas near the border. In the staff room, he'd listened closely to impromptu seminars on the mysteries of home plumbing given by the industrial arts teachers. Sales of sump pumps and backflow valves were way up. It was said to cost as much as $1,000 to protect the average home.

City Hall had announced that homeowners on vulnerable properties would be issued 800 sandbags. Diagrams in the newspapers indicated how the bags were to be placed. Overnight, everyone had become an expert. It was widely known that 5 feet was the practical limit of a sandbag dike.

Frank had found himself getting caught up in the whirlwind of survivalist preparation, although neither his home nor his workplace was threatened. The camaraderie and the energy that the flood preparations created were irresistible. He knew he wouldn't be sitting around his condo getting bored this weekend. He was going to spend both days on the hustle, diking at his buddy's place up on Scotia Avenue. It would be a good time. Chili and cold beer had been promised.

He chugged on toward the York Avenue underpass, loving the sun's warmth on his face. Only eight more short blocks between that subway and his building. The city council was currently brawling over the question of replacing the underpass before the Pan Am Games crowd arrived in the summer of 1999. *They're right,* he decided as he approached. It was ugly, dark, and forbidding. The giant wooden posts supporting the railway trestle looked as if they'd been there since the day Winnipeg was founded. It was definitely not an inviting gateway to the new Forks Park.

Slowing his pace to let a cabbie pass on the service road that ran parallel to the train tracks, Frank inspected the infrastructure with grudging respect for its engineer. There was no beauty in it unless you acknowledged the simple elegance of its serviceable design. He wondered if there were any trees of that size left in Canada.

High up on the dirty snow under the trestlework, a few crows pecked at something he could not see. A huge bird swooped down and scattered the flock. It caught one of the crows in mid-flight, then soared straight up and away. Frank thought he saw something dark drop from its talons. The bird continued to fly east and lift up toward the top of the Toronto Dominion bank tower at Portage and Main. He could see the silhouette of its curved, sickle-shaped wings. It had to be one of the peregrine falcons that nested on the bank tower. *Peregrinus,* he recalled from his high school Latin lessons. *Meaning foreign, alien, and exotic.* The birds were certainly all of that in the heart of this prairie city.

As he jogged closer to the subway, his eye fell on a second unusual sight. On the snowbank, spread out like a Victorian lady's fan, was a coal-black wing. He jogged in place, looking up to see where it had dropped from. Long rust-coloured stalactites of ice hung from the trestle. The wind caught the edge of a piece of blue plastic sheeting, which flapped back against the piling above one of the Y-shaped braces. The plastic flapped again, and he saw what the crows were after.

A pale face stared down at him. Frank closed his unwilling eyes for a five-second count. Opened them again. It was beyond doubt: she was there. He tried to climb the embankment to take a closer look but couldn't make much headway in his runners on the snowbank's icy crust.

Dead, he thought. *She can't be anything but dead.*

A long, oval face with dark bangs covering the forehead. Coated with a thin gloss of ice. Crowned by a darkened halo. Was it blood? He looked away and bent his knees to bring his head closer to the ground.

He looked up again. A dead woman's body. He told himself, *phone the police – you've got to call 911.* He raced through the subway and up onto Main Street. The train station looked dark, and so did the gas bar on the other side of the street. No pay phone on any of the corners. He crossed against the light and tore down the block and into the grand lobby of the Hotel Fort Garry.

"Pay phone here?" he shouted as he strode through the warm lobby.

A bellhop pointed toward the hallway along the side of the Oval room.

The serious voice at the call centre asked him to speak slowly and to repeat the location of the body. He was calm then and able to give that information and his personal data without stumbling. His call was logged in at 06:05 hours on April 11, 1997.

For nine cold minutes, he jogged on the spot on the road below the body until an ambulance arrived. One of the paramedics took the stethoscope draped around his neck and began twirling the bell in dainty arcs like a cowboy's lariat. "What'd ya see?" he asked Frank.

"First, I saw some crows or ravens, and then there was a hawk or falcon, flying away with one of them, and then that wing there on the snow, and then her." Frank gestured upwards and felt his stomach churning. He spat out some bile on the snow.

"Easy now," said the ambulance driver. "Take some good deep breaths. You won't have to wait long. News is already out on the police radio band. You better stick around and talk to the cops, though. They'll want your statement. There'll be plenty of cops here soon, checking it out before they go off shift." The driver turned to his partner, who had pulled back the plastic for a closer look. "What's it look like, Tom?"

Tom turned both his thumbs down. "No go," he said. "VSA. Vital signs absent. Looks like her lips are frozen shut. There's ice all over her face."

As the paramedic climbed back down the embankment, a police car pulled up. Two officers got out of the black-and-white and simultaneously slammed the car's doors. The engine was left running. They came toward Frank in what he judged to be slow motion. A tired, pale, overweight guy on the shady side of 40 nodded at them and then told his partner to go on up and take a look.

They all watched as the slender young Asian constable scrabbled up the icy embankment and lifted the blue plastic tarp. She shone her flashlight on the face briefly and then returned. Before speaking, she fished out a Kleenex and blew her nose. Frank saw she was on the verge of tears and took a step toward her. He thought of putting his arm around her.

"Pardon me," she said. Then she recited in a small voice that retained a hint of Tagalog rhythms, "Very dead, female, looks white, age 20 to 25, ice covering her face. She's wrapped up all in blue plastic. I think maybe she was dumped here. Not too much mess around." She looked back up at the bright blue tarp. "Could be she's Native. Or Métis. I'm not sure. It's hard to tell."

"Okay," the other cop said to the ambulance crew, "give me a copy of your run sheet. Then you guys can vamoose."

"So, Angie . . ." the cop continued. "Your first homicide, isn't it? First day on the job. Guess you're a lucky kinda gal. Start writing, constable." He nodded to Frank. "Okay, let's get in the car. It's below freezing out here. I bet it's your first homicide, too. I'm Constable Ed Shier, and my partner here is Angie Morales."

"I'll guard the body," said Constable Morales.

"You can do that from inside the car," he said in a patient tone. "Nobody's going to friggin' interfere with it while we're sitting right here."

"You going to call the Sergeant?" she asked when they'd all settled into the cruiser. "Also the Ident guys and Homicide," she added. "Or, no, I guess Homicide and then Ident. Does it matter who is first?"

"Yeah, I'll call. Christ almighty," he said. "Usually I like the overtime even though we're supposed to get off shift in forty minutes. Gotta call the wife at work. She's gonna be pissed 'cause I'm supposed to take her mom to the doctor this morning."

He began typing the scene location and details into the squad car's on-board computer terminal. By 6:25, police from three other districts had arrived. The officers all came up to Shier and Morales and got the skinny on the scene.

Shier continued to tap away at his computer. Morales recorded Frank's full name, home address, date of birth, marital status, occupation, and account of the grim discovery in her paginated blue leatherette-covered notebook. Her handwriting was girlish, neat and clear with rounded loops.

By 6:44, the first news photographer was on scene. He was big guy, in a beige parka with a fur-trimmed hood that closely covered his head, and he parked his car directly opposite them. He used a telephoto lens to take a few shots from that vantage point, and then started to cross the road, moving toward the police car.

Shier lurched out of the driver's side door and started lumbering toward the photographer, waving his beefy arms as if he were shooing away mosquitos. "Get the hell out of here," he bellowed. "Back off. Now!" He turned back to the car. "Snooping fuckers, you make me puke," he continued under his breath.

The Identification unit's van pulled up at 6:46. Will Sawatsky and Tim Petrie, two of the senior members, got out. Sawatsky took the details from Shier. He said Homicide was called out and detectives Jake Friesen and Rob Dunblane were on their way. Friesen was going to notify the Medical Examiner's office. Everyone was on board.

Frank watched from the back of the cruiser as the crime scene guys climbed up the snow bank to look at the body. He was going to be late for his school's in-service day at nine o'clock. That much was clear. He felt as if he were under detention, sitting in the back of a cruiser beside a door that had no handles. There was a thick, badly scarred Plexiglas screen with a grid of holes in it between him and the cops in the front seat. It reminded him of talking to the cashier in the ticket booth at the local Odeon.

"Well, teach," said Shier, "you're gonna be late for school this morning, but don't worry. I'll give you a note." He smiled. "It'll be a better story than 'the dog ate my homework.'"

Officers from the traffic division arrived next and blocked off access to the subway's east–west flow of cars. Some drivers honked at the sight of the roadblock, and some tried to circle around through the Forks Park to check out the source of excitement behind the bright yellow crime scene tape. The crime scene cops backed their truck parallel to the road to block off the gawkers' view. TV film crews and other photographers arrived. The word was already out over the local radio stations.

***

Maud Fallon awoke as Jake leaned over to kiss her cheek. She turned her head to give him a sleepy smile. The alarm hadn't gone off yet. Neither one of them slept well when on call; poor sleep was a well-known occupational hazard for people in their field. She envied Jake Friesen his ability to drop off as soon as his head touched the pillow.

As they lay entwined, they discussed their weekend plans. Jake expressed interest in going lingerie shopping with her.

"Thanks, darling," she said. "That's sweet, but I think I can handle it myself. You always *say* you like my taste in lacy things. I promise I'll get something you like."

"Okay. Remember, I like anything that's silky and skimpy and has garters. Or better yet, how about some of those thong under-wear thingies?"

"You know this desire of yours to go shopping with me – that sounds like a step forward on the commitment continuum." She hoped he realized she was teasing. Sort of. It wasn't the truth, she knew, but as soon as she'd said it, she'd started to believe it and so couldn't help feeling hurt even before he answered.

"Commitment? Me? I do keep extra shirts here now. There's a giant step, lover." He leaned over to kiss her raspberry nipples, the right, and then the left.

"*Lover?* You say that word like it is on your tongue and you can taste it." She ran her fingers over his lips like a blind woman searching for meaning. *And I would gladly eat your words,* she thought.

Her next thought was about how nothing worked out for her with men. She wanted to ask him that one question that was lodged in her throat like an unspoken prayer: *I know you love me, really, really love me, but do you like me?*

"Who invented the thong?" Maud asked after a few moments of quiet. She straddled his body and playfully pinned his arms. "It had to be a man."

"It was. I heard it was Jesus. Think of him hanging up there on his cross with that little rag over his crotch."

She broke up laughing and immediately felt guilty. Wasn't that remark blasphemous? Her grasp of the categories of sin was hazy now. It had been a long time since she'd given any thought to theological issues.

The urgent sound of a beeper going off interrupted their kiss. "I hate that sound," she said. "It's ruined *Beethoven's Fifth* for me."

"Mine," said Jake. He reached over her shoulder to pick up his pager from the bedside table. "Looks like the office." He squinted at the number displayed. Then he picked up the phone and punched the number in and spoke his last name crisply into the receiver. This was followed by a series of grunts and *yeahs* and finally a louder "Fuck me! Right. Okay, I'll call the medical examiner."

He turned to Maud. "It's gonna be a nightmare Friday, and you've got a case. A jogger found a female deceased up under the York Street subway. Consider yourself notified."

Maud groaned. A call out for a sudden death was the last thing she wanted to hear. She rolled over and pulled her duvet up over her head. It was 06:40, and she was stuck on call for another full hour and twenty minutes. Reluctantly, she dialled into the main phone line of the Forensic Sciences Centre. She listened to her own voice on the tape advising callers that police and institutions with urgent need of assistance page her and telling all other callers to leave a message at the sound of the tone. She quickly recited the spare known details of the homicide for the day staff and noted that she was going directly to the scene and would be into the Centre as soon as possible.

She watched as Jake, fresh from his five-minute shower, dressed in front of her. He put on a clean white shirt from the stash he'd started keeping in her closet after they'd begun sleeping together. He didn't usually stay overnight during the work week. He reached up to pull the collar down over his tie. The movement revealed a narrow triangle of bare flesh, bounded on two sides by the white of his shirtfront and on the third by the fabric of his grey trousers. His navel was dark, almost a wound on his lean torso. He looked vulnerable, his blond hair dishevelled, a shadow of beard on his chin. Like a young man engaged in the serious act of tying his tie.

Initially, Maud reflected, he did not impress anyone as being a strong guy. Barefoot, he stood 2 full inches shy of 6 feet. His frame seemed light, but there was no mistaking his strength. The hours he'd devoted to working out at the police academy gym had paid off in well-developed muscles that were clearly delineated even when he was simply swatting a mosquito.

She knew she loved him – all there was to him. So a few seconds later, when he belted on his gun, she was relieved he had that ugly measure of protection. It had been the source of their single quarrel. She had asked him not to bring it into her apartment, and when he'd said he was required to have it at hand always, she had compromised. They'd agreed that it was never to be in her bedroom. At night she liked to see her clock radio, her notepad and pencil, and her pot of herbal tea set out on her bedside table. His gun would look out of place – like a man perched on a peach velvet boudoir chair in a lingerie boutique.

"See you at the scene?" he asked. He smoothed the narrow lapels of his black wool blazer and clipped his gold detective's shield on the left side of his belt.

"Doubt it. You'll probably be gone before I get there. Did you get a cell phone number for the uniforms at the scene? What division is it?"

"No. We already know where it is. It's Division One. Down by the railway trestle at the subway into the Forks Park. What else do you need?"

"I like to call before I go, check in with the guys at the scene and find out how it's going. I don't want to be out in the cold a minute longer than I have to. It's been an ugly winter, and I've been cold since November. Besides, the mortuary service guys like plenty of notice for a body removal during regular hours. They've always got lots of bodies to move around the city. And I like to try to keep everybody happy. Don't you?"

"Later," he said and blew her a kiss.

"Love you," she answered. She counted off five silent seconds while she listened for the echo of her words. Her front door slammed, and he was gone.

Maud took a hurried sponge bath at the sink. She brushed her dark brown shoulder-length hair and clipped it back at the nape of her long neck with a large red plastic barrette. *I'm not in the mood for another homicide,* she confided to her reflection. "Calm yourself," she said aloud.

Although the weather channel advised that the wind chill factor was less than 1600, the thermometer was stuck at –18 Celsius. She decided there was no sense in taking a chance on frostbite. She pulled on tights, warm socks, black wool pants, and a black turtleneck sweater. It was nearly mid-April, and though there had not been fresh snow since the blizzard on the sixth of the month and all Winnipeg was talking about preparations for the coming flood, Maud was still in a winter state of mind.

People on the street looked glum in their well-worn cold weather gear, climbing over the dirty sand-encrusted snowbanks ploughed up at street corners. Everyone was longing for that intoxicating whiff of rich spring air and listening for the percussive music made by running water dripping off the eaves, for as soon as that sound was heard, the first voice of the new season, they all knew that the balance of the year had shifted. In a few weeks, the city's trees would be in bud, the city's outdoor cafés buzzing.

Maud dug out her old hiking boots from the oak hallstand and sat on its narrow seat to lace them up. Finally, she took a long look around her darkened living room. Her overstuffed chesterfield seemed to be inviting her to sit in its chintz-covered lap, and the sight of her stack of unread books on the coffee table made her wish she could crawl into their comfortable world. Groaning aloud, she reached for the phone.

She called downtown to the Sergeant Reader's desk and asked for an update on the scene. The sergeant said that Homicide and the crime scene guys were there and were still checking things out. She asked him to send word that she was en route. Her swollen black leather briefcase sat on the kitchen floor where she had left it yesterday. She had not been called out on a case overnight, so her supplies of government forms and documents did not need replenishing.

Was there a moment when I actually chose this? She could not recall. She must have.

Maud unplugged her trusty SUV's block heater and its interior warmer. The seat was cold, and again she wished she'd put out the extra cash to get cloth seat covers instead of the standard-issue leather ones. Little things meant a lot.

Slowly, she backed out into the lane and crawled along through deep icy ruts to the corner. It was like driving on the surface of the moon. The city's snow removal budget was shot. Nothing except the major arteries had been ploughed in the past six weeks. The sand trucks had not been around, either. Snowbanks towered over both sides of every street. She told herself that no winter challenge was too great for a true prairie gal. And besides, it was a dry cold.

All she could think of was getting through the next hour until she came off call at 8:00 a.m., too weary to think about the stack of files sitting on her desk. She'd been on call last weekend and had picked up thirty-two hospital cases. That was not an all-time record for her but close to that benchmark. Thank heavens this was the only homicide.

Many of the people she met and even some friends thought of her job as thrilling, replete with lurid insider details that she and her sexy detective lover discussed on their off hours. If only. If only they knew.

She drove north through Osborne Village, over the bridge, and east along Broadway past the Legislature. The light in the Golden Boy's torch was shining over the city like some low-rent Statue of Liberty. *Give me your murders, your suicides. Jesus, just give me a break.* She shivered as she got her first view of the police barricade from the T-intersection at Main Street. Maud pulled up behind a cruiser and put her Province of Manitoba parking plaque on the dash.

She introduced herself to the officer on guard, lifted the ribbon of yellow crime scene tape over her head, and walked toward the body. Sawatsky and Petrie from the police service's Identification section were deep in conversation at the foot of the embankment.

Maud smiled at the pair. "What have we got here?"

Constable Petrie spoke up. "Looks like a young white female. Can't see much of her except her face, and it's covered with ice. She's wrapped up in a blue plastic tarp, and most of her is buried under snow. Say, have you got a shovel in your car?"

"Yes. Doesn't everyone have a shovel in the trunk? This is Winnipeg."

"Ah, you girls are ready for anything, aren't ya?"

Maud nodded. "Frozen?" she asked. She looked up the embankment to the bright blue tarpaulin that was wedged up under the railway trestle.

"Yep, looks pretty solid," added Sawatsky. "There's nothing like an outdoor scene on a cold morning to keep the body cool and crisp. Scramble on up and take a look for yourself, Maud. I've taken all the shots I need for now, and I guess you'll want to take some, too. Pretty cold for your camera, though." Sawatsky tucked his 35 mm under his jacket and zipped it up.

"Okay," said Maud. "Does it matter where I step?"

"No, but watch yourself. It's pretty slippery, but you'll see where we've tramped it down."

Maud nodded. "Has Homicide been out here yet?"

"Been and gone back downtown," said Petrie. "We kicked them out – can't have them messing up our crime scene. They can look at the video later." All three of them laughed, because this was the way it usually worked out. The Medical Examiner's Investigator would take charge of the body and, with the Ident crew, document the mess.

She tucked her woollen gloves into one of her pockets and pulled on a pair of latex ones. Petrie handed her a set of the police service's standard issue white-hooded coveralls and booties. She took her time putting them on as she gave herself a pep talk. *It's not a decomp. She's frozen, so there won't be any hideous odour.* There would be something else – she was confident of that. Some days, the idea of opening yet another shroud, rolling the body, and catching a whiff of someone's very last post-terminal, already sour exhalation was almost unendurable. *Adopt a scientific perspective,* she instructed herself.

Maud looked up at the clear prairie sky and resolutely took a deep breath of the cold morning air. *You cannot be sick now. That would be way too embarrassing,* she warned herself as she carefully climbed halfway up the embankment. She stopped to take one Polaroid of the body from that vantage point. Someone had tucked the loose corner of the blue tarp back, so she was able to see the young face with its clear mask of ice. The birds had not broken through that thin layer. Maud knelt beside the body, placed her gloved hands on the cheekbones, and gently attempted to lift the girl's head.

Maud took two shots of the long oval face with its ragged black bangs. The body was lying on its left side with knees drawn up toward the chest. She felt delicately around the sides and back of the head. The chin-length hair felt brittle and as if it were coated with some kind of gooey hair gel. Or blood. Raw edges of a scalp laceration met Maud's examining fingers. A few particles of dark, quasi-metallic matter adhered to Maud's gloves. She rolled these between her fingers and sniffed at them. It was blood. No question. She noted a rill of frozen blood trailing down from the girl's right ear into the snow. Maud could see a silver-coloured chain running around the girl's slender neck, but the tarp hid the rest of her. *I wonder how he got her up here,* Maud thought. *And when?*

The icy crust of snow glistened as the sunlight glanced over it. Maud thought of Snow White in her glass-topped coffin. "Whose little girl are you?" she whispered. She quickly took two more shots of the once-pretty face, though it was too cold for the emulsion to develop properly. She knew Sawatsky would give her copies of his pictures for the file.

Maud tucked her Polaroids into the inner breast pocket of her jacket and inched her way back down the embankment. "What do we know about little Snow White?" she asked Sawatsky and Petrie.

Very little, Petrie admitted. A dumped body, for sure. Likely been there since before the last storm, which he recalled was last weekend, or five days ago. He said that she had slipped a little from her original position. "Sun is warmer every day, and snow's melting fast now." He pointed out a torn edge on the flap of blue tarp, and he found a tiny bit of the same material on a nail protruding from one of the struts about 10 inches higher. "You can see," he said, "that her feet are about that much higher. We're waiting for Barry Thomas to come out with a video camera to record the scene." That would take forty-five minutes at least, he said, and meanwhile they could think about how to move the body.

"Okay," Maud said. "I'll ask the service to bring a sheet and a plastic shroud pack. By the way," she called back over her shoulder, "for the record, time of death is 07:38. Today's date."

Maud tapped on the cruiser's window, and Shier popped open the back door. After introductions, she gave the teacher who had found the body her government department's brochure and a business card. She expressed sympathy for the difficulty his discovery must have brought him. Frank MacDonald tucked the card and brochure into his jacket and nodded when she suggested he call her pager number if he had any questions or concerns.

Back in her car, Maud turned the motor on and cranked the heat and defroster up full blast. The temperature was the same on the inside as outside. She dug into her briefcase and pulled out a preliminary report of death form and a toe tag, balanced her clipboard on the steering wheel, and began writing. Name of deceased: X – that is, unidentified; found under the Canadian National railway bridge on York Street; sex: presumed female. There were fifty spaces on the form, and about forty of them would remain blank for now. She recorded Frank MacDonald's name under the heading *found dead or injured by,* noted his *relationship to deceased* as "none," and wrote down his phone number. She added the date and time of his discovery from the information she'd received from the uniformed cops.

Maud wrote down the officers' names, their badge numbers, and their incident report number: 97/1/39611. She recorded Sawatsky and Petrie's names and badge numbers for the Identification section and listed Jake and his partner, Rob Dunblane, as the investigating officers for Homicide. Location of body at time of injury/illness: unknown. Position of the body when found: lying on left side. Appearance of clothing: unable to view at scene. Body - Appearance: wrapped in blue plastic tarp, frozen under 6 or 7 inches of snow, multiple bird pecks to ice over face. Hair: matted with blood. She recorded her own name and the time and date of death that she had pronounced. Activity accompanying death or fatal injury: unknown. Apparent manner of death: homicide. She omitted her impression that the darkened congealed blood on the white snow under the head suggested a halo. No saint she could recall had a halo of blood.

It was 8:10 now. Not too early to call the Chief. She dialled his private line at home. Dr. David Bekker answered on the third ring.

"Morning, sir. Maud here. I'm at a scene under the railway trestle at York Street and the CN station."

"What have you got there?" he asked. His voice creaked a little, as if his larynx needed oiling.

"It's an X, sir. Apparent homicide. Looks female, wrapped up in a blue tarp, likely dumped some time before the last snow. Birds have been at the ice covering her face."

"Oh. Birds. Crows, I wager. Close, I think, to the Forks Market. I know that place. The wife and I were there shopping on Saturday. Up under the trestle, you say?"

"Yes."

"Too bad he didn't put her on a freight train and send her out of town. Save us some trouble, wouldn't he?"

Maud did not respond. It was a predictable remark from the old fart.

"Blue tarp?" he asked.

"Yes."

"Army surplus type?"

"Hard to say, sir. Most of her, except for the head, is buried under the snow. It looks like the kind you get for going camping."

"How old?"

"Under 25, is my guess."

"Native?"

"Possibly."

"Okay." He grunted. "Send her in. Dr. Langdon on duty today?"

"Could be."

"Who's at the scene with you? Cops any good?"

"Don't worry. We've got a good crew."

"Want me to come out?"

"Not necessary, sir."

"Don't let the police screw the thing up. You watch when the body is moved."

Maud closed her eyes at that remark. The boss never said anything direct to her, but she knew that he knew she was sleeping with a cop and that he thought the relationship a liability that might compromise her work.

"Sir, it's going well. I wanted you to know what's going on. That's all. The media are here, and it's been on the radio news already. You might get some calls."

"Yes, the media. Give us this day our breaking news. They're always hungry. Thanks for, you know, putting me in the picture."

She was thankful, too. The last thing she wanted was the boss underfoot, causing a commotion. She hung up and dialled the number for the Assiniboine Mortuary, the body removal service. Then she carefully filled in the Registration of Death, the autopsy permission, and the toe tag. The same few known details were recorded on these documents, which must accompany the body.

The witness, MacDonald, was getting out of the back of the cruiser, and Maud overheard him refusing a ride home. He was exceptionally tall and lean for an older guy, she noted. A good-looking older guy. He nodded at her as he moved off toward Main Street. Not jogging now. Walking briskly.

Constable Shier rolled down his window, and Maud told him that she expected the body removal to take place within the hour. He and Morales and Tim Petrie from Ident would accompany the body to the Forensic Centre and see it into the lockup. Shier asked when the autopsy would be.

"Definitely not today," she answered. "I don't know for certain how long she'll take to thaw out."

Her pager beeped, and she saw the Homicide Division's number. She pressed speed dial, and Jake answered after the first ring.

"How's it going?" he asked.

"The usual."

"Can you get us an autopsy today?"

"Don't think so. She's frozen solid."

"How about the weekend?"

THE WEEKEND. Maud could see it spelled out in capitals. Her longed-for weekend off – but now obviously not one she was going to spend with Jake. Damn.

"Dream on," she answered. "What makes you think the pathologist is going to want to work on the weekend? They don't collect the same kind of overtime you do."

"I mean how long can it take? For her body to thaw, I mean?"

"My mom used to take the roast out of the freezer on Saturday night for our Sunday dinner."

"It's not the same thing as the Sunday roast, is it?" He sounded distressed at the idea.

"Close enough."

"How will they know when to begin?"

"They don't use a thermometer. It's a guesstimate. You know, a poke at the body with a finger. You know, the way Mom did to the Sunday joint."

"That sounds highly unscientific. Christ! See what you can do for us, will you? Right now we haven't got much to do besides comb through the missing persons list."

"Got to go," she answered.

Maud hung up on Jake and dialled through to the Forensic Centre's morgue. Robert Ferguson, the chief pathology assistant, answered immediately.

"Morning, dear," Maud said. "What's on your slate today?"

"Maud, girl, have you been out combing the back alleys and streets of this city looking for trouble? Trying to drum up business when you know very well that we don't want any more. It's Friday, don't you know?" He sounded relaxed – she could tell he had his feet up on the desk.

"R.F.," she said, "you know I never take on any work that isn't essential. Bit of a twist on this case. You're always willing to look at something different – admit it. The young lady is very, very cold. In fact, she's frozen. How long do you think it'll take before she's ready to examine?"

"Not today. We're all booked up, thanks to your office. How long has she been out in the cold?"

"Since before the last storm. We think."

"Five days at least." R.F. whistled softly. "Do we know her?"

"Not a clue at the moment. That's why Homicide is eager for some answers."

"Those fellas are always in a lather. I expect I could put it at the top of the slate for Monday morning. Even that will mean putting her into the main morgue until end of day and then moving her into the cage for the weekend. You get the cops to agree, and we'll do it that way. Lock her in the viewing room at the ambient temperature for the day. They can put their seals on the doors and sit watch all day if they want to. Tell the sergeant they can be back here for a 9:00 a.m. start on Monday."

Maud knew the police would never agree to that. They'd say they didn't have the manpower to put a guard on the body until the end of the day. Their focus had to be maintaining the chain of evidence. The girl's body would have to be secured in the wire cage within the cooler, and they'd all hope that it would thaw enough for examination on Monday.

R.F. lowered his voice to a whisper. "What did you see?"

"Not much. She's tucked up under the trestle by the train station. I only took a quick feel, but I'll put money on severe head trauma. Her hair is all stiff, and she has scalp lacerations." She looked up the embankment where the Ident crew was taking a video of the body in situ. It was the new guy. What was his name? She'd met him one other time. Was he a Brian? Another Bill?

"Head trauma," said R.F. "Okay, so how much are you into me for now?"

"Two dollars." Maud's feet were numb with cold now, despite her heavy socks and boots. She began to walk toward the warmth of the idling cruiser.

"Double or nothing?" R.F. sounded like he was sure of the bet. Licking his chops.

"All right. But I've got to see all the toxicology results reported before I concede and pay up on that other case." Black humour. That's how they got started with these bets. Besides, she remembered the cases she lost on, so it was partly educational.

"You drive a hard bargain, Miss Maud."

"We investigators are a tough breed."

"Don't I know it?" As usual, R.F. hung up without a goodbye. Cannot afford to get sentimental, he always claimed.

The Assiniboine Mortuary Service's dark grey van pulled up to the barricade and was waved through. Maud left Shier and Morales to their reports and walked over to the van.

"Morning, fellas," she called out.

"Morning, Maud," the two men, Mike and Jocko, chorused like schoolboys.

They all walked over to the foot of the embankment where the Ident crew was standing by.

"Video all done?" Maud asked the man with the camera.

"Basically, yeah," he said, "but I'll tape the removal since I'm here."

"Let me check this out," said Mike. He donned police coveralls and scrambled up the snow-encrusted surface. "Jesus, Maud! Why didn't you say to bring pitons?" He slipped and sank through the snow up to his knees on the way down. Petrie gave him a hand over the snowbank at the bottom.

"This is going to be a lot of fun. I've got a shovel and some rope in the van. We'll be right back." Jocko returned quickly with the gurney and pall. A black plastic shovel, a coil of yellow nylon rope, a shroud pack, and a white sheet stamped with the name of the laundry service of one of the local hospitals were piled on top. He suited up, and the six of them clambered back up to the frozen body.

"Doesn't look very old to me," said Mike, "but then we aren't seeing her at her best. I'll start loosening by the snow crust, say, about a half foot away from her, and we'll see if we can lift her up."

There was very little room up under the trestle. Maud stepped toward the outer edge of the scene where Sawatsky and Petrie waited.

Mike gently spaded around the body. "Now . . ." He pushed his glasses back up on the bridge of his nose with the back of a gloved hand. "Maud, you and the boys here" – he nodded to Sawatsky and Petrie – "spread out the sheet on top of the shroud. Hold them up like you're folding laundry, and Jocko and I'll try lifting her on it."

The constable doing the videotaping moved as high as he could go up under the trestle and trained his camera on their efforts from overhead. His 6-foot-plus frame was hunched over between a couple of the immense icicles that hung from the wooden trestle. "Anybody know when the next train is due?" he asked while following the others through his viewfinder.

"You take her feet," Mike said to his helper, "and we'll go straight up and over and lower her down. Easy now. *Un, deux, trois.*" He knitted his gloved fingers under the girl's head as Jocko slid his hands under the foot end of the crust of snow that surrounded the body like a visible aura. The transfer went as smoothly as hoped. The body removal guys danced their burden under the outstretched arms of Maud and the Ident officers and placed the corpse on the white sheet. Maud stepped back to let the men carry the body down.

"Careful as she goes," cautioned Mike. "I don't want to be seen stumbling on the TV news. That'd be bad for business."

"Look here," said the cop with the video camera. There was an imprint of a boot in the snow under the crust. He handed Maud his camera and with the plastic shovel delicately lifted away more of the crust. It was unmistakable: the imprint of a heeled boot with a pointed toe.

Paul Boudreau unlocked and carefully opened the door to his bachelor suite. The small square of cardboard he had placed in the jamb fell to the floor. Good. No one had tried to bust into his crib.

He unpacked the contents of his plastic bag of groceries – a litre of 2% milk, a loaf of day-old sliced white bread, two apples, a box of Kraft dinner, small jars of strawberry jam and instant coffee, and six eggs – and set them on the narrow wooden shelf that served as a counter. That stuff had eaten up most of the ten bucks the padre had loaned him. Things cost more at corner grocery stores than at the supermarket, but he'd wanted to check out the neighbourhood. He smiled a small happy smile and, with a flourish, pulled a package of bologna and another of tea bags from inside his bomber jacket. Presto! It was easy to lift things from Mom and Pop stores. That old Chinese guy didn't see nothing, Paul would lay money on it. He'd made sure he told the Chink he was renting a suite from the New Path Ministry people.

The New Path was an inner-city congregation whose members were among the city's most disadvantaged. The pastor offered counselling, a map of the path to eternal salvation, and low-cost housing. The housing was in an old building bequeathed to the church by a long-departed congregant. It had looked fine when the original tenants had taken up residence in June of 1940.

The dark brown brick three-story apartment block had the words *Maple Leaf Apartments* cut into the Tyndall stone lintel over the centrally placed front door. The building was set back from the street behind two spindly elms, each surrounded by a square of brown grass. The pastor had had the building cut up into bachelor suites and set up his office in the bedroom of a large suite on the first floor. His assistant, Martha Wiebe, managed the building from her station in its former living room, which did double duty as a meeting room in the evenings.

"How do we deal with the world?" Pastor Martin Kroeker would ask.

"Straight up," his congregation would answer.

Okay by me, thought Paul. He was good with New Path. He always worked out the rules on the first day at a new place. Found out right away who to suck up to. His story this time was that he was a construction worker, had been up in McMurray where he'd got messed up. He was off the booze and pills for a year and a half. Told the padre he needed to take a meeting right away.

He liked the way you could drop in to the Double A. Any place, any time. It was a good way to get connected in a new town. There always were a few rounders in the crowd. You could see their shaky hands trying to hold the Styrofoam cups of coffee steady.

He couldn't get his issue from welfare for another three days, so Martha Wiebe had given him the address of a food bank where he could get help if he ran short after using up the pastor's ten dollars. She'd gotten him to sign for the keys to his crib and handed him a copy of the New Path rules.

She was about the right age, he'd thought as he'd watched her fat white fingers write down all his fake info. Over 50. Plain face with a tiny squashed nose that looked as if it had been stuck onto her round face in a hurry. Her blue eyes were soft behind thick glasses, and the dull, thin brown hair that she tucked behind her big ears had no curl. He'd looked at her hard, wondering if he would see the sign he searched for in every older woman's face: a flicker of recognition, an acknowledgement that, yes, she was the crazy one who had borne him. His own mommy. He belonged, he was claimed. He hated all of them.

Sucking up to the good folks at the soup kitchen on Hargrave had been easy for him. That's how he'd met up with the padre. Kroeker had been trawling for lost souls at the soup kitchen, and Paul didn't mind pretending to get reeled in. He did need the safe, comforting arms of Jesus.

Paul had to keep a close watch on his cash, and he was feeling pretty low in himself. He wanted to move on, but he had no ride now.

The old man's classic '66 Dodge Polara had been Paul's inheritance. His sole earthly possession. His last foster dad, Charles Hardwick, had told him that he would give it to Paul when he turned 16. But Paul couldn't take it over then because he was already inside for setting fires. And that was no accident. Stupid sorry ass little fucker Brad Weston had ratted him out.

Charlie was the only one who'd believed Paul. Patricia Hardwick hadn't. That's why Paul always went back to the Hardwick place when he got out: to see Charlie and check up on the old bitch. After Charlie'd had a stroke, Paul hadn't trusted her to look after him good enough. And he'd been right. What he'd found the last time made him mad. She should never have left Charlie sitting out for hours on that crappy little glassed-in porch tied in his chair. It was grey and rainy every fuck-ass Nanaimo day. And that made the porch cold and dark as the hole. Paul swore he would have carted Charlie off with him right then, but he knew he couldn't have changed the man's diaper. They'd have both hated it. Besides, she'd had an orderly come twice a day for that.

When the old guy up and snuffed it, Paul had gone back to Nanaimo for the funeral. Ha, ha, right. No, Paul had been too pissed with her whining. Why would he go after the way she'd kept on ragging that it was Paul coming back into their lives that had sent the old man into the hospital, where he'd croaked? That was a lie.

Charlie had told Paul at least a hundred times that the car was going to be his. So when she had been away at the funeral, Paul had got into the house and taken the keys. He'd left that punk-ass town in style. The widow had been so upset that she hadn't even reported the car stolen. The old tea bag didn't have the nerve.

Paul hadn't been sorry to leave Nanaimo. It was the armpit of the Island. Forget parole. Fuck that shit. He'd done his time, and he was a free man.

The Dodge had flown along the Number 1 highway like Charlie had said she would. Only took Paul two days to make Winnipeg from Vancouver. He'd really poured it on until he got here. Winnipeg seemed safe enough. He didn't know anyone, and no one knew him.

He'd heard about Winnipeg from Pedro Fehr, his cellmate from his last stint. It had been Pedro's idea; he'd said it would be easy to cross the border there. He'd drawn Paul a map of a place where he used to cross the border near Gretna and given him a phone number to a cousin in Altona. Pedro had said, "Then you drive straight south to Dallas, then turn west to San Antonio, and keep on a-comin' to the Mexican border on the Rio Grande." He had said, "The police aren't looking for people trying to get into Mexico. It's the other way round. And once you're down there, it's easy to, like, disappear." He'd snapped his fingers.

Paul was going to hook up down there with Pedro, who had some good plans for them. They'd talked about it every night when they'd bunked together – lots of people there working with the Mexicans and getting pretty rich. Pedro had cousins there, and these cousins had a farm where they made cheese way out in the boonies that they could stay at between jobs. These dudes called themselves the Fehr Trade Dealers. Besides the cheese, they were dealing coke and had good connections.

Pedro had said it was near Chihuahua, where they had invented those cute little big-eyed dogs. Maybe he'd get one. Paul had always wanted a dog, but none of the foster homes would let him. If he had a little dog, he could take it with him all the time. Call him Mickey the Mouse Dog. Carry it in his pocket. Mexico. He was going to see lots of different shit there.

Nobody'd told him that this flood was coming, and it had fucked him up. He had to sit tight. He still had 583 of the 800 dollars he'd taken from Patricia Hardwick's secret hiding place behind the glass-fronted case that held Charlie's war medals. Served her right. She was the reason that Charlie had never adopted him. Paul had heard them quarrelling about it. That's why he'd never said the name *Dad* to Charlie out loud.

WWII. Besides the car, that war was about the only thing Paul and Charlie had talked about. And Charlie hadn't said much about that. "You don't know what it is to kill a man," he'd say. Charlie had been a gunner and was lucky enough to survive. Almost intact – except, as he would say, he could no longer live up to his name. Couldn't get his wick hard anymore due to unspecified damages. Gave his all for King and country. (That's why they'd taken Paul in, Charlie had confided. Always wanted a son.) Got a lot out of the war, he'd said: high blood pressure, trouble in the waterworks, and the France-Germany star for his trouble.

Charlie's car was rust-free, a two-tone beauty. Steel blue top and sky blue bottom. And now it was a loss. Christ, why had that girl refused? He'd thought she'd wanted a hot, sexy time. All her talk about vampires. He didn't fuckin' get it. She'd started off real friendly at the coffee shop, and like she'd talked so wild. Sitting close with him in the back seat of the Dodge, she'd traced the outline of the small triangle of beard he'd left unshaved below his lower lip with her round silver tongue stud. It had felt cold and smooth. She'd said she liked doing it, that he was cool. Like the Beats, she'd said, naming Kerouac, Cassidy, and Burroughs. He'd had no clue what she was yakking about. He didn't give a flying fuck. He'd just wanted to get into her pants.

After getting rid of her, he'd started driving east again on the old Canada Number 1. He hadn't even known why. He'd freaked out when he'd seen a RCMP cruiser that had stopped a pickup truck on the shoulder near the turnoff south to Steinbach. He'd tightened his grip on the Dodge's big chrome steering wheel. *Fuckers'll have me down next,* he'd thought.

There'd been nothing but the CBC coming in on the old AM radio, and he hadn't been able to stop thinking what a fuckup he was. No wonder old Patsy hadn't agreed to adopt him for real. Seven years he'd lived with them. He hated every one of her tight grey curls.

He'd never meant to do the girl like that. He'd picked her because when she'd smiled, she'd smiled a little like Linda, who had been his first. Linda had lived two streets over from the Hardwicks in Nanaimo. She was pretty and a hot little thing at 17, and she'd taken him into her bedroom any time she'd wanted it while her fat mother worked evening shift at the hospital. Linda had been nice to him. Sometimes, after, she had made him some food or they had gone for pizza. They had planned to go to Vancouver as soon as he had his 16th birthday at the end of December, but by then she'd died from meningitis in her brain. Pedro once told him that in Spanish *linda* means beautiful, and that's when Paul started thinking of her sometimes again.

Why wouldn't that girl open her legs and get it on? He wouldna had to hit her then. He hadn't wanted to hit her. He hadn't meant to hit her. Only when he'd seen she was afraid, he got mad.

Now he was in for it. If they got him, he'd be back in the joint in the range with the heavy dudes. Lifers. Some fucker was gonna want his pretty ass again. Or the Native guys would get to him. No way. No fucking way.

He'd been watching everything along the highway. Snow was bad. Coming thick and fast, whiting out everything in front of him. He'd been sweating heavy now and tightened up inside himself like a spring. Same as when he'd first got in the joint. Trouble could come from any side. And he was tired from being up all goddam night hiding that girl. Why'd she go with him if she didn't want it? The weather forecast had said it was going to develop into a blizzard. He couldn't see for the white shit. Had to drive real slow. He'd had the map spread out on the seat beside him. He'd seen that where the highway widened out close to a place called Richer, there were old roads leading off from the wide median. He'd followed one in and found some gravel pits and parked beside an old metal gate. He'd got out to stretch his legs and breathed in cold, fresh pine-scented air. The heavy snow cover had muffled all sounds from the highway. He'd seen a red-tailed hawk circling widely. Didn't it know that it was too early to return from the south? He'd thought of sitting it out there, but he'd been hungry and right pissed off. The cold had been too bitter for his thin old leather jacket and the Stampeders cap he had lifted in Calgary. He'd had on his Western boots and leather work gloves that were some better for snow. Not good enough, but he hadn't planned to stop anywhere this friggin' cold.

He'd hated to leave his wheels behind, but the back seat was covered with a sickening mess where her blood had frozen on the upholstery. He had chipped away at it, and a fair bit of the frozen stuff had lifted off. It was like pale pinkish ice. The outline of the stain was faint. He wished he hadn't made such a mess getting her onto the tarp. He'd never get it all out. Charlie would be furious if he knew the original upholstery had been ruined. He'd always kept his ride in mint condition.

Paul had dug a crescent wrench and a screwdriver out, removed the British Columbia licence plates, and hidden them in his toolbox. Maybe he'd get a chance to come back for his Dodge before anyone else found her. How else was he going to get to Chihuahua? He'd wiped his hands and his hammer off the best he could, using the snow beside the car to scour them clean the way he and Charlie used to clean their dishes with sand when they went camping. He'd scooped up more snow and scrubbed his face. The cold sting had been good, and Paul had felt more awake and freer than ever.

He'd picked up his toolbox, walked out to the westbound side of the highway, and headed into the blowing snow. It had been a goddam cold hike, and there hadn't been much traffic. Lucky for him, after twenty minutes he came to a crossroad with a gas station that had a café. He'd ordered a hungry-man breakfast plus coffee and a side of fries with gravy.

He remembered the girl had asked him what he liked for breakfast.

"Special K," he'd answered.

"Yeah." She'd felt his right bicep. "You like to lead a healthy lifestyle. I could tell that from your great build. I bet you work out every day."

"Yeah," he'd answered. There had been lots of time to bulk up in the joint.

She didn't know that his Special K meant ketamine. The cat tranquilliser. The breakfast of champions at Okalla. He was one more a-hole in the k-hole. He'd done a lot of drugs there – everybody did, to cut the boredom, short the time. As a goodbye present, Pedro had given him some of his stash of special little white pills. He'd said to slip a couple in some bitch's drink, and you'd get a piece of ass real easy. Said it was way better than booze. *They don't remember nothing. Not your name. Nothing. So you never have to pay for it. And pork her once for me,* Pedro said. In five weeks, he'd be out getting his own.

Paul paid for his breakfast with some of the money he'd stolen from her little purse. Thirty-two dollars and 83 cents she'd had. Besides her wallet, he took her driver's licence and university ID card (because it had a photo of her smiling nicely) and the keys to her apartment.

Paul had been sure he'd get to screw her. They'd left the coffee shop, and he'd driven them out to the ruined monastery she'd wanted to see. He'd got her into the wide backseat of the Dodge. No problem. But she hadn't seemed to get stoned the way Pedro had said she would. Maybe she hadn't drunk enough of her spiked coffee. Or he hadn't waited long enough.

She'd said it was too early for sex and giggled in a high-pitched nervous way. It was still daylight. She'd started to fight back when she'd felt his hard bone. He'd tried holding her down, but she'd been a wildcat. Tried to bite. He'd got her tight by the hair with one hand. She had been screaming and kicking with her feet at the frosted-over windows. He was the only one who heard her. He'd slapped her hard on the mouth, then reached down to the floor for his tool kit and got his hammer out. He'd wanted to show her he meant business and she had to give it up. She looked really scared and put her hands up over her eyes like the old bitch, Patricia. Cryin', whinin' *no, no, please, no.* His eyes had turned a hard blue metal. All he remembered was a brief steely flash, a glint that barely registered. She'd seen it coming. She'd had it coming.

He'd pulled open her clothes and looked at her. Red blood had been running out of her ear, down her neck and onto her chest. Her brownish pink nipples had looked soft. He'd touched them. He'd sniffed at her bush. She had smelled pretty clean, a little tangy from the fresh piss that she had wet in her panties. The hair had been way lighter than the black hair on her head. He had liked her smell and her warmth now that she was quiet, and he'd come all over her cunt hairs. He'd had his mouth over one of her nipples when he did it, and he'd bitten down hard. Then he had bitten the other one to even the score. He remembered it all real clear.

He had been way lucky to get back to Winnipeg on only the one hitch. Right outside the café he'd got on with a big old motor-mouth dickhead trucker in a Freightliner who was on his CB radio the whole way. If he wasn't on the radio, he was yakking about the storm coming up out of Colorado. "Ever been through the States? I been to every one of them at least once, 'cept Hawaii. They say the roads are bad going south today. You're not dressed for it, is ya?" The guy had looked over at Paul's leather bomber jacket and ball cap. "It's not too bad now," the guy said, "but the temperature's going into the toilet again. She's going to blow hard. Damn hard. I can't hardly believe you're out here on foot. And all's ya got are them cowboy boots? You sure lucked out when I come along. I pulled outa Thunder Bay at 8:00 this morning. Knew I had to lay the hammer down to get to the 'Peg before night. We are in for a good blow, I can tell. Our house got swamped in the

1950 flood, and I know what a bitch Mother Nature can be. She's goin' on one hell of a tear today. I'm taking my rig off the road. Getting' on home to hunker down."

Paul hadn't had to say much. It had given him a chance to think about his next move. He'd given the trucker a sob story about hitching in from Kenora. Said he was going to help his grandmother sandbag her little house.

"Where is she? Over in St. Boniface? I thought you looked kinda Frenchy. Fantastic," the guy had said. "I can put you down right on the corner of Fermor and St. Mary's Road. We'll be there in twenty minutes. You'll be almost on her doorstep. Say, does your grandma make an apple pie?"

She might. How'd I know? I never even met her, thought Paul. *She might.*

"Man, you are one lucky son of a gun."

"You betcha."

I guess I am, thought Paul.

He had dropped out of the cab at a red light on a busy corner. A bus marked #16 Osborne had come along to that corner within five minutes of the trucker pulling away. He'd hopped it because the girl (she'd told him her name was Georgie, but he wanted to think of her as *the girl*) had said, she'd said something about living near that coffee shop in the Osborne village, and he didn't know fuck all about Winnipeg. He'd taken the seat behind the driver so he could read the street numbers. They had been way the hell out. He had felt easier when they'd passed by a corner pub that he'd remembered seeing from their drive out to the old monastery. He'd leaned over and asked the driver how much farther to the Osborne village. "Comin' up in ten minutes or so" was the answer. The bus had rolled on past miles of three-story apartment blocks, the usual fast food places, past donut shops, gas bars, 7-Elevens, through an underpass, and up into the heart of the city.

Paul had stepped off the bus and into the same fancy coffee shop where he'd picked up the girl. No donuts here, so this time he took a blueberry muffin with his coffee and went over to sit on a stool at the counter in front of the window. This was good. He could watch the door and look out the window at the intersection easily. It had been a pretty busy corner for the middle of the day. He had watched people going in and out of the drug store, the bank, and the liquor store. No one had noticed him. The daily newspapers had been on the counter, so he'd looked through them. The news that the coming storm was set to hammer the Red River Valley had shared the front page with the report of a Native kid who had got swarmed and curb-stomped in gang-related violence. Singer Joni Mitchell had found her long-lost daughter, born in Toronto in 1965. No mention of a girl's body buried in the snow under a railway bridge.

He had picked up a bottle of rum at the liquor store across the street and asked the smiling security guard he saw outside for directions to Roslyn Road. Incredible fucking luck. It was one block away. He had headed for suite 14B, 21 Roslyn Road. It was a huge red-brick pile with turrets like a fortress and a green tiled roof. He'd slipped in the front door. It had been so easy he'd been laughing to himself. A young couple, both thin, both dressed completely in black, had passed by without looking at him. Fucking amazing! He'd found her apartment on the wing to the north of the central courtyard and, like she'd said, looking over the river.

Once inside, he'd set his tools on the doormat, locked the door from inside, put on the chain, and then eased his wet boots off and put them on the mat. Fuckers had been leaking bad. He was gonna hafta spring for new ones. Shucked his coat off and hung it on the inside doorknob. Jesus fucking Christ, he'd been cold, hungry, and tired. Lucky to be in where it was warm and dry. He'd taken his bottle out into the kitchen. The girl had had some Diet Cokes in her fridge. Lucky for her, because he was going to be in a bad mood if she didn't. He'd poured himself a big drink and looked through the fridge. There had been some leftover rice and other Chinese-type vegetable shit in a takeout container. Yoghurt, apples, wilted lettuce, carrots, brown bread, wrinkled potatoes with sprouts growing out of them, five eggs, skim milk, orange juice, tofu, and cheddar cheese. She must have been a goddam freaking vegetarian.

He'd found a pepperoni and cheese pizza in the freezer. Bingo! Not a vegetarian! He'd hucked that into the oven and gone to sit in the living room. He'd had a second and a third drink. He'd been hungry waiting for the pizza, so he'd rummaged through the fridge. He'd been really blasted on the rum, and that had felt fuckin'right, eh? He'd bitten off a big chunk of her cheese. It had been good. Cheddar. He'd chomped up about half the piece while the pizza cooked.

The ceilings in her apartment were very high, and the wooden floors had creaked with every step as he'd explored. If she'd had some cash hidden around the place, he was going to find it. There wasn't much furniture in her living room. A smallish red velvet couch with dark wood-carved feet, a 1950s brass floor lamp, an old TV sitting on the floor, and travel posters of some sunny beach stuck up on the wall. There were cold ashes in the old-fashioned green tiled fireplace. In the bay window overlooking the river, he'd seen a birdcage draped with a piece of blue cloth embroidered in gold with some kind of foreign letters. Maybe like Russian or something. He'd lifted the corner of the cloth and seen a little blue-feathered bird cowering on the floor of the cage.

"Hey, birdie." He'd said. "Polly want a cracker?" He'd made bright chirping sounds, and the parakeet had taken its beak out from under its wing. He'd spotted a package of birdseed on the window ledge and filled up the empty plastic dish that was fixed to the wire side of the cage.

"So she's got you in solitary, in the hole. You poor little guy, you need water too, don't you?" He'd carried the tiny plastic water basin to the kitchen, filled it, and carefully replaced it in the metal cage.

"Here you go. Let's see how you make out with that. Eat up, fill your belly, damn you. I want to hear you sing for your supper."

Her bedroom had been a real mess with clothes piled so high up on a chair he couldn't tell what colour it was. He'd found this disgusting. He could never live like that. He remembered how he had learned young that he had to keep his bunk neat.

A miniature dragon with a red bead in its mouth had been sitting right in the middle of her dresser. He had picked it up and thought about snatching it, but the little sucker was heavy. It was metal, not china. He'd put it down. She had made her bed; it was a futon, covered with a dark blue comforter and some frilly pillows and stuffed animals. One of those Indian dream catcher things of yarns and feathers had been hanging on the wall over the bed. Looked like an old spider web. Lots of Native guys he knew in the joint had them. They grew their hair long and got into that sweet grass mumble bullshit.

There had been a dark wooden desk and bookcase on the opposite wall. Most of the books looked like they were for school. Nothing he'd ever heard of. He'd picked the fattest one up from the top of the pile and flipped through the pages. That had been enough to give him a headache. Mostly writing, but with pictures of freaky people and stuff around the world. He had reached over, turned on her computer, and watched it boot up. A picture of Tom Cruise dressed in a vampire cape had come on the screen, and a dialog box requesting her password had appeared. He didn't know fuck-all about getting past that, so he'd gone to check on his pizza. The little blue bird had been cracking open the seeds now, and Paul had thought he looked a lot happier.

Some of the melted cheese had dripped on the oven racks because he hadn't been able to find a pan. The pizza had smelled great, and he'd managed to get the thing on a plate and hack it into four pieces. He'd carried the plate and another drink into the living room and put them on the floor in front of the couch. He'd put on the set and surfed through the channels until he'd found *The Simpsons*. Paul had watched that dumb asshole Homer fuck up again and scarfed down the pie. The dirty plate got dumped in the sink with the crushed Coke cans, and he had been so blasted he'd pissed in a high arc over all of it. His bottle had been almost empty and he'd been close to crashing. He'd felt great.

He'd pulled down his zipper of his jeans and loosened his belt buckle, being careful not to unfasten the silver earring with the pink stone that he'd pulled out of her pierced navel. He'd fallen asleep on her bed, rolled up in her comforter. It had been early, but he was used to early nights.

He'd almost shit himself when he'd woken up and saw where he had crashed. He'd thought he'd heard a knock at her door. Was it morning or night? The bedside clock had read 10:55. A brown velvet toy stuffed monkey with a red plaid vest and a black bow tie had been sitting beside it. The monkey had seemed to be grinning at him. He'd reached over and cuffed it, knocking it to the floor.

There had been another knock at the door. The second knock had been louder, more insistent. His heartbeat had sounded so loud in his ears it had seemed like his heart was about to jump out through his chest. Paul had felt in his pocket for his blade. Still there. Sharp prickles heated up his armpits.

A woman's voice had called out. "Hey Georgie, are you home? It's me. Chick. I saw your light on when I walked home last night. You sick or something? Why didn't you come to work? I froze myself coming over here lookin' to find you. Listen to your answering machine. I called you three times. Bruce is scorched. He's pissed about the storm 'cause he couldn't leave for Hawaii. And millions of people didn't return their freakin' tapes on time. It's hell out here. You might get fired. Call me. Later. At the store. After 3:00. I'm working late tonight, covering for you. I said you asked me to. Don't forget. Call Chick."

The clock on the bedside table had said 10:59 – a.m. or p.m.? He'd heard her footsteps go trip trapping down the hallway. He'd hunkered down and stayed like a stone until the hot prickling in his armpits had stopped. No more sounds had come from the hall. Fucking head was aching now. And he'd needed to piss.

He'd skated softly in his stocking feet down the hall to the can and taken a long piss in the bowl. A steady dark yellow stream. He'd blinked at his reflection in the white-framed mirror fronting the medicine cabinet over the sink. Same old badass there. He'd sniffed his armpits. He'd been rank. There had been a showerhead on a rubber hose coiled around the taps of the old relic of a tub. He'd stripped off his shirt and turned the water on. A weak spray had gurgled out. Not worth getting wet for. He'd walked over to look out the window. It was all white. He could see the back end of the Legislature building across the open river. The snow had been falling thick and fast. The wind had swirled it into drifts that covered the streets. A lone taxi had rolled over the bridge in the tracks made by a larger vehicle. He had been relieved to see that taxis were running. He could call one from the pay phone back at the corner.

He had put on the TV and flipped through to find the weather channel. He'd kept the sound down low. "Severe storm warning continues," the printing at the bottom of the screen had said. "Travel not advised," the announcer on the CBC had said. "Chaos in city streets as drifting snow blocks traffic. Thirty-seven inches of snow has fallen so far. The airport remains closed until further notice. Anyone with a four-wheel drive vehicle is requested to call the nearest police station to volunteer for emergency services driving."

The one smart thing he did was to move her. The snow would bury her and keep her hidden for a while. It would cover up the mess she'd made out on the ground at the old monastery when he'd moved her out of the car. Her blood had spread out around her head like a fiery crown on the snow. It was snowing. Fucking A. Give him time to figure out his next move.

He'd decided not to take a shower. It would take for fucking ever, and now he was thinking if he should get a room somewhere or head for a shelter. There must be a Sally Ann in this town. There were homeless and rubbies everywhere. He really hadn't wanted to bed down with the Lysol and hairspray crowd, but he had to watch his cash now or find some kind of work. Not what he'd had in mind. He was supposed to be on the way to Mexico. Wished he'd headed there a week ago. He had no driver's licence and no ID that wouldn't bring him a hassle at the border. He'd hidden his parole papers in the bottom of his toolbox and carried the social insurance card and birth certificate he had bought from that biker dude in the bar in Nanaimo. He needed a name he could get over the border with, be on his way to sunny Mexico and Pedro's farm. *No problemo.* Julian Russell. That's what he had to answer to. Buddy had guaranteed him this Julian fuck died as a baby. Who's the dickhead calls a kid Julian? Assholes! It was a hassle driving around without a licence.

He should have headed south right away. Not east. Fuck what Pedro had told him. Paul had heard the bikers say that there were lots of back roads in BC that you could slip over the border on. And keep on driving, straight on through to Mexico. This was a total fuckup. Paul liked boosting stuff. That was ace. Gave him a buzz that pumped him up. That little bitch had made him off her, and he hated her for it. The whole game was changed. He didn't want this. He'd never meant to kill her, for fuck's sake. He'd just wanted to get laid.

Paul had stared into his not-so-true blue eyes in the mirror and asked himself what the hell he was doing here in the fucking middle of the whole fucking country. He'd felt it, the hate rising in his gut like a river in flood. He'd pounded a good hard right shot straight at his reflection and hit the mirror dead on. His hand had been on fire, and blood had run back from his fingers. He'd smiled. He'd mouthed the word *asshole* at himself. Said softly, "You are one stupid asshole." He'd cradled his whole forearm in the tiny sink and run the cold water over it until it had numbed.

He had looked at his hair. It was shaggy shoulder-length at the back and short at the front. Hockey player hair. It would look better cut short. In the joint guys grew it long for many reasons. Like the Skins, they got into having it in one long braid, but for him, his hair length was pure laziness. Outside, long hair was more noticeable. He had looked in the medicine cabinet for scissors. He'd found a pair of manicure scissors and started to cut his hair off at his ear lobes. He'd dropped the wavy dark brown hanks into the toilet bowl and flushed each time the surface of the water had become covered. It had taken a while because he'd had to cut it in small sections. The result hadn't looked great. He hadn't been able to see the back. He wanted to shave his whole head. Better wait 'til it warms up. The tiny triangle of beard left directly under his mouth looked really stupid now. The girl hadn't had have any shaving gear in her cupboard. Stupid bitch. Didn't she know he was gonna need it?

A large colour photo of the girl standing with a man and woman on either side of her had been hanging on the wall opposite the mirror. In it, she'd looked about 12 years old. She'd had on a Native Indian costume and feathers in her braided hair. He'd thought maybe it was from Hallowe'en, but they were standing outside somewhere on grass that made it look like summer. He'd never guessed that she was a breed. Too pale. He'd thought maybe she was French. She did look like the mother, but the guy seemed too old to be her dad. All of them were smiling. But the girl was the only one who looked happy.

Paul had gone into the kitchen and looked through the fridge again. He'd taken out the eggs, milk, orange juice, and brown bread. He'd dug around in the cupboards for a pan and fixed himself a plate of breakfast. She didn't have no coffee in the place. He'd thought about washing the stack of dishes piled up in the sink and then thought better of it. That'd be too much like work, and it wasn't like she'd ever notice anyway.

He'd sacked out on the couch again with his legs hanging over the end, thinking about what to do until it got dark enough for him to leave. He'd had to be pretty fucking quiet, but he was used to that. Used to minding his own goddam beeswax. That was one of Charlie Hardwick's favourite sayings. Shame he'd had to miss the old man's funeral. Paul promised himself that the next time he saw a Legion Hall, he would go in and hoist a few beer in memory. Charlie would like that.

He had fallen asleep on the couch until he'd heard the phone ringing. The room had been in shadows. He'd listened as the answering machine picked up the call.

"Hi, Georgie," a soft male voice had said. "It's Uncle Markie. I thought I would find you snowed in like me and the rest of the city.

Wanted to know if you would pick up a couple of movies, come over, and keep me company. I have some of that great takeout butter chicken that you like from the Taj. Haven't seen you in a while. Wonder where you are now. Call me when you pick up this message. Okay. Bye-bye."

Paul had gone into the bedroom to check the time. It had been 4:57. Late afternoon. Like he'd thought. He'd picked up the little stuffed monkey and grinned back at it. He'd carried it down the hall to the front door and set it on his toolbox. Time to check out of this crib.

The place had been a lot messier than when he'd arrived, but the only clean-up he'd thought about doing was to go around and wipe his prints off everything he'd remembered touching. When he was on a job, he always wore gloves, but this had been different. He hadn't planned on ripping her off for any of her junk. He'd given more seeds and water to the little blue bird and covered him up again. *That might not last the little guy very long,* he'd thought. He'd dumped the rest of the box of seed out along the window ledge, turned back the cage's cloth cover, and opened the small wire door to the tiny cell. He'd never heard the little bird sing or even chirp. He'd decided to leave the girl's ID and keys on the table beside the bed. He had tucked the little toy monkey inside his jacket, then closed her front door quietly and headed down the stairs and along the street to the 24-hour drugstore to find a pay phone. "Chihuahua, Chihuahua, Chihuahua," he'd chanted, digging the way it sounded. "Choo, choo." Like he was a train gathering speed.

Winnipeg   April 13, 1997

Jake and Maud were in her childhood bedroom. They'd been carrying heavy boxes of her father's books and papers up from the basement for safekeeping. The sight of her four-poster canopied bed with its billowing girlish daisy-flowered duvet and skirts got him going.

He had Maud up against the closet door, his right knee parting her thighs and gently rubbing her pubic bone. Her face was in his hands, and they were hot kissing as she pulled his ass cheeks closer. He wrapped his arms around her, spun them 180 degrees, already thinking about walking her backwards over to the bed and quickly slipping it in. He was almost there. As he moved them past the door to the hall, ready to push it closed with his heel without breaking their embrace, he opened his eyes. Delia Fallon was standing on the threshold with clipboard in hand. She censured them with a cool glance.

Jake blushed. Colour bloomed upward from his chest and throat and stormed across his face and neck like a crimson meteor. He stepped away from Maud and turned his eyes to the maple floorboards. He heard a loud, dignified sniff from Mrs. Fallon. Then poof, she was gone.

Maud, bent double, hand over mouth, tugged on his arm. "Naughty, naughty," she whispered.

His blush was fading but not his annoyance. Busted. And Maud giggling and making big eyes at him. How could he win in this house?

He wasn't bitter about giving his only day off to helping Maud's mother prepare for the flood. Mrs. Fallon had asked him to be present, and, if necessary, to supervise while a Provincial Jail work gang did community service by laying sandbags for a dike along the river behind the family home on Kingston Row. He had no worries about his own parents, who were safely out of the floodwater's reach, up high and dry on the family farm near Altona. They had opened their hearts and the doors of their home to folks from the beleaguered town of Morris and made themselves so busy with flood relief work that he hadn't been able to speak with them in over a week.

Neither he nor Maud had any illusions as to why he had been invited to help. He found it a welcome distraction from the case that was in a stall while they waited for the body to thaw enough for autopsy. He hoped the pathologist would uncover some trace evidence that would lead to real results. Maud didn't seem to want to talk about the case either.

Before he'd even had his foot over her threshold, Mrs. Fallon had asked him if he was, as she put it, carrying a sidearm. "I understand that you are a fair marksman," she'd added. He knew that was faint praise. Delia Fallon did not approve of her daughter's work, nor of him. Jake had tried to please Mrs. Fallon but finally recognized that she would not permit that. It seemed she would barely tolerate him, and approval was out of the question.

Her vigilant blue eyes had followed his back as he carefully carried box after box of her late husband's books and papers up from the basement to the second floor bedrooms vacated by Maud and her brother, Liam. The entire contents of the main floor, including the appliances, had been moved out and into storage three days earlier, leaving only the ghostly footprints of chairs, tables, and the chesterfield on the broadloom. Mrs.

Fallon said she was pleased that she'd had the foresight to do that, "as you know, every moving truck in town is booked solid now."

She was in a poor humour because she was suffering from a flare-up of her shingles. This annual irritation was further inflamed by the city's request that she sign a no-liability waiver. "That Mayor is a nervy thing," she'd declared. The city was not so much as offering to help erect dikes. Mrs. Fallon had attended a seminar at the Fort Rouge Community Centre on the topic of dike construction and become an expert overnight. She had clipped a diagram of a correctly constructed dike out of the newspaper and secured it to a clipboard that she carried like a shield before her modest bosom.

"It will not do," she told them. "Our esteemed Mayor, that fool, thinks that having 240 works employees working twenty hours a day filling sandbags is adequate. It is not. Even at seven days a week, it will never do. The sooner the army is called in, the better for all of us."

The Fallons were among the residents of Kingston Row who had breached the secondary ring dike along their property so they could have an unobstructed view of the river. It was not advisable to remind Mrs. Fallon of that now.

The Fallons had come to Winnipeg from Dublin in the early '60s when Maud was 2 years old. Michael Fallon got tenure at University of Manitoba where he lectured on twentieth-century Irish poetry and gave an honours course on his personal favourite, W.B. Yeats. Their home overflowed with his students, who came to lounge on sofas in their library or, on warm days, out on the lawn by the river; listening to Fallon tell his stories of mystical love and Irish mythology, evoking the glamour of spiritual poets who made visions of unearthly beauty. Delia would watch from the sidelines and provide refreshments. Few knew she had been a promising scholar of history whose undefended doctoral thesis had been languishing in a leather-bound trunk in their attic since their son Liam was a toddler.

Delia rarely missed an opportunity to let it be known that Winnipeg's unforgiving climate was difficult for her. In her fine Dublin accent, she claimed the prairie winters had ruined her complexion. She took this year's threatening floodwaters as a personal affront.

Maud had tried to convince her to go back to Ireland for a holiday, but Delia would have none of that. Delia was adamant. Her sole diversion was voice coaching for the cast of the local Irish theatre company's productions. She said that she and Michael had talked of going together in his next sabbatical year, but now it was out of the question. How could she go back home alone? "What is more bitter than to recall happy times when you are low?" she often asked.

Delia did not approve of her daughter's line of work. It could hardly be much further removed from real nursing, could it? She termed it *déclassé*, meaning it was incompatible with her background. That word was a favourite, recalling associations she, Delia Heaney, had enjoyed through her family's rank in Dublin society. The Heaneys were well-known as cultured people. Distinguished academics. She had so frequently remarked that this police business, this Nancy Drew work was making Maud look older, harder than her years, that her comments now sailed by the ears of their intended target without remark.

Maud and Delia Fallon did not discuss Jake. Instead, Delia said, "I thought you would want to associate with educated people." She set high standards for what was worth accomplishing and what she classified simple amusing pastimes. Schoolboy achievements.

Maud was thankful that she had moved out of the family home while her dad was alive. It would be far more difficult to escape the obligations of that lacy motherly embrace now.

"My mother, bless her heart, is a tyrant," Maud had explained to Jake. "And an unhappy woman to boot. These days her sole topic of conversation with me is the institution of marriage and its perfections." Maud had given him a wry smile to indicate this was not her own view. Nor her father's; he would have said that she was entitled to make her own mistakes.

It troubled Maud that Jake and her mom were so cool to each other. She was angry with both of them, though more with Jake for not making any larger effort to charm Delia. He was being stubborn about it, and that made Maud wonder why, but she had not asked.

A flotilla of creamy cloud puffs sat at anchor in the blue yonder north of the city, out over the lake. The sun warmed Delia's shoulders and brought up the pungent smell of freshly turned earth. It confused the senses, made the threat of rising water seem less urgent. Overnight, the actual level of the river had crept up almost two more steps above the lower deck, and now the lapping water was a single step away – a mere 8 inches – from the upper level. Now it threatened to carry off her beloved vine-covered gazebo with its white wicker furnishings, including comfortable chairs, book-laden tables, a fern stand, and Delia's chaise lounge. She and Michael had retreated for their pre-prandial drinks and what they called "a few minutes of civilized conversation" to this island. The gazebo was her refuge now, where, with the day's cares blurred by a couple of stiff gins, she relaxed in a silent tête-à-tête with her late husband. No one, not even Maud, knew that she had buried a handful of his ashes there.

"We remain under siege," said Delia, gesturing toward the muddy waters. She furrowed her brow under her short, straight white bangs and licked her thin, dry lips. She had the Heaney family face, lean with a long-bridged pinched nose that looked as if she only inhaled.

Her determined, clear, blue-eyed gaze gave the impression that she imagined she could defeat the force of rising water through steadfast exercise of her will. Canute reincarnated.

She directed Maud and Jake to carry the furniture from the gazebo up onto the lawn close to the house and away from the provincial work gang that was piling sandbags under her direction. She declined to speak to them and gave her orders to their keeper, such was her displeasure in being at the uncertain mercy of exigent circumstances and having "criminals" on the property.

At ten minutes to 9:00, Jake pulled his car into the Forensic Science Centre's parking lot. A squad car and the Ident team's van occupied two of the six spaces reserved for police vehicles. He signed the visitors's book at the glass-enclosed counter and flashed his shield at the receptionist, a second cousin of his mother's, Audrey Klassen, who sat behind the front counter and presided over the comings and goings of visitors, the courier deliveries, and all telephone inquiries.

Audrey was yakking away with officers – Shier and Morales, the uniforms who had attended the frozen girl's crime scene – about the local newspapers's misinformed coverage of the story. This murder was not a big enough story to knock the flood news off the front page. Jake listened to Shier discussing the latest report that the heavy-equipment operators (and Shier's brother was one, so he had it on good authority) were under such intense government pressure that they were working around the clock to build the new Z-dike near Brunkild to protect Winnipeg's western flank. ASAP. The job was so urgent that they were not given work breaks, and it was expected that they urinate into bottles. It was more of a brag than a complaint. After all, they were getting double overtime every shift.

Jake went directly upstairs. He knew the uniforms had come in early to meet the pathology staff at the morgue. In compliance with the need for a secure chain of evidence, Shier and Morales retained the key to the wire cage in the main morgue, where the girl's body had been secured over the weekend. Now that the body was on the table, they were delaying going in to witness the autopsy. Jake really didn't blame them. The sights and smells were hard to get used to. The nauseating odour of blood. The shockingly bright cheap-margarine-yellow of body fat. And especially the cloying odour of formalin, present like an invisible fog in the autopsy suite's cool air.

Dr. Jeremy Langdon was already suited up in operating room greens. He was talking with Maud and making notes on his clipboard. "Is this it?" he demanded when he saw Jake. "What time are the rest of your crowd going to be here?"

"The scene officers are on their way up, and Ident is ready to go, I see." Jake nodded his head at Sawatsky and Petrie, who were busy at a side table organizing their camera gear, notepads and labels, and plastic evidence bags.

"Do we know who she is?" Langdon asked.

"Not yet," said Sawatsky. "I'm ready to print her as soon as you give the go-ahead."

"Not so fast," Langdon murmured, "not so fast. First things first. Are you sure she's thawed enough to begin?"

"Yes, guv," said Robert Ferguson. The diener poked the girl's right deltoid muscle with a gloved finger to prove his point.

Jake thought her body looked paler, slighter now, laid out on the stainless steel autopsy table. The plastic shroud, the cotton sheet, and the blue tarp had already been bagged and labelled for closer examination. Her left hand was crossed over her right, and her left foot over her right. Yellow polypropylene rope bound each set of limbs. The knots were simple bowlines. There were faint indentations and minimal abrasions under the ligatures. She looked so young, so cold under the concentrated beam of the bright arctic light of operating room lamps.

"Where is the permission?" Langdon scowled at Maud as she handed him the official paperwork that requested the post-mortem examination in legalese. He had slept poorly last night. Was it the leftover lasagne he had snacked on before bed or the thought of this morning's first case that troubled him? A mystery. He had woken before 6:30 from a dream in which Her Royal Majesty, Queen Elizabeth, sitting at the table in his breakfast nook, ravenously ate a sticky bun while she complained to him that she detested her husband's smile. The Prince stood by watching. He was dressed in a Boy Scout uniform. Did the dream suggest that he should go back to Avonwick to see his old mam? He would have to page Dr. Freud. That had been the end of his dream and his sleep.

"Is there any requirement that you girls dress in black?" he asked Maud in an aggrieved tone. "Every day I see you here, you look like an Italian widow. Never out of mourning."

"You're right, Jeremy, I am not," Maud agreed dryly. "But I'll let you in on a secret," she said. "I'm only wearing black until they come out with something darker."

Langdon snorted out a suggestion of a laugh.

They watched as R.F. and the other diener cut the ligatures, straightened the girl's limbs, and removed her clothing. She, too, was dressed in dark clothing: a knee-length charcoal-coloured men's overcoat and a black scarf with a design in maroon paisley. No gloves. Two black sweaters, a long black woollen skirt, and a black sports bra. Her badly torn black tights were pulled down below her buttocks. Constable Sawatsky photographed every step of this unveiling. Each article was wrapped in brown butcher's paper and labelled. The clothes would be dried and examined at the department's forensic lab.

Her silver-coloured chain and nickel-sized medallion enamelled with the black-and-white yin-yang symbol and her dangling silver filigree oval-shaped earrings were noted, photographed, and removed.

"Those earrings look rather Celtic in design, don't they?" Langdon said. "And see this, too." He indicated a band of intricate tattooing that encircled her right upper arm. "That's a Celtic type pattern, as well." He jotted that detail on his blank set of autopsy records. *Tattoo on right upper arm, in greenish ink, approximately 3 inches above the elbow, Celtic pattern in a 1-inch wide band encircling entire arm.*

"What percentage of the young cases we see now have some form of tattoo?" he asked. "I think it's got to be close to 40 per cent. Both of my boys have one. Giles has a big green scorpion on the back of his calf, and Rod has a band something like this girl's on his arm. They call themselves the *bod-mods,* while I say they are members of the Tattoo nation, the sons and daughters of us Baby Boomers, the Birkenstock nation." He laughed and pointed to his shoes.

"Or maybe they're the Download generation, the Downloaders," he added. "That would describe my lot. They can spend the whole bloody night on that Internet."

He asked R.F. for the height and weight and said, "She doesn't look that chunky. Are you sure you make it 59 kilos?"

R.F. gave him an exasperated look. He had little tolerance for Langdon's habit of second-guessing. He thought that, by now, his uncompromising attention to detail would go unquestioned.

"Want it done again, guv?" The dieners were already reaching under the girl's shoulders and ankles to swing her body back on a stretcher to be taken to the scale.

"Never mind." Langdon dismissed them with a wave. "She's pretty tall though, isn't she? Did you say 180.3 centimetres?" He went back to his notations. "Never mind, boys. I'm merely thinking out loud."

Her hair was clotted with dried blood. A rivulet of it ran dark down her right temple and into her ear. Langdon delicately palpated the dense mat of bloodied hair over her right temple.

"This feels promising," he muttered. He recorded that her hair was dyed jet black.

Jake was also taking notes. He recorded the start time of the examination and the names and ranks of all present and Langdon's remarks as the external examination of the body continued. He had swapped his navy blazer for a long yellow isolation gown and was busily mimicking Langdon's notations on a cadged set of schematic drawings of anterior and posterior views of a human figure.

"Slow down, boys," Langdon said to the dieners. "I need a consult with the forensic dentist."

There were the bite marks around the pale pink nipples on each breast. The police officers present all took a step forward while Langdon's Bic pen hovered over the four semicircles as he traced their incomplete outlines. No one spoke for a few moments as they contemplated the nasty looking marks.

"All you guys have to do is connect the dots to the right guy's mouth and bingo, you'll have your man," said Langdon. He turned to Maud. "We do need a dentist. Will you call Dr. Scurfield and find out if he can come and how long it will take?"

He turned back to the body on the table. "Too bloody early to break for lunch, isn't it? Let's keep on with the external examination."

There was remarkably little to see. Lividity was present. It was pink in tone. Exactly as expected, given she was found in the cold. It was fixed in a pattern that indicated she had been placed on her left side for maybe about eight to twelve hours after her death. No scars. R.F. pointed out a perforation in the fold of skin above her navel. And a fresh tear from the tiny hole and right through the fold of skin. There was no ring in it now. Not surprising. Did her killer take it as a trophy? Jake moved in for a closer look.

Maud watched Jake's face as he looked at these twin discoveries: bite marks and the tear. His lips curved up slightly in a suggestion of a smile as he made notes. She knew that meant he was concentrating and that he was pleased by the discovery of these carnal wounds. Something else to work with. One more piece of the unsolved puzzle, like the boot print found in the snow at the scene. She found this evidence, and Jake's reaction to it, frightening and disgusting. She knew he would say that she needed to adopt an objective stance to the bites, but she could not. Bitterness sharp as the taste of tin flooded her mouth. The girl had died because she had angered a man.

Maud wondered if other women felt as uneasy as she sometimes did about the potential for damage that lurked below the surface of their lives with men. Did they ask themselves, as she did, whether some marginal evidence of cruelty in an otherwise good man represented an aberration or the tip of an iceberg?

The bites, the tear would not have been painful, she reminded herself. Dr. Langdon said the wounds appeared to have been made post mortem, and his cytological examination would support that opinion. She went out to R.F.'s office to call Dr. Harvey Scurfield. He was in his operatory, his receptionist said. She waited until he came on the line.

Maud knew forensic odontology was more than a hobby for Scurfield. He taught the basics of the subject to the dental school undergraduates. His protocol for analysis had set the gold standard in the field when he published it early in the '90s, and his expert opinion was in high demand by Crown counsels and the defence bar in jurisdictions from St. John's to Victoria.

He answered Maud in calm, precise tones. It would take approximately one hour for his examination. They agreed to book his examination to follow the autopsy.

Maud went back into the morgue to tell Langdon about the arrangement.

"Okay then, boys," said Langdon to the dieners. "Let's finish the external."

They rolled the girl over and held the body balanced on her side to allow Langdon to see the back. There was general silence in the room when she was turned back and Langdon rotated her left leg outward and pointed out the lettering. **No matter what happens I love you Waylon Spence** was written in blue ballpoint pen on the medial surface of her left calf. A line in the same blue ink encircled the words so it looked like a cartoon character's speech. Or like a dark edged cloud. Sawatsky stepped in front of the doctor to record that final message on film. It was enough to break any human heart.

"*Spence,*" said Langdon. "Isn't that a Native name?"

"Yes," Jake said, "it may be. Often is. There's a lot of them up around in the Interlake."

"Okay, everybody see that?" asked Langdon. "She doesn't look Native, does she? Rather pale, eh?" He took a probe and lifted her right eyelid to check the colour of the irises. They were dark brown. "You can't tell with these people nowadays. Could be treaty for all I know."

"Heads up, friends," cautioned R.F. "Look out for low-flying stereotypes."

"Well, then, how about the 'off-white people'? Do you prefer that? Off-white people. Is that politically correct enough for you?"

No one offered any further comment on Langdon's theory. No one said aloud that this murder was non-Native in character. Those murders typically involved knives and alcohol and, generally speaking, were within the family circle. The victims did not turn up gift-wrapped in a blue plastic tarp under a railway trestle. Everyone knew that these were politically incorrect views and, if one supported them, it was prudent to keep quiet.

Langdon decided they ought to break for lunch while they waited for the last of the freezing to go from the girl's torso. R.F. removed his mask, gloves, and scrub gown. He draped the long green gown over the girl's body, covering her from head to ankles. Only her long, slim, pale feet were visible. The pathology staff and police witnesses agreed to exit together and lock her body inside with a single guard at the door.

Maud went upstairs to the staff lounge and made herself a fresh cup of drip coffee. She drank it there while leafing through one of the back issues of *People* magazine and eating a slightly stale Mars bar from the stash of snack foods she kept in her bottom desk drawer. She wished she had prepared herself a tasty lunch. Why was she so indolent, so disorganized? As usual, none of the other investigators were present, all of them either out on a case or off duty. There was no one to listen to her complain about life. Or to mooch food from. She considered sending out for a club sandwich but did not, as she felt confident that it would arrive at the moment she was called back to the autopsy suite.

She kicked her shoes off and stretched out on the couch. *You cannot have it all,* she cautioned herself, *but sometimes a nap is all you need.* She fell asleep instantly and was in dreamland when something began tickling her in the ribs. She rolled over and reached for the pager vibrating in the depths of her sweater pocket. She took a look at the number on the LED display and returned to the morgue.

"Okay." Langdon gestured to the dieners. "Let's get a move on. Floodwaters are rising, the cooler is full of bodies, and I have a planning meeting on the other side of the river at 2:30 sharp. Somebody flip on the down draft. Please. And Mr. Ferguson, let's begin."

R.F. proceeded to take six swabs each from the girl's oral, anal, and vaginal orifices. Scrapings were taken from under her black painted fingernails. He plucked hairs from her head and pubis, which was combed to recover any foreign hair. Constable Sawatsky took possession of all these specimens.

"Pubic hair feels slightly crunchy," R.F. said. "I'll take some more swabs in case there is something else. No bruising, however. It doesn't look like she was interfered with."

He turned to ask Maud. "Or have girls started using hair gel on that part of your anatomy?"

"I speak only for myself and the answer is no," she said. In the background, she could hear Ella Fitzgerald snaking her way through "Ain't Misbehavin" on the department's sound system. Then there was the harsh plangent grating of metal on metal as R.F. put his knives to the sharpening steel. She shuddered.

"Cold?" asked R.F.

"No. It's that sound. It gets to me, every time, like fingernails on a blackboard."

R.F. grinned and carried on with the honing to finish up with a symphony conductor's flourish.

Constable Petrie stepped in to take a full set of finger and palm prints. He asked young constable Angie Morales to run them downtown for a rush comparison. You never knew, they might get lucky with identification. Morales had spent most of the past hour intently examining her notebook at the desk near the door with her back to the room. She gave him a small happy smile at the prospect of a task that would take her away from her unwelcome assignment as invigilator.

R.F. used a 5 c.c. syringe to withdraw samples of vitreous fluid from both eyes. At the same time, Langdon took up a right-handed #4 scalpel and made the standard large Y-shaped incision that opened the body up from stem to stern.

He began to remove the breastplate, ripping through the costal cartilages with a rib hook, while R.F. withdrew specimens of urine, peripheral blood, and bile. Once the breastplate was lifted out and set aside on the body's thighs, he drew cardiac blood. Tim Petrie assisted with the labelling of all these specimens that would be submitted for toxicological analysis.

Langdon then dissected the bowel out from the duodenum all the way down, stopping barely distal to the ligament of Treitz. He took samples of breast tissue and a section of lumbar spine for a bone marrow specimen. Langdon carried the plumb to the end of the table and began to reverse and reflect the aorta away from the oesophagus. He was singing softly now in counterpoint to the jazz piano coming over the speakers, and some of the words to his song echoed in Maud's memory. *Bang, bang, Maxwell's silver hammer came down upon her head. Bang, bang, Maxwell's silver hammer made sure that she was dead.* She gave him a look, and he stopped mid-phrase.

All Maud could hear in the room now was Oscar Peterson at the piano and, at irregular intervals, R.F.'s soft burr as he called out the weight of the specimens. Langdon sectioned and checked the tissues for unusual features. He measured the thickness of their walls, made cuts in the coronary arteries every 2 millimetres, and put samples from each organ into the twin jars of 4 per cent buffered formalin that would fix the specimens and avoid development of artefact. A good-sized chunk of liver and the stomach contents were examined and plunked into separate white plastic containers identical to the ones takeout foods go home in. These would be labelled and frozen for future analyses.

Maud started toward the door of the morgue. Jake raised his eyebrows as she passed him. She did not speak, merely shrugged her shoulders. They had not seen each other or spoken since late Sunday night.

Jake remembered that Maud's mood had seemed down as they'd kissed goodnight last Sunday. He'd asked her if she was thinking about the murdered teenager, though all she'd said about it was "You can sing of a king's death, not a child's." He didn't get it. It sounded like Shakespeare, didn't it? He had no idea. He was preoccupied with the known and the unknown in the case and how far apart these poles were.

Dr. Langdon continued to hum softly as he weighed, examined, and sampled every organ. "A lovely, healthy young thing, wasn't she?" he remarked to the others. "What do you think? A student, maybe?"

No one responded.

R.F. put her head up on the block. He gently and carefully washed away all the dried blood from her hair. The visible damage was confined to the right side. He made his incision behind the right ear just below midline and carried through across the top of the skull to the left side. He lifted the scalp free of the skull and began to reflect it forward down over her pale face. He used a clamp to stabilize the head and then cut through the calvarium twice with a butcher's hacksaw and removed the bone skullcap with a surgical mallet and chisel.

"Take a gander at this," he called to Langdon. All the observers crowded round.

Langdon reflected the dura, cut the carotids and spinal cord at the base of the cerebellum, and lifted out the brain. He gingerly examined and weighed it.

"Cut or fix?" asked R.F.

"Fix."

R.F. ran a length of cotton thread under the major vessels and suspended the brain in a plastic pail of formalin to rest for two weeks until it was suitable for sectioning.

"There is your answer, lads," said Langdon, gesturing at the bloody empty brain box. "Severe craniocerebral trauma." All crowded in to see what he would later describe formally as a circular depressed fracture over the right temporal-parietal suture.

Quepos, Costa Rica   April 16, 1997

Rona Kay-Stern paid Ishmael the four dollars in U.S. funds. Four singles. The minimum charge for using the Internet at the International House of Pancakes in Quepos. She counted them into his pink-palmed, grimy left hand. He grinned and bobbed his head in thanks, his dreadlocks writhing in the stifling air like Medusa's locks. Rona was relieved to see that he was not doing the cooking. The thought of those braids waving over the stove was nauseating. The culinary duties were the province of his cherubic, bronze-skinned wife, Eugenie, a *zaftig* gal who was singing joyfully in Spanish over her batters.

Ishmael and Eugenie had come from San Francisco. "Long ago now," they said in unison. Their café was crowded for its hearty breakfasts served out on the narrow cement-floored patio at the side of their house. It closed for lunch and re-opened at dinner. When Rona had asked, Eugenie was vague about the time and the menu for the evening. "We do offer a special every day," she'd said. "Depends," she'd added with a laugh. "Who can say what will be provided?"

The Internet access was set up on an old kitchen countertop in what must be their living room when the café was closed. On three sides of the room were low, hard couches arranged in what Rona thought of as waiting-room style. They were upholstered in turquoise vinyl and softened by fabric-covered pillows in African prints that featured elephant heads and giraffes running through grassland. Fearsome-looking dark wooden masks glared down from dull gold-coloured walls. Black and brown zebra stripe draperies hung from floor to ceiling and screened off the back half of the room.

Ishmael swanned back and forth between the folds of these drapes with menus and trays of water glasses and cutlery. Eugenie herself came out to mark down the food orders with a rundown pencil on a notepad made of stapled-together paper scraps. She looked her customers straight in the eye and nodded her approval of their selections. She greeted all she knew with a beaming face and a cry of "Let me hug you up!" These regulars were clamped to her bosom with a delight that made other customers feel second-class. They spoke in jargon like some esoteric religious cult.

Rona overheard them talking about Gurdjieff and sufistic dancing. *Sunnies rather than moonies,* she thought. While she waited for her turn at the computer, Rona watched a thin 20-something *Québécois* who was typing at a furious pace. When stuck for a word, he rhythmically slapped his bare tanned thighs, right hand over right thigh, left hand over left, and sang *merde, merde, merde,* running up and down a familiar scale as if trying to harmonize with himself. She remembered seeing him the day before with a group of kids at the kayak rental place on Manuel Antonio Beach.

He took so long, Rona had to ask to use the bathroom. It was surprisingly clean, though she knew her standards had shifted after seven months in the Third World. The rough stucco walls around her were a rich, vibrant pink. It was like being inside a watermelon. She examined her angular tanned face in the mirror. No major damage visible after months of tropical sunlight. She wet the tip of her index finger on her tongue and smoothed her high arched eyebrows. She had let her hair go while they were travelling. It had grown out to grey at the temples.

Ben had cut it once, and now it was grazing her shoulders again. She had lost 10 pounds over the winter and looked slender in her long cotton skirt. She admired her full breasts and smoothed her pale blue t-shirt over them. She pulled out the tortoise shell combs that held her hair and twisted it back with her hands into a French roll. She turned around and examined the back of her head by looking into the mirror over her right shoulder. Maybe she would try that look. She winked at herself in the mirror. *Not bad for a 51-year-old,* she thought.

As soon as they'd crossed the border into Costa Rica, she had felt safer. It was a relief not to worry about the drinking water. She felt content, happier perhaps than she'd imagined she'd be. She had slowly worked out a routine in this nomadic sabbatical year, where every familiar comfort was absent. She kept her journal and sketched and helped Ben as much as he wanted, which was little. She missed her studio and kiln and Georgia Lee, but it was good to get away with Ben after long, dutiful years of parenting. It wasn't like when they were first together, the hot and heavy early years. Now it was mellow and rich and tender between them.

Rona had persuaded Ben to have brunch at the cyber café so she could check her e-mail. She hoped for one from Georgia Lee, at home in Winnipeg, far away in frozen Canada. When she got online, it took only seconds to see there was nothing from their daughter. She sat trying to calm herself, recalling that she and Ben had agreed, as he said, to back off and let their daughter live her own life while they were away. Georgia Lee had refused their offer of a gap year in Israel, saying, "That's only a really big reservation for Jews, isn't it?" She had quite a mouth on her.

They'd set Georgia Lee up in her own funky apartment before they'd left Winnipeg early in September. Ben had a full sabbatical year from his position as department head in Anthropology, and they had spent these first months, as planned, touring aid projects in Belize, Honduras, and Nicaragua. All places associated, in Rona's mind and now in her experience, with life lived not without dignity but under primitive and chaotic conditions unlike anything she'd ever seen.

Costa Rica was their last stop, a chance to relax. And though Ben was working on his notes, it felt like a holiday. Or, more accurately, a working holiday. This was a designation that Ben enjoyed. "We live in oxymoronic times," he'd declared. They'd rented a small white stucco bungalow – set in a riotously coloured garden of tropical plants outside the town of Quepos – that had a primitive kitchen and a functional bathroom. It did not matter. Rona liked drowsing in the hammock with the afternoon breeze clicking in dry palm fronds, marking time. They had managed their money easily in the Third World and now had lunch and dinner out each day and a more varied diet. Not beans and rice, rice and beans, beans, rice, rice, beans.

She could see her husband out on the patio of the cyber café hunched over one of his notebooks on the glass-topped table amid the leavings of their brunch. She wished she'd brought her sketchbook. She would love to capture him now with his bull neck and square Roman skull rising above the collar of his shirt. He had a heavily muscular torso and short, powerful arms and legs that ended in wide square feet. His balding head was deeply tanned, and his broad shoulders were prominent under the thin fabric of an old white dress shirt stretched tightly over his back. His longish white fringe of hair and full beard marked him as a man in his early 60s. In his 63rd year, to be precise.

She hurriedly sent an e-mail to her brother Mark at his office. She tried for a casual tone. "Have you seen our little *bubeleh*?" she wrote. And added, "You know, NO NEWS IS NOT GOOD NEWS FOR

MOTHERS." He had promised to be in contact with Georgia Lee every week. Mark was not an ideal choice as guardian for their daughter, but as their only close relative in Winnipeg, he was their obvious option. And his condo was only a few blocks from her apartment. To delay telling Ben that Georgia Lee had not written, she looked up the Winnipeg weather. She knew that this would please him, both the idea that she could easily find their hometown newspaper's web page and the sweet knowledge that the temperature in Winnipeg was in the minus range. That their city was firmly in the cold grip of winter while they idled in the sun. She knew it intensified his pleasure to know that they were escaping the city's familiar communal miseries, that they were not among its shivering citizens with their nostrils frozen together. Granted a reprieve from block heaters and wind chill.

"How sweet it is, he'd said." His delight in having twelve months of warm weather was constant. He'd announced that this suited him. "I've always thought that, psychologically, I needed to experience the four seasons. I am happy to acknowledge," he'd added, "that I was wrong."

Why hadn't Georgia Lee written? Rona made up a list of possible reasons for the absence of the promised weekly letter. Too bogged down with end-of-term reading or papers? Was there a new boyfriend? All she wanted for her girl was the best. She was young. Hadn't turned herself inside out for love. Where was her cousin Waylon Spence? In Japan? Rona had agreed to go on sabbatical partly because she'd known he was going to be away from Winnipeg, too. Him and his fast motorcycle gone, gone.

There had been a nine-day gap in their communication over the Christmas break when Georgia Lee had a bad dose of the flu. Rona was so worried that she'd sent Mark over to check. Ben had downplayed her anxieties then, too. He'd been right. *A silence can mean any number of things.* Rona told herself to consider only innocuous reasons. An 18-year-old should be, was, capable of looking after herself.

Rona mentally reviewed Georgia Lee's daily schedule. The weather network had reported that that Winnipeg's skies were clear; the temperature was a tolerable −1 degree Celsius with a predicted overnight low of −3. Daylight saving time was making Georgia Lee's mornings brighter. The snow the blizzard had dumped on the city ten days ago had quickly melted, and the annual threat of spring flooding was under daily appraisal. Dikes were being constructed, and the swollen Red River was reported to be an ominous sight as it flowed toward the Manitoba border. The potential for a deluge of biblical proportions was greater this year, due to the heavy rains that had supersaturated the ground late in the previous fall.

Rona imagined Georgia Lee dressing in layers to walk from her apartment over the bridge across the frozen river, past the statue of Taras Shevchenko brooding over the side lawn of the Legislature grounds − a lone crow perched on one of his thick white epaulets of snow − and on to her classes at the university. She imagined her daughter in long underwear decorated with hearts and flowers covered by two sweat tops, skinny-legged blue jeans, her down-filled parka, tuque, mitts, and a scarf tied over her mouth. The sky was clear and bluer than any sea, that clear prairie light seen only in the winter cold.

Mothers can't know everything, and Rona didn't know that Georgia Lee had reinvented herself soon after her parents had left town. Changed her name to Georgie. Cut her hair in a chin-length bob with short bangs and dyed it jet-black. Long black skirts and black sweaters had replaced jeans and sweat tops. Casual went punk. A dime-sized silver hoop set with a piece of rose quartz dangled from her pierced navel. Doc Marten boots replaced moccasins. An old grey Persian lamb coat from a thrift store topped off her new look. Value Village chic.

Her extra-curricular activities had changed, too. No more dance classes at the old church on River Avenue. Now it was dancing at Die Machine (the after-hours club in the Village) and, most weekends, a session of theatre improv with the new friends she'd met through Chick Fontaine, the skinny platinum blonde who worked with her at the video rental store kitty-corner from the coffeehouse at River and Osborne.

Chick had the palest skin; you couldn't see anything Native about her. She'd said it was her grandmother who was Métis, and she liked that. "I'm like a long-lost cousin to Louis Riel." It was cool. She was an art school student, and she had made dozens of videos, including a series on the seven deadly sins. Georgie had starred in the one about lust.

Rona looked out through the doorway again. The intense sunlight bleached the patio of colour; she had to squint to see Ben. Now his body appeared foreshortened, his face in deep shadow. He was engrossed in deciphering and transcribing his handwritten notes, an onerous task usually accomplished by his patient secretary, Helga Neustaedter, who could easily turn what he called his "snail trails" into intelligible English. Rona watched him tapping away on his laptop for a minute or two before she went to tell him that there was no word from their Georgia Lee. She had not written since April 5th. Eleven days ago.

He looked up, and she felt his deeply set golden eyes assessing her. Could he see the ache that sat behind her breastbone?

Rona knew that if she brought up the topic of returning home earlier than planned for Passover, Ben would refuse to discuss it. Before they left Winnipeg, they'd debated the fact that, in this sabbatical year, they would be away from home for all the major holidays. September 1996 to June 1997. It was only one year of many.

"We'll take a year off," he'd said. "In circumstances like these, the Lord forgives."

"What do you care?" she'd countered. "Aren't you an atheist?"

"I am not interested. As you know, other concerns shape my life, my world. Rationality should be your guiding force, not religious superstitions." She knew Ben prided himself on the limits he placed on his Judaism. He had reduced it to a loose cultural affiliation of humanistic traditions and seasonal feasts.

He'd smiled at her and continued. "You won't be able to find any *matzah* in San Jose. No matzah, no *charoset,* no *gefilte* fish with fresh *chrane,* no carrot *tzimmes,* no *farfel* kugel, no *chremsleh* with prunes inside, no compote, no macaroons, no Red Rose tea with lemon, no nothings. That sounds like a punishment worse than the ten plagues, doesn't it? But you do realize that you cannot carry your house with you on a trip like this."

That was his way: to smile and look away from her sorrows. These discussions had been going on for the full extent of their married years. Twenty-seven years of compromise but no real consolation. She knew that she was not being entirely fair. Not realistic. No one thing could fulfil all her needs. He usually listened patiently as she talked about her feelings. He gave as much as he had, and when his sympathies were exhausted, he became quiet. She knew he cared.

Ben knew Rona believed that he did not understand her. What he did not understand – and he knew this – was her need to factor her sorrow into every day of her life.

He had two fine sons from his first marriage. Avi and Lior were strong like their mother, Rivka. Neither of them needed any mothering from Rona. Over the intervening years, the boys were polite but aloof on the rare occasions when they were all together. They had made *aliyah* to Israel with their mother twenty years ago.

He had found a refuge in Canada and made a new life with Rona. There was no point in looking back, no point in missing other places, other people. When he accepted the job offer from the Winnipeg university, he'd thought he was going to a place so remote from New York; it would be like being in exile on the Russian Steppes. To his delight, it was like being on a bustling island in a golden sea of wheat. He'd loved it from the first day of sunshine.

That Rona was unable to bear a living child did distress him for her sake. Being barren had a deeper meaning for her. She said she was not a real woman. The potent spirits of their two unnamed stillborn sons lingered in the shadows of their marriage bed. Two pale wraiths that mocked their union. And she longed for them, her lost babes. Born asleep.

Ben was interested in finding workable solutions. That tenet was central to his carefully drawn *Weltanschauung*. He was a product of his 1960s doctorate from Columbia University, and he fully endorsed the All-American idea that know-how and a can-do mind-set will overcome any obstacle. He had appreciated that their problem required a solution and embraced the most viable, and then currently popular, option suggested. He'd proposed that they adopt a child. This had seemed to him to constitute a form of *tikun olam* – the repair of the world. A restoration of balance.

A number of his colleagues at the university had promoted the idea of adopting aboriginal children from bleak inner-city houses or the northern reserves. They firmly believed that this was a good thing, offering the benefits of the middle class and making a safe home for children who otherwise would lead impoverished lives. These earnest professors had hoped to strengthen the birth communities by fostering a generation of leaders who would use their talents to help their own kind. Native communities were to be helped like Third World countries. It was an avenue for social change that appealed to the domesticated '60s radicals now safely ensconced in tenured positions on pacific Canadian campuses.

He did not imagine then that Rona would live in constant fear that something would happen to their child. He did not know that that child would be the centre of their world.

She was eight days old when she came to them. The little girl they named Georgia after Ben's favourite song, *Sweet Georgia Brown*. That was the first song he'd learned to whistle successfully. He did it to annoy Cousin Moishe, his aged guardian who detested popular music. Lee was her English name for the Hebrew Leah. She looked a little like Rona, whose Russian ancestry was evident in her broad, high Slavic cheekbones and crimped black hair. Strangers who noticed Georgia Lee's warm olive skin and dark hair presumed that she and Ben were her natural parents. "Why didn't your mom give you any of her curls?" they asked.

The illusion of likeness had lasted until she was 12 and puberty brought her its astonishing changes and indications of her aboriginal ancestry. Over her teenage years, her skin tone had faded to tan, and she'd grown tall enough to look down on both of them. She had developed a graceful way of carrying herself thanks to her dance lessons and had grown her straight hair down to her waist.

After learning she was adopted, Georgia Lee had informed Ben and Rona that she was finished with Hebrew school. "There is no point in going," she'd told them in a new, definite tone of voice. She'd said she didn't know who she was, but she knew she was not Jewish. There would be no *bat mitzvah*. Voices were raised, and hot accusations made. Rona had had the menu for the *oneg* after the *bat mitzvah* planned, and all her friends were scheduled to bake their specialities for the pastry table. She'd make her delicious *Shmoo* torte. It was world famous all over Winnipeg.

Rona would not admit, even to Ben, though he certainly knew, that she had been living out her fantasy. It didn't feel that way to her. It was her private dream. She was so accustomed to her version of their story that she almost forgot it was not the only one. Not the true one. Georgia Lee's birth story could not be completely erased. Rona had always agreed to tell their daughter the truth – but not just yet. She wanted the timing of the revelation of her daughter's origins to be perfect. So perfect, with her Jewish identity so well-ingrained, that there would be no thought of her seeking anything, anyone else.

Ben had intervened, and a cool truce was made over the roiling, sulk-filled chasm of regrets and resentments that could not be spoken aloud. He shuttled between them: talking with Georgia Lee in early evening over a game of chess, then later translating selected bits of their conversation to Rona under their warm covers, then back to Georgia Lee next evening and so on as he blessed each with generous portions of love. These dialogues continued every day for weeks. Or was it months?

Georgia Lee had convinced Ben that she needed to see her adoption papers. When she'd found out that old truth, that her mother was Ruby McKay, a Cree girl who had moved to a city she had never seen with a dream as big as Winnipeg, Georgia Lee had asked to visit the reserve at Footprint Lake. Ben had taken her the following spring. Rona had refused to go with them.

They'd found some remnants of Georgia Lee's birth family: a granny, her mother's uncle, a few cousins, and an aunt who remembered that her beautiful niece Ruby had had a child in Winnipeg. None of them had thought about that baby in many years. They did not recall that the child was a girl.

Her granny's eyes had filled with tears – dark brown, almost black, soft eyes moist with her sorrows made fresh again.

"After a while . . ." the aunt had said, "well, not to say, you forget. You keep it deep in your heart." She'd smiled at Georgia Lee. "We would have loved you if we knew where you were. We never saw you." They did not know the name of her father.

Ruby had been dead for thirteen years by then. She'd gotten drunk and sniffed up and was found frozen in a snow bank outside her own front door on her 22nd birthday. Harvey Spence, the band councillor, who had added this last piece of information, also told Georgia Lee that her mother had been a lively girl who had made friends with the wrong crowd. She had gone south to Winnipeg to study at the beauty school on Portage Avenue. That was all they knew. Georgia Lee already knew the space for a father's name was left blank on her birth certificate. Not literally blank, but the word *unknown* had meant the same thing to her. She'd never felt half so lost as she did then. That's what she told Ben. "I'm a lost member of a lost tribe."

After the autopsy was described in meticulous detail and the final diagnosis given, the case stalled out. Nothing more came from the scene investigation. The Ident staff took all the specimens to the forensic lab, where they joined the very lengthy queue of exhibits awaiting analysis. Estimated wait time: six months. Sawatsky and Petrie carefully stored the casts of the boot print in the police evidence locker, where they would remain until some future day when the Ident team had a boot to compare them with. They ran further comparisons of the girl's palm and fingerprints. They found no matches for either.

The homicide team was thwarted as well. Jake and his partner Rob Dunblane knew the cause and manner of her death. What her blood type was. The colour of her hair and eyes. How many fillings she had in her mouth: none. They thought that she was part Native, though the excellent condition of her teeth argued against that conclusion. Perhaps she was a runaway from some northern reserve or from one over the border in Ontario. One of the hundreds of young people who floated between city and reserve. They came to the city to spend the winter where the climate seemed warmer due to the little-publicized fact that life can be tough on some reserves if you are not related to the chief or anyone sitting on the band council.

The police had no idea who the deceased was.. They continued to refer to her as "the girl," though her apparent age was closer to 20. She had never been pregnant, and she was not known as a sex trade worker. She did not match the description of any person reported missing. The body remained in the Forensic Centre's morgue. Unclaimed. An answer had to be found within thirty days, since provincial law stated that no body could remain above ground for longer.

Constable Will Sawatsky sifted through his negatives until he found one that showed her face after it had been washed. Then Len Donaldson, the chief of police, held a brief news conference. The photo and a statement from the chief asking for the public's assistance in identifying the girl were released.

The media outlets sent single representatives to the Medical Examiner's Office to pick up the press release and copies of her photo. Their staffs were occupied with two other simultaneous press conferences. At the second one, on the dock at the forks of the Red and Assiniboine Rivers, the harbour master was warning schoolchildren to stay away from all flood-swollen rivers and creeks. And at the third one, at the Legislature, the Tories were predicting that a bonanza of jobs and money would flow into the province with the Pan Am games in 1999. This was a calculated attempt by the spin doctors to divert public attention from the worrisome flood news with a feel-good news item, but not even the glitter of 267 million loonies could knock brutal death and Mother Nature's news off the front pages.

WHO IS SHE? asked the banner headlines in the two local dailies. "Female, age 15–20, possibly Native, found murdered and frozen in the snow beneath the York Street underpass." Constable Sawatsky's photo of the girl ran above the fold, side-by-side with an image of the harbour master inspecting the footings of the Provencher Street Bridge.

Over the following days, the homicide was the subject of editorials and feature articles about the decline of civilized living and the plight of the urban aboriginal population. Radio phone-in shows debated the safety-in-our-streets issue and the freedom of young women to dress and act as they wished. Women's groups, victims's rights groups, and the sex-trade workers's support group made pronouncements on the prevalence and fury of male violence.

The Victims of Violence lobby group and the Aboriginal Women's Coalition held a joint candlelight vigil on the grounds of the Provincial Legislature. The marchers carried homemade placards with the names of women who'd been killed. One of the placards had the words **JUSTICE FOR HER** over a large photo of the unidentified girl and **Not Just Ice** under her photo. Many people broke down in tears as the list of names of the other victims of violent crime was read aloud. Slowly, the marchers paraded along Assiniboine Avenue beside the river to the York Street underpass, carrying candles and singing along to the solemn beat of a rawhide drum. Some were holding hands, some pushing children in strollers. At the crime scene, they placed a wreath with an enlarged, laminated copy of the girl's photo in its centre and they said prayers in English, French, and Cree and Saulteaux. They scattered single red flower petals, bright as fresh blood, on the gritty trampled snow.

Edna Spence saw the protest march on the TV news. The girl in the picture looked like Rosie but she was not sure. She had so much sad feeling from looking at the photo and her heart swelled up with longing. The moose hide, muskrat fur strips, sinew, stroud, and coloured beads for Rosie's moccasins were set out on the card table with the scissors and glover's needle. Rosie had already made her pattern by tracing her feet on the brown paper bag from the grocery stores. She was good at learning the way to cut the hide and wool for the lining. Edna waited every day for her granddaughter but Rosie had not come round to see her for more than a week.

Granny thought she wanted to tell somebody, but no one was coming to see her now except the driver of the HandiTransit van that took her to the hospital for her dialysis. He was always in a hurry. She dried her tears and opened her Bible to stop the worrying.

Frank MacDonald watched the marchers from the sidelines. He had not been sleeping all that well since he discovered the girl and got caught up in her story. The police clearly were not making much progress, and he could not help wondering what would happen to her if she were not identified. It simply did not seem possible that no one knew her. He had left two messages with that pretty young woman from the Medical Examiner's office but had received no response. Not every night, but on too many nights, dark thoughts invaded his dreams and he woke up startled, longing to call and hear his daughter Emily's sweet voice reporting the happy details of her travels, but it was never the right time. She was so many time zones away in Thailand, and he could not speak about his troubles or his worries over the phone.

Winnipeg   April 17, 1997

Mark Kay feigned surprise when his secretary buzzed him to say that two policemen were in the office and asking to see him. "You're kidding me, aren't you?"

Wasn't he expecting the police to contact him after he'd called the Crime Stoppers hotline? He'd thought they might, since he had left his name and office phone number on their answering machine. He wasn't sure how it all worked.

He'd decided to call Crime Stoppers from a pay phone at the Charter House restaurant during his lunch hour. He had given himself a pep talk as he ate his usual daily lunch, a toasted salmon salad sandwich. *It's the least you can do, you schmuck. Call up and try to find out if it could be her. The first step is the hardest,* he thought, recalling his father's words. He had dialled the number he'd recorded on a sticky note and then crumpled it into his sweaty left palm. On the telephone, he had lowered his voice and told the police answering machine that the dead girl in the newspapers might be Georgia Lee Kay-Stern. He had said she might be a student at the downtown campus. He'd never liked dealing with the police. That's why he had gone into corporate law. He preferred dealing with corporate welfare bums more than regular bums. After he had hung up the phone, he had heard his father's voice whisper the rest of that old Russian proverb: *The first step is the hardest; the last one, even harder.*

He thought he had recognized that it was Georgia Lee from the frightening photo in the morning paper. It showed only her head and neck, but he could tell the girl was nude. Her eyes were closed and her hair appeared wet, as if she had recently showered. It was Georgie. The black and white yin-yang symbol and silver chain she had showed him so proudly the last time they had met was around her neck.

She had looked so spooky then. Dressed in black from head to toe and sporting a steel stud in her tongue. He knew he'd grimaced in distaste when he'd seen it.

"Go ahead, Uncle Markie," she had prompted. "Say it. Say what you are thinking." He had wrinkled his nose. "Wait until you see my belly ring," she had teased. "It's a really pretty one."

"You know what your mother will say, don't you?" He'd made a face that looked like Mrs. Estelle Costanza tasting sour milk. "'That's a lovely belly ring. Excuse me, darling, while I put my head in the oven.'"

"Come on, Uncle Mark, admit it. You really like it." And they'd both laughed.

"Feh," he'd said. "In your *pupik* yet!"

She'd smiled again. She'd gotten the reaction she wanted, and so she was willing to sit through lunch with him. She'd told him he was okay as an uncle, as uncles go. He'd switched to calling her Georgie as soon as she'd asked. Anything to please her. She was still his little sweetheart.

That was early in April. He had not spoken to her since. Nearly two weeks ago. Before that last storm. That was not going to sound good to the cops. He could say that he thought of her most days as he drove by her apartment block on his way to his office. That really was not the same as calling. She hadn't called him back when he had left a message, had she? Instead of calling again, he had rehearsed the argument he had known he would have with Rona and had e-mailed Georgie a joke when he'd gotten to the office. How could he confess that to the cops?

He wanted his secretary to believe that this call was a bolt from the blue. She had not commented on the photo of Georgia Lee that the police had published in the newspapers. She knew his niece through her phone calls but had met Georgie face to face only once, so little wonder Bev Cunningham had not recognized her; she looked so different. He had said nothing to Bev about his suspicions.

Mark ran a damp forefinger around the collar of his pink linen shirt and adjusted the knot in his grey silk tie. There was no reason for him to feel nervous, but he did. He was terrified that it was Georgie. How could it be? Rona would kill him.

He carefully filled his fountain pen with blue-black ink.

"Did you say *detectives*? Two of them? Bev, come on. It's Thursday and, officially, remember, I've left for the day and the weekend. And I'm helping with the sandbagging around my condo tomorrow. Did you say they're from Homicide?" He carefully put the lid back on the ink bottle, wiped the nib with tissue, and recapped his pen. "Did you tell them I don't do criminal work? Okay. Guess I'll have to see them. Show them in, and then you head for home. Yeah. You have a great evening, too."

As soon as he switched off the intercom, Mark stood and picked up and opened the copy of the Starbucks annual report that had arrived in that day's mail. He stared at the page. He knew his stock was up, but he could not read the graph. The type was blurred by his tearing eyes.

Bev escorted the two men in and indicated to them with a nod that they seat themselves in the two leather tub chairs facing Mark's antique mahogany desk.

He continued to look at the page, willing it into focus. The detectives sat down. Mark held his right index finger up to indicate silence.

As he stood running his eyes down the columns of figures, his torso moved in a gentle back and forth motion as if he were *davening*. He held the pose for less than ten seconds before tossing the report face down on the desk and looking up.

"Thank you, Bev," he said. "You can leave now. I won't need anything else today."

Mark walked around to stand directly in front of the detectives and said, "Good afternoon, gentleman." He did not extend his hand to them. His hands were undersized and fine-boned, and he disliked the practice of shaking hands as a greeting. There were so many kinds of malevolent germs in the outside world.

"What can I do for you?" He leaned back against his desk, resting his *tuchis* on its sleek surface. He noted their off-the-rack suits, their crappy ties, and, bless them both, their black tasselled loafers. Their jackets cut slightly boxy to cover the sidearms they wore at the waist. Their shields displayed on their lapels. The well-dressed dick look.

Jake Friesen introduced himself and his partner, Rob Dunblane. Simultaneously, he and Rob reached inside their jackets's inside left breast pockets. Friesen produced a Polaroid photo of Georgia Lee taken at the hospital after her body had been washed. Dunblane dug a regulation notebook and pen out of his.

"This photo was in the papers today. Did you see it?" asked Friesen.

Only the head and neck of the young woman were shown. It was unmistakably the portrait of a young, dead female. Eyes that would not open. Lips that would not smile. Wounds that would not heal.

Mark stared at the photo. His face was expressionless, but he paled as if an unjust sentence he could not bear had been passed against him. He did not want to believe it. He thought it *was* Georgie, but why was her hair wet? It didn't make any sense to him. He'd received another e-mail from Rona about her this morning. Georgie was not keeping in touch again. *Kinder.* She had not called since before the big storm. And he had gone to New York on business right after the blizzard and before he had thought about it again, another day or two had passed. He should have called her, should have gone to see her before he'd left. He sighed. He had called her number twice already today. He had planned to drop by to see her at the video store on his way home. Rona was going to have his head on a plate.

"Where was this taken?" he demanded.

"Do you know her?" Friesen asked. His voice was soft; the four short words offered an invitation.

Mark coughed, flushed, and coughed again. "It looks something like my niece. I don't see how it could be, but it looks a little like my niece." He shivered as he handed the photo back to Friesen.

"Is it? Is it your niece?"

"I think so," replied Mark. "It might be. She was adopted." He added this last as a way of explaining that this sort of thing did not normally occur in his family. "I haven't been able to get her on the phone lately."

"Then, and correct me if I am wrong, her name is Georgia Lee Kay-Stern," said Friesen. "Two calls were made to the Crime Stopper's hotline today by people giving that name for her after this photo was publicized."

Mark nodded. "What happened to her?"

"When did you last see her?"

"I haven't seen her – that is, haven't seen her face to face – since early in March."

Mark thought of how angry Ben and Rona were going to be. He was supposed to be looking after their daughter. But. But. But Rona had insisted, don't crowd her – she needs to be independent. "But I have spoken to her almost every week, and she e-mails me, too."

Friesen and Dunblane continued to stare. Mark thought he read contempt in their cool gazes. He figured they were thinking that he didn't care that much about his niece. They were wrong. He cared, but he didn't know what to do with it. He had no experience in raising children, never mind with young girls. The person he didn't care that much about was her mother. His younger sister gave him a royal pain in the *tuchis* with her feminist attitudes. No point in going into that history with these people.

Mark remembered when Georgie had moved into that massive old red block that towered over the Assiniboine River at the corner of Roslyn and Osborne Streets. She had been so delighted with her first suite and its dusty hardwood floors, the working fireplace that she was forbidden to use, and the antiquated kitchen that she hadn't seemed to notice the lack of closets. The building was full of students and other questionable artsy types. The last time he'd invited Georgie to lunch (was it in the last week of March?), she had said that she didn't have time to go with him. She was busy with school and working at the video store. He'd had meetings up the wazoo, too. They had agreed she would check in with him by phone. She had. She had left voice-mail and e-mail for him at home and chatted with Bev when she had called during office hours. She said her classes were interesting. And everything else was fine. That was agreeable to him. He'd had no idea what to talk to her about anyway. Called herself Georgie now. Always changing something. He had thought that they both were fine with each going their own way. And their exchange of messages had fulfilled the letter of his promise to Ben and Rona.

He tried to remember the name of the guy who had given her the yin-yang medallion she wore. It was that guy she had stayed with when she had run away. *Waylon.* Didn't she say he was a cousin? One of the ones from the reserve up north. There was some story about him going to Japan. Mark never could keep them straight. Nothing about Native culture interested him. It wasn't as if they had much to offer. Not even great music like the American blacks who gave the riches of jazz, soul, gospel, and the blues.

"It is her," he said. "Georgia Lee. I recognize that medallion she is wearing. Did she have a silver belly button ring with a pink stone? Like a big earring through her navel?" Mark heard his own voice in a high-pitched echo.

Friesen said he didn't think a belly ring was found. He'd double-check.

"I'll try to phone my sister now. She and Ben, her husband, are on sabbatical this winter in Costa Rica. They e-mailed me a number for their landlord there. For emergencies, they said. I'll see how soon they can fly back to Canada. She can't be buried until they get home."

He walked around behind his desk and sat down on his ergonomic black leather chair. He tucked the phone under his chin and pulled his electronic day timer out of his breast pocket. His hands were shaking, and he held his elbows close to his sides to help conceal this. He put the phone down, placed the day timer back on the desk, and sat staring at it. Without looking up, he asked the cops again to tell him what happened to her.

Friesen described how and where she had been found. While he was talking, Mark got up and walked over to the south-facing wall of windows that overlooked the rail line and the Forks Park twenty-three stories below. He could see patches of melt, dark against the bright of snow. It looked like rot at the old heart of the city. "Do I have to go to a morgue to identify the body?" Mark looked at the detectives. Their expressions stayed neutral.

"Yes, that will help our investigation," said Friesen.

After a minute or two, he asked the detective to continue. Assurance was given that her death had been immediate and pain free. The question of sexual assault was unsettled. Test results would resolve that issue. They asked about birthmarks, scars, and tattoos. And who did her dental work.

Mark found himself eager to talk then. Eager to explain how Georgia Lee had become a member of their family.

Who was Waylon Spence? they wanted to know. There was nothing in their system on him.

Seven urgent phone messages were Scotch-taped to the door of Maud's office when she arrived at 8:30. She pulled them off and looked through them, then stuck them one by one onto the metal spindle beside her phone. There were two from Frank MacDonald – that handsome teacher who'd found the girl while out jogging.

The topmost message had the notation "very N.B." written on the top edge and highlighted with blue marker. It detailed a phone call from a Bernice Spence, lawyer for the Manitou Repatriation Association, who requested an urgent call back regarding the case of Rosie McKay. That name did not ring a bell with Maud, but the Manitou Repatriation Association did. They were among the groups that had participated in a candlelight march and vigil to the site under the old train trestle where the girl's body had been discovered. The query had to be about the frozen girl.

Her call was answered on the second ring. A woman answered abruptly, "Bernice Spence here."

Maud identified herself and asked how she might help.

"You can begin by authorizing the release of Rosie McKay's body to her family for burial." Her voice was calm, a sweet alto. "I speak for her and for our family in making this request. We believe the girl who was murdered is our Rosie, and we request to see her body for confirmation."

"What is your relationship to the deceased?"

"Rosie is a cousin to me. She has been missing for more than a week. None of us have seen or heard from her since before that last blizzard. No one knew at first, except her grandmother, Edna Spence, who lives here in the city these days. Rosie was to take her granny to see the doctor for her diabetes check-up at the hospital last Thursday, but she never came. She saw something about the girl frozen in the snow on the TV, but she doesn't speak much English and she doesn't keep a phone, so she waited until one of our cousins came to town. That was yesterday when they called me. We would like to see this girl as soon as possible. Mrs. Spence will make the identification since she knows Rosie better than I do."

Maud arranged for a viewing of the body within the hour and, after the two women arrived, escorted them to the morgue. She asked them to stay for a moment in the hallway and went in alone to check on the body. Maud was pleased that, as she'd requested, the dieners had put the girl's body in a blue gown on the hospital bed in the viewing room. She took care to fold the white sheet closely around the girl's neck so they would not see the roughly sewn incision on her trunk. So it seemed that she was sleeping. Then Maud opened the door and asked the two women to come in.

Bernice Spence was a short woman, probably in her mid-30s, dressed in a black suit jacket worn over a red, full-skirted shirtdress, and she had pulled her long, dark hair back in a single braid. A fringe of straight bangs curtained her forehead above dark eyes. She walked arm in arm with an elderly Native woman. The lady, introduced as Mrs. Edna Spence, seemed frail and wan. Her thin body was lost in baggy brown trousers and a white blouse and cardigan buttoned up to her neck. A few wisps of grey-streaked black hair escaped the colourfully printed floral babushka that covered her head. She hesitated a few steps inside the heavy steel door. She looked around the room at the rows of stainless steel body lockers set into white walls and up at the buzzing fluorescent lights. She said something in Cree.

Bernice Spence answered yes with a gentle smile. She met Maud's questioning glance and translated, "Like on the TV." Then Bernice put her arm around the petite elderly lady's shoulders and spoke a few sentences to her in Cree. Mrs. Spence nodded and wiped her eyes with the back of her hand. Their conversation continued, and Maud watched silently as the grandmother reached out and stroked the girl's cheek.

"She wants to know what happened to Rosie," said Bernice. "And why is there water on her face like that?" Bernice indicated the clear drops of moisture on the girl's forehead and cheeks.

Maud explained that it was condensation formed when the body was placed in the cooler. "Tell her it is like the dew that comes on the grass at night," she added. *Why didn't I think of wiping her face?* she silently admonished herself.

This answer was translated, and it seemed to please both women. They continued their private conversation. Their small nods and exclamations and resigned sighs suggested that they were sure of the girl's identity.

"Was she wearing a black and white medal around her neck?" asked Bernice. "Granny says she got it from her cousin Waylon. It's from a Buddha temple. He's been living and studying in Japan for a while now."

"Yes," answered Maud. "It is being held for safekeeping in our office. The family may have it returned to them."

"Then this is our Rosie, our granddaughter and cousin," announced Bernice. Her voice rang out clearly and definitively in the cool air, as if she was beginning a summation in court. She repeated this in Cree, and Granny nodded slowly and reached out to touch the girl's cheek again softly. Her old eyes glistened, but no tear appeared.

The words hung in the air, solemn as a benediction. Maud felt something give way inside her like a fist unclenching. She had been waiting for this moment when a name was pronounced, to begin to put the frozen girl's case into the past tense, in a file with a name and a number.

"What can we do now to have her body for burial?"

Good, thought Maud, *this is the easy part.* Now that the girl's identity was known, the family would begin to grieve their loss. She wished she could put her arms around Mrs. Spence, but she was not sure that gesture would be welcomed.

"I'll tell the medical examiner, Dr. Bekker, that you are willing to claim her body. And when you have decided which funeral home you want to use, have the director call our office and we will release her body to them." She offered her condolences again and her business card and escorted them on their slow progress to the main entrance.

The phone rang loudly as she walked through the door to her office, and Maud regarded its blinking lights with deep displeasure. The possibility that the caller was anyone she wished to speak with was unlikely. She glanced over her stacks of files at the call display screen; the number there was a familiar one. It was for a cell phone the police Ident unit used. But the caller was Jake.

"I have a probable name and address for that girl now," he said.

"You do? Well, I have news for you. Your timing is off. I just finished doing a viewing, and those people want to claim her. Her grandmother from Footprint Lake and a cousin who, by the way, is a lawyer with the '60s scoop repatriation movement. What name do you have?"

"Georgia Lee Kay-Stern – that's with a hyphen between the last two names. Age 18, DOB 1979, July 14th, adopted in Winnipeg as an infant, birth mother was a Cree from up north and father unknown. We took her uncle, Mark Kay – he is a lawyer – in for a viewing last night, and he gave us a positive ID and the name of her dentist. I'll give you that name so you can seize her dental X-rays for comparison. She has no prints in the system, so we need the dental. She was a university student, worked part time at the video rental place at River and Osborne, and lived in suite 14B, 21 Roslyn Road. We are heading over there now. Want to join us?"

The sense of relief that Maud felt only moments before when the Spence family confirmed the girl's identity vanished. Her churning stomach told her that solution was all shot to hell now. The Native birth family versus the adoptive parents: Where did these parties rank on the list of the Medical Examiner's Office's preferred order of claimants? Which group had the legitimate claim to bury this one dead girl? Dr. Bekker would have something to say about this mess. Most definitely.

Both she and Jake had thought she looked part Native, though Georgia Lee Kay-Stern was a name that sounded distinctly middle class. Very likely Jewish. It evoked a comfortable life lived somewhere in the south end of the city with caring parents and their ordinary dreams. In a clean and well-maintained house that was close to good neighbourhood schools, a life filled with music lessons or art classes, perhaps dance lessons, summers at the family cabin or summer vacations abroad to give the child a chance to experience other cultures.

"Jake, that is not such good news. There's going to be a problem. I just did a viewing for a Manitou Society lawyer for the McKay family and the girl's grandmother of the Spence family from Footprint Lake. They identified her as Rosie McKay, who had a Cree mother and unknown father, and they are requesting that the body be released to them for burial. Dr. Bekker is not going to like this. He will not agree to play King Solomon."

"That's a helluva tangle," he answered. "But it's for your office to decide. I can't help you. I've got a murder to solve."

"Did you say that her apartment is on Roslyn? In that the old red block on the corner? With the green Mediterranean style roof tiles?" Maud drove past it every morning on her route to work.

"Yeah, that is the one. The Roslyn Arms. Are you going to join us?"

"Think I will," she said. The towering stacks of files on her desk would keep.

Maud nosed her Jeep along Broadway and turned south at Osborne. From the top of the bridge, she could see the crews of volunteers placing sandbags around the base of the glass walls at the ground level of the thirty-story condo building on the south bank of the river. Another group was reinforcing the dike that ran along that bank of the Assiniboine. She made a mental note to check with her mother about the state of affairs at 192 Kingston Row and thanked her lucky stars that her own apartment was a third-floor walk-up.

A patrol car, an unmarked car, and the Ident team's van were parked beside the Roslyn Avenue entrance to the apartment block by the time Maud pulled up. She parked behind the van and slapped her government issue parking plaque on the dash. The boss would not be pleased if he knew she was stopping off like this. Investigators were supposed to concentrate on the medical side of their cases and leave the police work to the police. It was not an official policy but a preference. Dr. Bekker would not make it a policy, because under certain circumstances, like the murder of Miss Kay-Stern, the governing legislation allowed an investigator to declare a place where death, or injury leading to death occurred, a crime scene. When such circumstances arose, the investigator worked more closely with the police. That might be the case here. She justified it to herself because it was on her way home and she was on her own time.

She wanted to delay her entrance. Continued exposure to death scenes did not bring her any greater degree of ease in approaching them. The most difficult part was getting through the door and confronting another corpse. Each time, she found herself rehearsing the list of data to be collected, of forms to be completed, of phone calls to be made. Today, there was no body to examine, no grieving family members waiting, nothing to satisfy but her curiosity. Even for that, she needed to feel calm. She sat in her parked vehicle doing her deep breathing exercises and listening to the news headlines on the radio.

She heard that the Provincial Justice ministry had fired the first volley in the war on local gangs with court orders to prohibit the association of members. Neither the Indian Posse nor the Manitoba Warriors had issued a response. The military were on standby for flood relief and, to Maud's complete surprise, the announcer said that the Coast Guard was readying a sizeable fleet of watercraft, including large barges to rescue livestock in outlying municipalities and help the farmers move them to higher ground. The Coast Guard operating in the middle of the prairie. That idea amused her, though perhaps it shouldn't have. There was a real possibility that a wall of water would flood in to fill the ancient seabed of Lake Agassiz. The level of the Red River had come up 2 feet in downtown Grand Forks, North Dakota on each of the last two days.

Maud went around to the main door on Osborne and rang the buzzer for suite 14B. The date on the building's cornerstone was 1909. Then it had been an elegant address. Now it sat in faded splendour, a great red-brick dowager solidly planted riverside with the tatty downmarket shops of Osborne Village crowded round her skirts. Maud gave her name and that of her office to the male voice that responded from the answerphone of suite 14B and got directions to take the ancient, wheezing brass cage elevator up to the second floor. A uniformed cop standing on guard halfway down the hall waved her forward.

Jake stood inside the door. He raised the strip of crime scene tape so she could scoot under. As she bent her head, he leaned forward and she felt his lips softly graze the top of her head. They smiled at each other, and he led the way down the long entrance hall toward the kitchen.

"Wow." She stopped to gesture upward with her right arm as she turned in a slow circle in the hallway. "Look at these wonderful high ceilings. This place is amazing. I've always wanted to see inside." She was babbling, she knew, but she did not want to cry, so she didn't look at him. Why was she on the verge of tears anyway? The dispute arising from the claims of the girl's two families was not her concern. *Get a grip,* she lectured herself. "Did you see the main lobby? That's real oak panelling on the walls, and that brass cage elevator, isn't it a beauty?"

Jake turned back and gave her a quizzical look that asked if she was okay or losing it.

"It's not bad unless you prefer a place with more than one closet to hang your clothes in," he said. "Cheap rent, so it's full of students, weirdos, and lefties." His flat tone told her he was completely uninterested and that the building's official heritage designation did not impress him.

Maud fished in her oversize purse and hauled out a pen and a file folder with her preliminary report of the girl's death. She filled in the section marked *address of the decedent.* What to record as her name? She decided to enter both in alphabetical order with a slash mark in between them. Kay-Stern, Georgia Lee/McKay, Rosie.

Maud followed Jake down the entranceway into the kitchen where Sawatsky and Petrie from Ident were going over the scene in their patient, methodical way. Tall Tim Petrie, whose nickname, predictably, was Tiny, was hunched over the ancient white porcelain kitchen sink. He was humming the theme from *Bolero* softly and clicking his tweezers like castanets as he peered through his reading glasses at the rinds of pizza and food-encrusted plates.

"Are you finding anything helpful?" Maud asked.

Jake answered. "Number one, the suite was not secure when we arrived. The door was closed but not locked. Her wallet, her ID and keys are on a table in her bedroom. There's no money. Not a penny. I don't know where he did her, but it wasn't here. A little partying is a definite possibility, judging from the mess. The guys are looking for trace. I'm heading back downtown. "You" – he nodded at Maud – "you are going to sort out the family business for us, right?" He wasn't interested in the conflicting family claims. He did not wait for her answer.

"The uncle," he said, "Mark Kay – and he's an odd dude – the uncle's contacting her parents. They're somewhere down in Costa Rica. Academic types. Went to Central America for a year on a sabbatical. Not due home until the end of May. Daddy is paying the rent here 'cause their place over in the West End is rented out for the year."

"Okay," said Maud, "I'll talk to Dr. Bekker and the families."

He leaned over to brush her cheek with the back of his hand. "You okay?" he whispered.

Tim Petrie looked up from his crouch over the sink and grinned at them. "Pay attention, you lovebirds. This sink is loaded with potential evidence. Looks like somebody pissed over these dishes. Smells like it, too." He wrinkled his nose, and his handlebar moustache peaked up in a dark bow over his thin upper lip. "She must have invited a bunch of party animals over. That is not consistent with what the uncle told us about the girl's usual habits. So, either she has very rude guests, or it's a commentary on her poor cooking. Then there's this empty rum bottle I find – after the uncle told us that she never takes a drink. Makes you wonder. And look at this cheese here. Someone took a few bites and left the rest to dry out. That's very bad housekeeping, and that does not sound like our girl either."

Will Sawatsky came through the doorway from the living room. "Like I say, if you lie down with dogs, you get up with fleas. Sounds like she was more of a Spice girl than a nice girl. She was Native, wasn't she? Check out the picture of her in her pow wow dress on the bathroom wall." He shook his head. "Most parents don't know what the kids are really up to. And that includes me. The uncle said she did never, not ever drink, and yet we find an empty rum bottle. My illusions are shattered."

"I didn't think you had any left," said Jake. "Except about your golf game."

"You betcha." Petrie grinned. "That's our motto. We are men without illusions. That's why we are sampling a little of this interesting stinky yellow fluid from the kitchen sink. And everything else we decide to like. We gotta cast a wide net 'cause you never know . . ." His voice trailed off as he concentrated on collecting the fluid in question.

"That means you're seizing the cheese?" asked Maud.

"You betcha!" said Sawatsky, his baby blue eyes alight with the thrill of the chase. "We're getting it all tonight. So far, we have a few good prints from various surfaces throughout the suite. The best are a partial palm and three digits from the wall beside the medicine cabinet. And a lot of blur in places and that makes me think the place has been wiped.

I found two long brown hairs with some curl on the girl's pillow, cut hairs on the floor of the bathroom that appear similar, to my naked eye, and I took three more from under the rim of the toilet bowl. Also, there was the faint smear of blood I got from the bathroom wall beside the medicine cabinet. We'll be seizing her computer, too."

Somehow things in the girl's suite were not right. Maud did not know exactly how to put it. She disliked this necessary sorting and sifting through the detritus of the girl's life. It felt as if the team were making a further invasion of her privacy. She remembered that the girl's hair was short, straight, and dyed a deep black. Maud stripped off her jacket and draped it over her shoulders, since there was no place to hang it up. The air was heavy, overheated, and stale. A headache-inducing atmosphere, and within that stultifying quality of staleness, there was something feral. It was especially noticeable in the kitchen, where the disgusting mess of dirty dishes crowded the sink. Beside it was a sealed plastic evidence bag that now encased the large hunk of dried yellow cheese with prominent teeth marks.

The greedy bite marks in the cheese distressed Maud more than the mess of dirty dishes in the sink or the empty rum bottle. The gnawed cheese spoke of deviations from the norms of polite behaviour and reminded her of the angry bite marks around the girl's nipples. She caught another whiff of the rank odour of stale urine. She felt ill. Was she losing it? She watched the guys at work, searching for trace evidence with their powders and brushes, their solutions and lights.

She wandered into the living room. A student's first apartment with the parents's cast-off red velvet sofa that looked as if it belonged in Proust's salon, an older model TV sitting on the floor, and travel posters from Israel stuck up on the wall. There were ashes in the old green-tiled fireplace. A tiny blue parakeet was hopping around on the floor of a metal cage hanging from a stand over in front of the window that overlooked the frozen river and the controversial statue of Louis Riel. The bird's seed dish was nearly empty, and the cage floor was very dirty. There was a mess of empty shells and bird droppings on the windowsill and the floor around the cage's stand.

"Hey, you guys, what about this little bird?" she called out. Petrie ducked his head around the kitchen doorway and said, "We found him hiding in the folds of the drapes. I gave the little fella some food and water. He seems kinda weak to me. Haven't heard him sing yet. I'm thinking of taking him downtown."

"Downtown? What's the charge?" teased Maud.

"Jake wants to question him. We figure he's seen plenty, and if we can get him to sing, I bet he can tell us a whole lot."

"All right," answered Maud. "Go for it!" She smiled at his silly joke, but that queasy feeling came back.

She checked the girl's bedroom. It was about 12 feet square, and the walls were painted a rich lemon yellow. A dark blue denim comforter and some frilly pillows and stuffed animals were balled up on the unmade futon bed that was pushed up against the wall opposite the door. The late afternoon sun shining slantwise through the mini window blinds threw zebra stripes of light and dark on the heap of clothing draped over an old armchair under the window. A dream catcher of yarns and feathers was hanging on the wall over the bed. Sitting centred on the top of her chest of drawers, a miniature dragon held a glowing red crystal bead in its mouth.

There was a wooden desk with a desktop computer setup and bookcase on the opposite wall. Maud glanced at some of the titles: *Introduction to Cultural Anthropology, Introductory Psychology, Bury My Heart at Wounded Knee, An Actor Prepares,* even that Canadian girls' favourite, *Anne of Green Gables. Intro Anthro, Intro Psych, Anne of Green Gables:* she had those same titles on her bookshelves. Anthro. She had taken that as an elective in first year. Really liked the course. She picked up the text, flipped through it, and put it back down on the desk next to the computer, whose cream-coloured case was dusted with black fingerprint powder. Petrie said he'd found two long curly dark-brown hairs on her pillowcase. Evidence. They all knew the girl had short, straight hair dyed pitch black.

She walked back into the kitchen.

"Tim," she asked, "how much longer do think you'll need to be here?"

"Hard to say. Another hour or two, and we should be through. What'd ya say, partner?" He called out to Sawatsky, who was working in the bathroom.

"Time will tell."

Maud watched as the beefy constable, who was squatting, rocked back on his heels in the narrow bathroom and continued scraping up minute amounts of trace evidence from the old-fashioned white hexagonal floor tiles.

"Pretty interesting stuff in here. It's going to keep the lab busy for days. Not much in the rest of the place. Looks like it's been wiped down."

"No surprize there," she answered. She was staring at a large framed photo hanging on the wall opposite the medicine cabinet. A large colour photo of the girl standing with a man and woman on either side of her was hanging on the wall opposite the mirror. In it, she looked about 12 years old; she was wearing a Native Indian costume and feathers in her braided hair.

"Oh," said Maud. She was staring at the photo.

"What's that?" asked Sawatsky.

"It's the dad." She pointed to the photo. "Her dad. He's a prof at the university. I took a course from him in first year. Anthropology 101. Haven't thought of him in ages."

"Well, they say Winnipeg is a small town."

"Sure is," she answered. Stern, that was his name. Professor Stern. He was so knowledgeable in his field, so interesting that she remembered that she had considered changing her major. Couldn't be, could it? She moved in for a closer look. It was him.

"Okay, I'll leave you to it," Maud said. "You're going to get the builders out to put on a new lock, and you will have the scene sealed, right?"

"You betcha," said Petrie. "I'll clean up a little if I can. And we'll take the little birdie back to the station for safekeeping."

Maud nodded her thanks. He was a good cop and a kind one. She made a mental note to advise the family to hire a janitorial service to clean the apartment before they entered the premises. There was no horrifying blood-drenched evidence for them to see, but she knew from experience how distressing even the sight of the various powders the cops used to dust for fingerprints could be, the powder smudges like bruises blooming all over the girl's belongings. The family did not need to know who had been there.

En Route: San Jose to Houston   April 17, 1997

"We'll get a cab out to the airport and get the first flight home," Ben said.

He'd run uphill to the landlord's house to take the phone call from his brother-in-law, Mark, and he'd run all the way back to their bungalow and was panting so heavily with unaccustomed exertion that he huffed the words out. "Pack. Pack. Please," he'd sobbed, "pack now."

He'd repeated the gist of the phone call.

Rona heard his words rattle over and over in her mind like tumbling dice. She could hear each one separately, could visualize their correct spellings, yet the message seemed nonsensical. Georgia Lee was in an accident, she had been taken to the hospital, and her condition was poor. She had a head injury. It did not look good. Rona began to feel an intense cold at her centre. She sat on the side of the bed and rocked back and forth.

Ben took out his wallet and checked the contents: $150 in US currency, plus the $1,000 he carried in his money belt and some of the local currency. He stared at the dense wad of the multicoloured, ornately designed *colones*. They'd stood in line for forty-eight minutes that morning at the bank to get the banknotes. He remembered how they'd joked as the brawny cashier had held each American $50 bill up close under his moustache and scrutinized it with prudent eyes and then snapped it between his deliberating fingers. It seemed comic, a routine from a Marx Brothers's movie. Exactly what you would expect in a banana republic. The multicoloured bank notes of local currency were faded and limp yet silky from the talc applied at the bank.

The taxi fare to the airport would require at most one-half of those hard-worn *colones*. Where could he exchange the rest?

They arranged to charter a flight to the capital and then sat waiting for it for over three hours. To pass the time, Ben calculated and recalculated the distance and possible speed they could make if they'd had a car. Even if they had to wait five hours for the charter, it was still far quicker than driving back to San Jose. He knew he was incapable of negotiating the mountain switchbacks, potholes, and washouts in the state he was in. Whatever trouble Georgia Lee was in, it was bad, a very unfortunate ending to their otherwise gloriously successful sabbatical.

He turned to Rona. She looked wan. Absent. For reassurance, he counted the number of pieces of their baggage several times.

The frail-looking four-seater propeller-driven plane sailed up and away from Quepos, swiftly leaving the sea and the coastal town below in the mist. The drone of the engines had a hypnotic effect. Rona stared out the oval Plexiglas window and down over the mountainsides, glossy green with coffee bushes. Ben held her hand loosely. His strong fingers were cool and steadying. She was wearing all the articles of warm clothing she had with her – a white cotton cardigan and her red fleece vest – but she felt chilled despite these layers. *The air must be thinner up here,* she thought.

Rona had forgotten to ask which hospital Georgia Lee was in. Was she at the Women's Pavilion at the old General Hospital? That's where she was born on July 14, 1978. The 14th of July was Momma's birthday, too, and that was the hospital where Poppa had died, leaving them alone in the world. She and Beryl and Mark had stayed on in the old suite above the store for the first year after their Poppa died while Beryl, being the oldest and very bossy, tried to run the deli and finish her education degree. After graduation, Beryl had negotiated the sale of the business, gave their longtime housekeeper, Mrs. Mary Klymkiw, her notice, and handed Rona and Mark each a cheque for a one-third share of the profit. Then she had split for Vancouver with Zach Levin. They never did get married.

Mrs. Mary Klymkiw had given them the only mothering they had in those years after their own mother died. Mrs. Mary, who arrived at 7:00 a.m. on weekday mornings and Saturdays, with her round smiling face, her fresh housedress neatly pressed, and her thick, varicosed legs encased like wurst in lisle stockings. She took charge in the kitchen and of the mops and brooms and, after giving the children a rough inspection each morning, shooed them out the door to school. Mrs. Mary kept their house in good order, their clothes clean and mended, and their meals deliciously satisfying. She taught the sisters their needlework and cooking as if they were her own daughters and fed little Mark special tidbits by hand to build him up. She marched them into Oretski's every October to be fitted out in new snowsuits and galoshes and provided them with warm mittens knitted by her hands. She was so much theirs that when her son, Gregory, pushed Rona down on the icy schoolyard and insisted that she was his mother alone, Rona refused to believe him. When Rona heard the word *mother,* she saw Mrs. Mary's wide gold wedding band bite into her plump widow's fingers as she kneaded their *challah* for *Shabbat.*

On the day Ben and Rona were notified that their adoption request was granted, Rona had hurried out to Eaton's to buy a layette. What delight she had taken from the sight of those dozens of white cloth diapers and tiny pale pink sleepers and soft receiving blankets with cuddly teddy bears printed on them. To have her own receiving blankets and all the deep pleasure those two words conveyed. *Receiving blankets.* Ready to receive her heart's desire.

Their hastily organized nursery had met with the smiling approval of the social worker who brought their little girl to them. Like a fairy godmother, she'd arrived – sudden in her appearance and with a benevolent shower of gifts. She had brought them a perfect baby girl, tins of formula, disposable diapers (convenient for trips to the shopping mall, she'd advised), and official certificates and papers. Rona had barely given these documents a glance before scrawling her name. The child's future with her was more important than the past sorrows recorded there. Rona had informed the worker that Ben would take care of the *details.*

She'd imagined that they would be called to the hospital to pick up their baby and was slightly annoyed by the appearance of this social worker. She'd visualized a young, sweet-faced, white-clad nurse handing her a tiny sleeping infant; then Rona would walk out of the hospital with this babe in arms while Ben smiled and held doors open for them, as if in a scene from a 1950s movie.

When they were alone on warm afternoons of that autumn, after she had given Georgia Lee her bottle and knew she was not hungry, Rona would put the child's little doll lips to her dry breast and pretend to nurse her daughter to sleep. Rona knew that she would not have milk despite the assurances of the La Leche League. She decided that her pink nipples were better than an old rubber soother. Better for both of them. On that first of many golden afternoons, all her yearnings were satisfied in those few quiet minutes of closeness that were for

Rona the most intimate she had ever experienced. The pale spirits of her stillborn sons lounged at her feet, like two putti in a Renaissance tableau of Madonna and child. Like all dead children, they would not leave. She felt their warm breath on her bare legs.

As her baby suckled, she'd invented the whole story of her pregnancy. Her two-and-a-half difficult months with morning sickness (how happily, how bravely she had endured it), the thrill of feeling this child's first movement, and the drama of her twenty-six hours of natural labour and delivery. The deep pleasure of hearing "It's a girl!" and holding that sweet, soft dark-haired little doll. She knew it was a fantasy, her favourite – that she could replay and whisper in those perfect little ears. A secret shared by only these two. At five and a half months, Georgia Lee had begun to break off the nursing. She would look at Rona, then gurgle and smile.

A few times over the years, Rona had found her daughter making faces at herself in the mirror. She'd say she was different. *How can you be different?* Rona always exclaimed. *Why ever say a thing like that?* Rona would rush on to avoid hearing an answer. *You have a mother and father and a home like everyone else.* Georgia Lee had accepted that crisp reassurance while she was young enough to believe whatever explanation her parents offered. The happy life of their family had gone on behind Rona's imaginary white picket fence.

Ben was exhausted when they got to Houston. They could not get a flight out to Toronto until the following morning, and although it was now 9:00 p.m. and he longed for a bed, any bed, he did not argue when Rona refused to leave the airport terminal to go to one of the nearby hotels.

Their few fellow travellers ignored them. Two women (a pair of buxom blondes whose faces said they were mother and daughter) and a thin boy of perhaps four had bedded down in a corner of the lounge. They were snuggled up with their heads resting on a large red piece of soft-sided luggage. The younger woman had her arms around her son. Her mother was snoring but obviously not loudly enough to awaken the others. The boy was on his back, his right thumb stuck in his mouth, his arm snuggling a purple dinosaur, both of them sheltered between the women's curving denim-clad thighs.

Five male students spent most of the later part of the evening drinking beer and watching the NBA semi-finals on the TV in the bar opposite the lounge. Ben was amused by the way they exchanged insults and loudly called each other down when their favourites scored a basket. When the bar closed, they flopped out on rows of chairs in the lounge and replayed the game until they passed out.

Rona sat through all of their noise without protest. She wanted nothing to eat and had a cup of tea only because Ben insisted. He ordered a clubhouse sandwich and fries. "Wheat or white?" the wait-ress asked in a baffling accent. He could not figure out what she meant until she showed him the breads. He offered Rona a couple of french fries on the end of his fork and she chewed three or four times and then opened her mouth like a toddler and he saw the half-chewed fries were sitting there on her tongue. He reached over the table with his paper napkin, and she pushed the warm mush out into his hand with her tongue and closed her eyes.

She complained of being very cold yet rebuffed him when he tried to put his arm around her shoulders. Finally, he got her to curl up with her head in his lap and draped his windbreaker over her shoulders. Only twenty-four hours earlier, they'd been in Quepos sitting in *La Vaca Loca*, a small rustic bar run by expatriate Americans. The air had been warm with the scents of oleander and frangipani, and soft rain fell on the unpaved street. They had held hands, talked, laughed, and drunk down the good cold local beer and eaten delicious *quesadillas* while a trio of musicians sang sweetest harmonies that even made corny old songs like *Besame mucho* sound fresh. The club had been full of sun-bronzed 20-something surfers who joined in loudly with the musicians on the choruses and kept time by banging spoons on their empty beer bottles. Their shy local waitress, a slim girl of perhaps 16, had giggled at the older kids. Later, after a moonlit walk to their little house and their contented lovemaking, he and Rona had slept in peace under the whirling blades of the ceiling fan.

They spent their night in Houston stretched out on a long row of hard, orange molded plastic chairs with unforgiving 2-inch gaps between the seats. It was slightly less comfortable than a wooden park bench. Ben was glad that Rona had taken some travel sickness pills that finally knocked her out around one in the morning. He dozed off and on during the long night while the airport staff walked back and forth past them without interest.

They landed in Toronto at one o'clock the next afternoon. Rona had not closed her eyes since they'd left Houston. She'd paced in the aisle on the plane until the stewardess asked her to be seated. They had offered acetaminophen for her headache and motion sickness tablets for nausea but had nothing that would quiet her nerves. Ben had called Mark from a payphone in the Air Canada departures lounge at Pearson to give him their arrival time in Winnipeg.

The last and shortest leg of their journey home was the most wearisome. Ben was in the window seat. They were flying westward, somewhere over northern Ontario. He watched frozen lakes and barren ground inch by outside the oval Plexiglas window. The plane lifted above the clouds and the uncertain heavens, and the wild blue yonder filled his view. His world, their world had shifted. Of that he was sure. Georgia Lee was in the hospital. Had there been an accident? Mark had not described the circumstances clearly, and now Ben could recall only phrases of their disjointed conversation. Found in a snow bank. Head injuries. These two phrases blinked off and on in his mind like neon signs: red letters on a background of night sky.

He remembered the wallet-sized card that had been presented on his American Airlines breakfast tray. It showed a beautiful sparkling river, flowing from a distant mountain range out to sea. The scene was bathed in the warm golden orange light of a sunset. The opening verse of Psalm 107 was printed in the sky above the mountain range: *Give thanks to the Lord for He is good; His love endures forever.* This unwelcome intrusion of the hollow promises of religion infuriated him, and he resolved to write a letter of complaint to the airline's management. *No bargaining,* he told himself. *I will not be caught up in that superstitious drivel. No bargaining,* he said, repeating the words over and over like a prayer.

He looked at Rona. At last, she was sleeping. Unlike him, she had not had a religious upbringing. After her mother died, the housekeeper had continued to keep a kosher kitchen, but that was the extent of family observance. Rona's ideas about religious observance consisted of preparing traditional foods for the holidays when she, a slave to her superstitious nature, made everything kosher, but only for those eight days. During the '80s, she had joined the women's minyan (dubbed Lesbians for the Torah by some local critics) that held alternative services on the holidays and new moons and went in for using Obie's steam baths or the lake at Winnipeg Beach as a mikvah.

She and Ben had never discussed what praying meant. She went in for superstitions and the age-old nuggets of wisdom reclaimed and recycled in trendy New Age rituals. Some of these he agreed with. *Say whatever prayers you like,* he told her. *But,* he said, *if prayer did any good, we would be hiring people to pray.*

His thoughts were interrupted when the pilot came over the loudspeaker and announced that they were twenty-five minutes out of Winnipeg and that the air temperature there was plus 10 degrees on the Celsius scale. Ben turned his watch back an hour. There was nothing to look forward to.

Ben found Mark standing at the foot of the escalator by the baggage carousel. As soon as Mark saw them, he waved his hand in greeting. He smiled, but then his face registered a note of panic, and his smile fell off and he looked away.

Warm coats and scarves were draped over the luggage cart and, strangely, the sight of them made Ben's spirits rise. Home. They were home. Rona brushed past him and confronted Mark.

"Where is she? Where is Georgia Lee?" she demanded. "I want to go to the hospital now. Let's go see her." She tugged on his coat sleeve, and her breath assaulted his nostrils with its sour strength. "Now."

Mark hesitated. Beads of perspiration stood out on his temples, spoiling his otherwise immaculate appearance.

Rona repeated her question. Mark hesitated until Ben was beside them.

"I am sorry," Mark said. "I have bad news."

"What do you mean?" whispered Rona. "What news?"

"Tell us," said Ben. He saw that Mark was trembling and put his arm around his brother-in-law's thin shoulders.

"This isn't a good place to talk about it," Mark answered as he stepped away from Ben. "Let's go to my house."

"Did she run off with Waylon again? Is he in Winnipeg now?"

Mark shook his head.

"My God, my god, she's dead, my god." Rona was shrieking. "She's dead. Isn't she?"

Ben pulled her close to him and whispered to her. Then she began crying with loud carrying sobs. Other travellers gave them quick, curious glances and looked away.

Rona staggered as she walked toward the exit. The men took her by the arms and walked her over to the automatic door. Mark whispered to Ben that once they got her in the car, he would go back to get their luggage. They walked Rona out into the sunlight and over to Mark's BMW and bundled her into the back seat. Ben climbed in beside her and waited for Mark, who slowly settled himself in the driver's seat and switched on the ignition and turned the heater and fan on to high. Immediately, a Miles Davis trumpet solo blared from the CD player. Mark punched the stop button quickly, embarrassed at this unexpected indication of his less-than-total absorption in the matters at hand.

"Look," he said, "I think we'd all like to get away from here as soon as possible. I'll get your bags. Then we are going to go to my house, and I'll tell you what I know." He turned to look at them. Rona's tanned hands screened her face. Ben nodded to him. Rona's intermittent sobs echoed in the car. A jagged lament that proved that something terrible was admitted. Ben held her head close to his chest and gently stroked her back.

After a lengthy interval, Mark returned. He angrily thumped the luggage into the trunk and pushed the cart aside, leaving it adrift on the gritty snow. No one spoke on the ten-minute drive to Mark's building on the riverside or in the mirrored elevator as they rode up to the penthouse.

The air in the condo was very warm. Mark kept it at a humid 75 degrees Fahrenheit, ideal for his rare orchid collection. His elegant suite was professionally decorated with sleek couches in tan suede, chrome-and-glass tables, brushed aluminium lighting fixtures, and bleached wood floors that gave it a high-tech look. His Ivan Eyre landscape was centred precisely over the couch. His orchids were displayed in his collection of celadon and black porcelain jardinières. Both Rona and Ben disliked the effect. In private, they'd joked that it was as cosy as a Star Trek set or some posh intergalactic hotel suite.

They settled themselves on one of the soft couches, and Mark made them tea. He told them about the visit from detectives Friesen and Dunblane. Georgia Lee had never been in any trouble, so she had no fingerprints on file. The detectives had requested that Mark go with them to the Forensic Centre to visually identify Georgia Lee's body.

Mark tensed as he struggled against the urge to blurt out the whole nightmare of identifying the body. He and the detectives had met an orderly who had the keys, and they had gone to the morgue, a room that he found was as frightful as anything he had ever imagined. They went through a heavy steel door into a cold room where the bodies of the newly dead were stored, wrapped up in crinkly white plastic shrouds. There were nine of them, misshapen bundles of various sizes, displayed there on stretchers like unclaimed batches of laundry. The diener had gone over to one in the corner. One bare big toe with a lick of green polish on the nail peeked out of the plastic wrapping. A tag was tied around it with a thin wire fastener. It read *female, unknown, found at York Street and the Canadian National railway trestle.* That is what finally got to him: the thought that she had been down there in the snow and he had walked by the large plate glass windows in his office and looked out over that ugly old railway bridge dozens of times in the last few days.

The detectives had asked if he knew of any identifying marks or distinguishing characteristics that his niece had. All he could think of was the tongue stud she had shown him the last time they met. They had asked him about dental visits. They wanted him to look at the body but said they planned to do a comparison of dental records to be certain.

At the morgue, the diener wanted to know if he was comfortable with looking at the body. Mark had never felt less comfortable. In addition to being cold, the room had smelt of strong bleach. And there was another sharp sour organic odour, a dark stink under the chlorine that he would forever recall as the stench of death. He nodded in assent, eager to discharge this grim duty, and the diener moved to the head of the stretcher and with gloved hands quickly folded back the white plastic sheeting covering the face.

"And this person definitely has a silver metal stud through her tongue? My niece had one of those put in before Christmas. I saw it when we had lunch together." He winced at the memory of that disfiguring adornment. "Also, she had another earring with a pink stone through her navel."

"Yes, this girl has a pierced tongue," answered the diener. Mark's mention of the navel piercing was noted, and they told him that the girl did not have a belly ring there at autopsy.

It definitely was Georgia Lee. Her eyes had been closed and she'd looked very dead – even waxen, like a damaged mannequin – under the morgue's harsh florescent lights. *Murder* was such a dark word that he had pushed it away immediately, perspiring profusely despite the air in the cooler. After he got home, he'd had to wash his hands to the elbows for eight minutes (which he understood from Lisa, his second ex-wife, the doctor, to be the requirement for surgery), and he bundled and took all his clothing to the cleaners.

He'd thought of Georgie on summer weekends out at his cottage at West Hawk Lake. He pictured her curious ten-year-old self, picking wild blueberries and helping Rona make a pie. On August nights, they would lie on their backs on warm rocks to watch the Pleiades shoot across the pitch-dark sky. "Look," she'd said, "the man in the moon is smiling at us." He and Ben had taken her on canoe trips exploring the lakeshore. She had been certain they would find a new place, where no one had ever been. "How can you tell," she had asked when they'd beached their canoe, "if any people have been here before us? I claim this land for the people of the Kay-Stern tribe," she had said resolutely as she planted her miniature Israeli flag left over from that spring's Independence Day party at *cheder*.

Mark had been married then, if memory served, to his first wife, Marsha, the concert violinist. He was not sure he ever wanted kids, and that was what had broken up both of his brief marriages. He never managed to stay with any one woman. He had told his shrink he was afraid of being swallowed up. Like by all the old auntie types who pinch your cheeks and say you look good enough to eat while they squash you into their enormous bosoms. It was like being smothered by two soft pillows. It was very frightening for a small boy. Eventually marriage, for Mark, came to the same thing.

Mark had enjoyed those long-ago summers with Georgie. The drive out to the lake was what he liked best. The promised pleasures of leaving work at noon on Fridays, loading the car with books, clothes, bathing suits, bedding, and towels, and swinging by the deli to pick up the weekend's groceries. Their caravan of cars left behind the city and its responsibilities and the heat, driving east over the Ontario border into the heavily forested wilderness of the Canadian Shield.

The warm air in his condo made Mark feel drowsy. He could not think of anything safe to say. He decided that he would keep the story of his visit to the morgue quiet for now. He would have to tell someone. But who? Being single had its drawbacks. His trumpet-playing psychiatrist had moved on to California, and the thought of starting over again with another shrink was insupportable.

Mark looked across the table at their now-empty teacups. No one took any of the cookies he'd set out. He watched Ben and Rona through half-closed lids. She had her long legs drawn up under her chin; her bare feet were digging onto the nap of the tan suede upholstery. Loose strands of her hair fell over her cheek. She was massaging the middle knuckle of her left ring finger with a vigorous motion. He imagined she might suddenly pull her wide, gold wedding band off and chuck it across the room. Ben sat close to her; he was rubbing the nape of her neck in small contiguous circles with the tips of his fingers.

"Did you call Beryl and Zach?" Mark asked. He knew that their older sister would have a steadying influence on Rona. And he looked forward to putting the arrangements into her capable hands. He had confided the awful details to Beryl but had sworn her to secrecy until Ben and Rona arrived home.

"Yes," Ben said, "I called them from Houston to let them know she was in the hospital."

Mark thought that remark sounded sarcastic. He didn't want to get into an argument; he was too exhausted to defend his position tonight. They should all go to sleep. Talk it over in the morning. Rona was upset Mark had not mentioned Georgia Lee's job, which he had known about because it was at his neighbourhood video rental place.

He had shrugged when Rona had grilled him about their daughter's activities. "You said to leave the kid alone," he had reminded her, "so I did."

There were no funeral plans. According to their religious law and custom, Georgia Lee should have been buried within twenty-four hours of her death. Who knew when she died? There had been an autopsy. It seemed that fate had blown them so far off course that they were at a loss about where to begin. Mark thought of calling the place, the place you call for that, but he could not remember who it was you called. He looked over at Rona, who was now relaxed in the circle of Ben's arms.

"Earlier today," said Mark, "I was thinking of her out at the cabin. Remember how she loved to go canoeing? Once she told me that she liked being there more than anywhere else on the whole planet. When she said that, she was only 5 years old, but you could tell she had some idea of the size of the world."

"It's an ugly world!" Rona shouted. "Dammit, Mark, don't give her eulogy now. I won't allow it." She burst into sobs again. Ben tried to put his arms around her, but she pushed him away and went out onto the balcony. She stood out there in the cold air looking down on the dark, swollen river.

Winnipeg   April 19, 1997

Rona sat quietly, slumped over in the 1963 red Mercedes two-seater. Mark had lent them his prized car to use in lieu of their own that sat, de-insured, in his garage so Ben could drive to the main police station to pick up the keys for the special lock the police had installed on the door to Georgia Lee's apartment. The police insisted that he come to be interviewed and collect this key before going to the suite.

Rona rolled down the window to clear out the stale sun-warmed air inside the car. They were parked downtown in the warehouse district beside a triangular parkette, a browned scrap of trampled city grass that was partially fenced in by black wrought-iron railings. A warm breeze carried the piquant aroma of fried onions, hot dogs, and chips from a lunch cart parked on the terrace of interlocking bricks that surrounded a small wooden stage. She saw a few lean, pale-skinned, dark-clothed arts types, uniformed city workers, and regular bums, all sitting on the park benches enjoying the sun.

Ben had left the radio on auxiliary power when he'd turned off the motor. She heard the announcer say that the temperature was now up to 7 degrees Celsius. The warm sunny weather was expected to continue through the weekend. Then he announced the sounding of the official time signal from the National Research Council in Ottawa. A series of short beeps, followed by ten seconds of silence, then one long dash. That meant it was ten o'clock Central Daylight Time.

The news came on, and the excited announcer almost tripped over his tongue as he described how the mighty roaring Red had rushed over the dikes guarding Grand Forks, North Dakota, leaving that city's whole downtown underwater. And, he added, that included the well-known Whitey's Bar and Grill, a spot dear to the hearts of generations of Winnipeggers who liked to go across the line for a long holiday weekend. Rona tried to picture all of Grand Forks underwater. All of the places she and Ben and Georgia Lee liked to go to shop and eat out. And, the announcer added, whatever was above water in downtown Grand Forks was on fire. He spoke quickly, keen to share the amazing details of this fresh disaster.

She thought about the lost city of Atlantis and the legions of fishes populating its watery depths. She began to wish that the water would hurry, hurry up the Red River Valley and cover all of Winnipeg. She longed to surrender to an irresistible current, to be borne away on a cleansing flood that would free her, carry her onward to peaceful days in a garden of unearthly delights, beyond the confining frame of her own mind. She was eager for the peace that the waters would bring, covering all with a cool, muddy deep.

Rona heard the announcer read out appeals for volunteers to sandbag in Elmwood and West Kildonan, Fort Gary, and St. Norbert, but the names of these familiar areas of the city scarcely registered. She felt the force of dark waves rolling up against her, lapping at her shoulders. She put her head back on the seat and let the waters pull her down into the quiet.

Ben received a nod of sympathy when he gave his name and Georgia Lee's to the officer on duty at the front desk of the police station. He was escorted upstairs to the second-floor offices of the Identification unit. He presented the business card that Jake Friesen had left with

Mark to another uniformed cop behind that desk. A phone call was made, and Detective Friesen appeared with a uniformed officer he introduced as Constable Tim Petrie.

They led Ben to a nondescript office with bare walls painted in high-gloss tan-coloured paint. It was furnished with a grey metal desk and two side chairs upholstered in black vinyl. A narrow rectangle of bright sunlight poured in through the dirt-streaked window, and the light harshly illuminated the scrapes and dark scuffmarks on the battered furniture. Never did Ben expect that he would be inside a police station listening to the words *homicide* and *your daughter* in the same sentence. He watched as they took up their positions.

The lanky Constable Petrie sat down and tucked himself in behind the desk and placed a legal-size manila file folder on the bare desktop. Friesen remained standing until Ben took the chair indicated near the window; then the detective perched himself on the edge of the desk at Petrie's right elbow. His dark suit jacket fell open, and Ben saw a beam of sunlight glinting off the gold metal of the detective's shield, which was clipped over his black leather belt.

Detective Friesen asked if he or Rona had been able to come up with any more names to add to the list of Georgia Lee's friends. They had not, and it troubled Ben to have to admit that they were not more well-informed. He reiterated that she had not mentioned any particular names of new friends or classmates in the last number of months. Nor had she told them about her part-time job at the video rental store.

Georgia must have met other students in her classes at university, but he did not know any names. This lack of information was worrying. It added to growing list of things that they did not know about their daughter. Things she had changed. Her hairstyle, her punkish clothes, her pierced navel – about this, they'd also heard from Mark.

The detective asked Ben to tell them more about the time Georgia Lee ran away from home. Friesen said that though they knew the story and had read the Missing Person's report filed at the time, he wanted to hear Ben's version of the events.

It was true that at 14, Georgia Lee had bolted after a quarrel with Rona over giving up on her traditional dancing classes. Ben said Georgia Lee was confused then. It was not unusual for kids who were cross-culturally adopted to have a rough adolescence. Everyone knows it's no easy time. That was the explanation given to them four years ago. Many of the families they knew through their adoption support group had experienced similar and even worse episodes of rebellion. ("Don't say those words," Rona had cautioned him then. She meant drugs, booze, and unwanted pregnancy. "Don't call them down.") Rona had grumbled about the lessons for months. She did not want Georgia to take the dancing lessons, nor did she want her to quit the lessons, once begun, in midterm. She sparked a huge quarrel when she told Georgia Lee that she must learn to finish things.

Georgia Lee had walked out and was gone for ten days. She had stayed with friends on "sleepovers" for three nights and then moved into her cousin Waylon Spence's apartment in a roach-infested house on Qu'Appelle Avenue. His bachelor suite was not big enough for both of them. She had been sleeping on his beat-up couch, and Waylon had camped out on the floor in a sleeping bag. The landlord had been unwilling to have her, and Georgia Lee was refused the social assistance needed to pay her share of the rent.

Waylon had telephoned Ben and explained the situation. Ben was able to persuade her to return home and to agree to some new house rules. Things were not quite the same between Rona and Georgia Lee after that. Rona was blind to the fact that Georgia Lee had been rebelling against their authority, not their love. Their family therapist had said they should accept it as normal teenage behaviour.

Ben heard Constable Petrie clear his throat with a sound like a front-end loader dumping gravel. Petrie took off his glasses and opened the file. He paged through the contents with long fingers and evened out the bottom edges of the differing sizes of papers by tapping them on the desktop, as if trying to dislodge some minor piece of information about the case that he had overlooked but that would prove helpful in its solution.

As Ben watched this performance, he found himself wondering if the guy played piano. He had long, slender fingers with clean, very short-clipped fingernails. Why was Ben even thinking of such a thing now? The idea so discomfited Ben that he flushed and looked at his lap as if the weave of his trousers held some sudden fascination. He looked up at the officers again and saw in their flat facial expressions that both cops were disappointed by the contents of the file folder.

Petrie closed the folder. He admitted that the investigation of the scene and of Georgia Lee's apartment had not produced anything that could generate an immediate arrest. They had received few tips despite the considerable publicity the case had generated. He alluded to microscopic examination of evidence collected at the railway under-pass, during the autopsy, and in her apartment. There was likely going to be some delay in processing at the lab, but this should not hamper their investigation unduly.

The investigators needed to keep certain of her personal effects for the time being, including her computer. Police department experts were analysing her computer files and e-mails. The parents were probably unaware of her online journal. (They were.) "Here," Petrie said, passing over a sheaf of pages. "I had a copy made for you."

He continued speaking, referring to complex crime scene analyses, toxicological examinations, and DNA tests. Certain aspects of their investigation must remain known only to the investigators for the time being. He repeated that the main problem was that although eight days had passed since the discovery of her body, little new information had been uncovered.

Detective Friesen presented their theory that the fatal assault, as he called it, had taken place at a location other than where she was found. They had not established where that was. No witnesses had come forward. They had interviewed her friends, other students, the staff at the coffee-house, the clerks at the video rental place, and people in her apartment block. She had no connections to any of the street gangs. Neither their informants nor the tip line had yielded any intell. Ben watched the detective's lean, impassive face for clues about what had happened to Georgia Lee. They gave him little direct information about her injuries.

The detective told Ben that the family should contact an investigator named Maud Fallon at the Medical Examiner's office for what he referred to as the "medical details." They knew how Georgia Lee died but would only say it was immediate, implying that she did not suffer. Both cops maintained a manner that was kind and sympathetic about his loss and allowed no show of emotion other than a fierce appetite for information as to the where, why, and whodunit.

"I swear to you that we will keep on searching until we find the man who did this," said Friesen. "We will find him."

"Please. That's like taking on a whole world," said Ben as he put up a hand to silence him. "Don't promise that. I know this world. So do you. I know that you will try."

Constable Petrie cleared his throat again and asked how the family was doing.

Ben thought of Rona's tears, her inability to eat, the way she sat in Mark's apartment and stared out at the river for hours. She refused to try to speak to friends who called. The true answer was that their world had imploded and they were sifting through the ashes of that bleak landscape like two survivors of an atomic-size blast. No one wanted to hear that kind of talk. What could he say to people other than that she was in shock? That was what Murray Fine, their family doctor, had said when he prescribed the sleeping pills that gave Rona a small measure of peace.

Detective Friesen asked if the family would like to be referred to the police department's Victim Services branch. He indicated that counselling was available, plus compensation for the criminal injury sustained and sometimes assistance with burial expenses if the family met certain requirements.

Without looking at it, Ben wearily accepted another business card for the contact person in that department and added it to his collection. He had one with the police incident number, others with phone numbers for the detectives, and other scraps of paper with numbers for the Forensic Centre morgue, *Hevra Kadisha* (the Jewish burial service), and the reform rabbi's pager.

Constable Petrie then produced a playing-card-sized envelope with various notations scrawled across the seal. He looked carefully at these, then tore the envelope open and shook out a single brass key. He passed it to Ben as he explained that it was for the temporary lock that he had ordered installed on Georgia Lee's apartment door after their examination of the premises. He said he was relieved that he could tell Ben that Georgia Lee was not assaulted there. The only other person to enter her suite had been the man from the janitorial agency Ben had hired to clean up after the police had visited to seize evidence. And one more thing, the constable said: they had been looking after the bird they had found in her apartment and, if it was her bird, they would like to return it now.

Ben was shocked that neither he nor Rona had given a thought to the fate of little Nikolai Vasilyevich Gadol. Nikolai was not quite a member of the family but was certainly held in sufficiently high standing, not like some boring old-country third cousin whose name easily slipped the mind. Ben felt tears well up in his eyes when the tall cop carried the dainty ancient brass cage into the room.

Rona's grandmother had been the original owner of the original Nikolai and the little cage; on its faded pale blue cover, she had hand-embroidered the bird's name in Hebrew. Sonya had kept a songbird since she came to Canada from Yalta as a 5-year-old girl in 1910. The cage had sat between the *bawbi* and *zaida's* blue plush-covered easy chairs in the living room of their tiny white frame cottage on Charles Street. Little Rona, Beryl, and Mark had sat on the worn tan-leather ottoman between the chairs and listened as the *bawbi* told old-country stories. This Nikolai was Nikolai Gadol the Sixth, and Rona had entrusted him to Georgia Lee before they had left on their sabbatical.

The policemen stood, seemingly ill at ease, and nodded in silence as Ben tucked the small key into his inside jacket pocket and stood up. He felt dizzy and knew he should sit down again, but he was eager to get out of the airless room. There was a tightness in his chest that increased with every breath. He hooked two fingers through the ring on top of Nikolai's cage and waited as Constable Petrie opened the door for him to pass by. In silence, they escorted him to the elevator and even pressed the button for him, as if he were some feeble old man. Befuddled. He was perspiring and felt faint, and since both hands were busy with his sheaf of papers and the bird cage, he wiped his forehead with the sleeve of his old, tan raincoat and thought of how distressed Rona would have been if she'd seen such an uncouth move.

When he came out of the building, he saw two inebriated Native men wavering as they tacked their way across the triangular park. They could be anywhere from 25 to 40 years old. It was difficult to say. They looked exhausted, and careworn, like refugees camped out in a city that denied them its freedoms. Their old red-and-white-and-black Chicago Bulls team jackets were dirty and torn, and the men seemed oblivious to the bustle and the heightened rhythms of the city and the encroaching floodwaters. Hadn't they heard the rumour that the river water might rise up over the Forks, flooding out Louis Riel's grave in front of the old cathedral in St. Boniface and swirl on through the downtown streets to inundate the concourse and shops at Portage and Main?

Ben thought about Georgia Lee's birth family up at Footprint Lake. He should try to contact them. *Who was left?* he wondered. The band office would know. What about Waylon? He was closest to Georgia Lee. He should be told. A touchy subject. Was he still in Japan? Before he'd left, he and Ben had suspended his restored 1966 Harley by ropes and pulleys from the rafters of their Canora Street garage, where Ben and Georgia had figured that Rona would never catch sight of it. Rona was not to know until later about Georgia's campaign for a gap year and the road trip the kids had planned. Ben had told Waylon and Georgia they would delay that talk until he and had Rona returned from sabbatical.

As he approached the car, Ben saw Rona sitting where he'd left her in the front seat, her head lolled over against the window frame. Was she sleeping? He hesitated to disturb her. She needed rest more than anything. He sat down on a park bench about 5 feet in front of the car and let the sun warm him. Ben looked at the letters of the Hebrew alphabet embroidered in golden thread on the faded blue cover of Nikolai Gadol's cage. He could barely tell one from the other. Like a blind man, he ran his fingers over the surface of the letters. *Nun, koff, lamed,* and *gimel.* The tilted old lettering like pale ghosts from his childhood days in the *shul* beside his father. He knew that the letters spelled out the bird's name as Nikolai Gadol, which was as close to his full title as the *bawbi* could manage at age 12. Later, she had added a tiny crown over the letters and surrounded them with French knots.

The little bird was silent, but a beautiful aria, the *Dome épais le jasmin* by Lakmé, began to play in Ben's head. He heard it as pure and true as he had first heard it at the Met, when Joan Sutherland and Jane Berbié had enchanted him with their silken voices. He sat there listening as each angelic note played and eased him with a healing balm. He felt that he understood something, though he could not specify what it was.

Ben wished that Rona could hear what he heard, feel what he felt. The song rose from a forgotten part of his heart, and he also wished that he could open his mouth wide and let the golden words pour out comfort to her. He thought of the phrase "with a perfect heart." He could not recall its source, except he had a faint notion that it was part of a long-forgotten prayer. He wished he could speak with his mother, and at the same time, he was thankful she was not alive to see his despair. He regretted he had forgotten how to pray. He covered his face with his hands and let tears run down his cheeks, wetting his fingers. They felt as warm as blood.

Each day since Mark had called them in Quepos had brought another dilemma. They had rented their Canora Street house out until the end of June, when they planned to return from Central America. Yesterday afternoon, he and Rona had gone to call on the tenants and pick up some personal articles and books. They'd walked up to the oak front door, past the shelter of sentinel elms covered with green buds that in a few days would leaf out to full canopies to shade their second-floor windows. Faithful and bright, yellow, white, and purple crocuses were in bloom at the hem of the cedars's skirts in the front flowerbeds.

Ben had reached to press the doorbell and noted the laminated note card fastened above it. In firm handed italics, the card read: Dr. Charles and Mrs. Caroline Nash. Their renters were Brits, a visiting oncologist from Liverpool and his tense, blonde, years-younger, and now heavily pregnant wife. "Come this way," she'd said. "We'll take a detour through the sitting room." Caroline Nash had waved her hand dismissively at their living room sofa and led them quickly through the familiar layout. She had given Ben the impression of a snobbish real-estate agent showing a property that she felt had little potential. He half-expected her to begin making comments on possible redecorating schemes.

Ben noted with a pang that the French ormolu clock Rona had inherited from her grandmother was missing from its usual place on their mantel. Then he remembered. Before they had gone away, they'd taken an inventory of their most personal and precious belongings. The pretty clock had been sequestered, unwound, with their other cherished things in a locked third-floor room under the eaves.

To Ben and Rona's surprise, Ruth Oddy, the retired schoolteacher who lived next door, was in the sunroom; she'd looked up quizzically when they'd walked in. Her stocky little Hobbit's body had been backed up into the corner of their beige linen-covered love seat, and she had been leafing through a back issue of a magazine on the Royal family. One of her voluminous scrapbooks, the Princess Anne archives, had been open on the wicker coffee table. Clearly, Ben and Rona's visit had interrupted a heart-to-heart session on the Royals. While Miss Oddy had greeted them in her usual lukewarm manner and expressed her sympathy for their loss, she had looked at the Kay-Sterns with mild disapproval, as if she was hoping they would not be too colourful in their grief.

"I must be off now," she'd announced, cutting Ben off in mid-sentence. "Will you be able to manage, Caroline?" She paused. "Shall I bring the tea in before I go?"

"No, I'll be fine. Thank you so much for your kind advice."

Miss Oddy had given the Kay-Sterns a bob of her brightly hennaed head and a tight-lipped smile and slipped away through the side door that opened off the kitchen.

Caroline had served tea to the Kay-Sterns in their sunroom. She had added milk and sugar lumps to their cups as they'd requested. When the rattling of silver spoons and small talk had ceased, Ben had asked if there was any possibility that they could get back in the house sooner than the end of June.

Caroline had said she regretted that was impossible. There was no immediate likelihood that she and Charles could change their arrangements. It was, regrettably, out of the question. Certainly she realized that they were in an awkward situation. She and Charles had got some of the details out of the paper. And some policemen had come round, once they had learned who the girl was, to ask if she and Charles had seen or heard from her since they had moved in. Caroline's answer to the police had been a definite no. The same definite no that she gave to members of the press who came around with requests to see the interior and, more strangely still, the girl's bedroom. She had put them right on that question.

The bedroom that had been Georgia Lee's looked out into the crown of one of the elm trees in front of their house. Her room had been dismantled when she'd moved into her apartment. Her stuffed animal collection had gone into storage on the third floor. The walls had been repainted a mild sage green to complement the simple linen drapes and the brown and cream French mattress ticking of the slipcover on the new hideaway bed and the accent pillows covered in vintage French fabrics. The transformation from bedroom to guest room had been complete. There was nothing for the journalists to see.

"I am sorry." Caroline Nash had said this in a clear tone that suggested she was spelling it all out for them in uppercase letters. "You let the house until the first of June. We regret that you are having difficulties, but where are we to go?" She had shaken her sleek blonde head. "Surely some of your friends or family connections will take you in."

Ben offered to put the Nashes up at his expense, in a hotel of their choice, but Caroline would have none of that. Too disruptive for Charles, she claimed. With his heavy workload at the hospital, he needed a calming routine after hours. And for someone in her condition, they would understand, another move at this time would be most difficult.

Rona had been speechless. From the sunroom, she could see through to their warm, yellow-painted kitchen with its white cupboards, the open shelves of her own carefully glazed hand-thrown dishes, her collection of bright Mexican pottery, and her own colourful weavings hanging on the wall of the breakfast nook. She told Ben later that she'd felt so poor then, so let down at being denied a return to her own home.

As they were leaving, Caroline had asked if the house had a sump pump. Charles had reminded her that morning to clarify the matter.

"Everyone tells us that these are essential to avoid the flooding," she added.

Rona and Ben had stood on their front steps looking up Canora Street toward Wolseley. The warm sun had shone on them as they walked along, brushing by the pea green fuzz of new leaves on the caragana hedges that overhung the sidewalk. Without speaking, they'd begun to walk south toward the river. They had turned west at Wolseley and continued on in that direction to Laura Secord School. The light was shifting behind that old cream-coloured brick building, and the façade was in dark shadow. It looked dismal and forbidding as any government ministry in any provincial town. They had stood on the sidewalk watching the children on the playground. This had been Georgia Lee's first school and where they had dutifully attended meetings of the CCAP, the cross-cultural adoptive parents support group on the second Tuesday of each month.

Ben felt a sweet rush of closeness to Georgia Lee returning as they walked along her familiar paths. He could hear her excitedly calling out to them as she came into the house on the run, her long, dark brown veil of hair flowing behind her. The screen door banging closed. The broken halves of a robin's pale turquoise egg shell cradled in her small hands. He had believed that the love in their family provided a saving grace from the troubles of this savage world, and that grace was what you could depend on.

What then, had gone wrong with the love in theirs? In his? He had no memories of his family in Berlin and few of Charlotte, his delicate mother. Of her glorious nimbus of golden hair that grew thinner each day until, to her horror, her shapely head was smoothly bald and she began wearing a *sheitel,* not out of any religious feeling or pious duty but to conceal the shame that signalled her illness. It was like a coarse, shapeless mouse-brown hat, and it dulled her beauty as sickness took her strength. The Nazis had killed his father and the rest, his entire family. Ben had had no reason to go looking for them in Germany; no one was left. The photographs he had inherited might as well be of strangers.

His mother had died late in spring of the year of the war's end, and Ben had experienced an ever deeper version of the feeling of abandonment into which he's fallen as she lay dying. Although he did not understand it at the time, as a boy of 12 with his bar mitzvah unsung, he later realized that the unhappiness building up inside him had destroyed his faith when he needed it most.

Life in New York with his mother's elderly cousin Moishe had continued, a narrow round of school and *shul*. He'd married his first wife, Rivka, in his freshman year at Columbia. He was ashamed to admit to himself that one of the reasons he had proposed was so that he could join her large, noisy family. In the constant embrace of familiar arms, an instant *mispoche*.

Ben had fallen in love with Georgia Lee and Rona (all over again) from the moment he saw them together. It was his third and last chance for a family life. He'd gladly become the *paterfamilias* of the Canora Street house. He revelled in his domestic duties, his Saturday mornings devoted to household maintenance. On a seasonal schedule he cleaned windows, emptied gutters, raked leaves, shovelled snow, and checked the mortar in their chimneys. His lawn was a paragon of green velvet. He built a treehouse for Georgia Lee in the low-branching arms of the old cedar out back. His home became his temple, his worship of the mundane wholly satisfying.

And he, an urban Jew, who had never before planted a seed, put in a splendid vegetable garden. His radishes, carrots, beets, onions, potatoes, string beans, tomatoes, and herbs stretched in orderly 15-foot rows down to their back fence. The airy fronds of asparagus ferns swayed on spring breezes. His spades, shovels, edgers, trimmers, rakes, and clippers were neatly arrayed on pegboard in the garage. If he could have distilled all his happy labours into a single moment, it would be that one of joy when he brought his vegetable offerings to their table, heard his wife and daughter exclaim over their flavours, saw the two of them glow with health, and believed he was finally blessed with a time of true happiness.

The word *family* had always confounded Ben with all its attendant mysteries and miseries, its fervid rhythms that shape lives, with its sometimes spurious promises of comfort and sanctuary from the savage weather of the world. But he had not been truly aware that its structure was so enormously frail, that their peaceful kingdom could be so easily toppled.

Ben found Mark waiting for them in the lobby of his building when he and Rona returned from the police station. Mark was staring out through the glass front door to where a dump truck was dropping a load of sand off on the boulevard and an able-looking group of volunteers stood by, ready to fill sandbags. The security staff was buzzing around in their lobby office behind him, and other tenants were rushing in or out, or going to the parking garage. City works trucks dumped three more loads of sand on the side lawn, and the crew of volunteers began bagging it and carrying the bags through the lobby and out the riverside door. Mark was watching as the steady tramp of their shoes ground sand and mud into the lobby's pale grey carpet and scoured the marble floor. A new dike was going up behind the back of the building, down on the bank of the Assiniboine River, so swollen now with pressure from the Red that in a reversal of the natural order, it was flowing backwards from their confluence at the Forks.

"What took you so long?" Mark demanded as soon as he noticed Ben and Rona. Mark's forehead was dripping with sweat. "I need your car keys. The basement is about to flood, and I've got to move the cars up to the street. And I don't care if yours is de-insured. It has to be moved. And now! This is a real hoo-ha. The city is trying to stop us from using the street because it's an emergency route. Where are we supposed to park? Up in the trees? I paid a fabulous premium to live in this building with its extra-fancy reinforced walls, and do you think I can find that contractor today?

"By the way," he continued, nodding at his sister, "Beryl is arriving in forty-five minutes. Zach is finished teaching, so he came with her and so did the twins. Barbara and David can take time off from school, but Daniel is in the middle of his final exams so he's staying in Victoria.

"And Rabbi Sol Berman from Temple Israel called. Says he can do a graveside service on Sunday at 10:30 in the morning." Composure regained, he rattled all these items off in even-toned clipped speech, as if he were dictating a memo to his secretary.

"Okay, okay," Ben said. "I'll take Rona upstairs so she can lie down. Her headache's back. I'll call the rabbi and the *Hevra Kadisha*. We'll arrange to bury Georgia Lee next to your mother and father. You will have to go out to the airport and pick up the family."

Ben fished in his pants pocket for the borrowed car keys. He saw in Mark's sulky expression that he was balking at this suggestion, so he clamped a hand on each of the shorter man's shoulders, pinning him to the ground. That made it much easier to keep his right hand from slapping Mark's face. Anger was boiling in him. Such a boy Mark was – he knew when it was useful to play the baby brother. He couldn't even acknowledge any degree of responsibility for Georgia Lee's death. Why had they trusted him?

"Don't say another word, you little *putz*. I don't care. You are going to have to put everything on hold for the next few days. Do you understand? Your sister needs you to do this for her. I want Rona to rest. We have an appointment with the Medical Examiner later today."

***

Dr. David Bekker flipped quickly through the grim photos from the girl's file which he had spread out on top of his desk. The doctor quickly scanned the police department's photo contact sheets from the crime scene and the autopsy and selected enlargements showing the girl's damaged head and face. This was what made the job real for him. Bekker felt the return of that very familiar sense of unease as he steeled himself to review such photos analytically, hoping, always hoping, not to see a familiar face, not a face he had known smiling. After giving each a careful examination, he shuffled the photos into a loose, uneven pile and stuffed them back into the file pocket.

"Don't show them these," he instructed as he tapped the blue cover of the file with the eraser of his lead pencil. "I don't want the parents to see these." He looked up at Maud, who stood on the opposite side of his wide desk. "Have you nothing else? What about the one that was in the newspapers?" He leaned back in his chair and pulled off his black-framed reading glasses. He massaged the bump on his narrow, high-bridged nose.

Maud handed him her print of the police photo that had been in the newspapers. He put his glasses back on to inspect it.

"Okay, that one, it will be all right. But no more. By the time the pictures can be released after a trial, the family may not want them.

And don't tell them about the bite marks. Don't let that get out. The cops like us to hold something back. That helps them weed out any crazies, any fruit and nut bars that try to confess to the thing. We'll say that she was not raped, I mean not violated. Tell them that they, eventually, they can have a full report, but emphasize that they should remember her as she was." He paused, waiting for Maud to acknowledge these directives.

She nodded.

"And, did you left to me, ah, leave for me, a message about another group that wants to claim her?"

"Yes, sir. A Bernice Spence. She's a lawyer for the Manitou Society and a cousin to the girl through her birth family. She contacted me yesterday afternoon, and she brought the grandmother in to do a viewing. They identified her only by her birth family name and status as a member of Footprint Lake Cree nation. At that point, I was unaware that on the previous evening, the police had taken an uncle from the adoptive family into the morgue and he made a positive ID under the other name. The uncle, Mark Kay, who is also a lawyer, told the police that his sister and brother-in-law adopted her when she was a week old and she has always lived with them."

"This is astonishing. Claimed by two families, you say? Do these people know each other?"

"I can't say what that story is. The lawyer for the Manitou Society didn't mention anything about an adoption to me."

"What are they saying then? That the claim for the girl's body is based on the mother's, and I mean natural mother's race? Do you know? I thought that Native status was based on a link to a band that signed a treaty with the British government. Not the mother's status. And what about the father? Is he known? I have never heard that about

Natives here. We know about the Jewish people. I mean among themselves, that is how they tell – if the mother is Jewish, so is the child. We do not like to ask those questions. I know that if one parent is French and one is Native, the child is Métis, but is that in the law? I didn't know we had identity legislation here in Canada. I thought I left all of that behind me in South Africa."

"I understand that the lawyer did say that the girl's father was unknown. I mean it's hard to say; he could be Native, too. Or Métis."

Bekker tipped back further in his chair, and with his hands clasped behind his neck, he rested his head on his knitted fingers. "The police have nothing so far?" He raised his eyebrows as he raised his voice at the end of his sentence.

Bekker had never mentioned Maud's relationship with Jake, but she suspected he knew and didn't approve. If he approved, he would mention that he was aware of it. Instead, he referred to her "contacts" in the CAPU, or Crimes Against Persons Unit. He had good contacts, too; everyone understood that. The number for his private fax machine was widely known.

"Did you ask the lab to rush the tox report?" he asked. "I have suspicions she was on something." He paused to give Maud a piercing look. "Don't you?"

"Anything's possible, sir."

"Ja. But what is likely? She's not your average Jewish girl, is she? She is maybe an Indian princess, not a Jewish one." He chuckled at his joke and passed her case notes back. "Waylon Spence – that sounds like a Native name, doesn't it?" At this, his stomach grumbled loudly, and they both checked the time on the wall clock: 11:35. Twenty-five minutes until his lunch meeting with the Rotary Club.

Maud shrugged. "Could be, sir."

"I wonder when she wrote that message on her leg. Seems odd, doesn't it? Maybe she was planning another visit to the tattoo parlour?"

When Maud did not respond to his musings except by raising her eyebrows, he continued. "You did want me to sit in when you meet with the family? What time are they coming? You said after lunch?"

"Yes," she answered, "they're coming at 2:00 p.m. You'll be back from lunch by then, and I'll call if I need your help." She did not mention that she had taken a university course from Professor Stern. That was fifteen-plus years ago, so it was unlikely that he would remember her.

Bekker's direct phone line rang, and he punched the speakerphone button. "Yes," he grunted.

"It's Audrey Klassen down here at the front desk, sir. The security guard is escorting some people up to see you." She was wheezing, and her voice sounded slightly hoarse. "Some aboriginal people, sir. They say they are the family of that girl who was found under the railway bridge. And they want to claim the body. I told them that she was already claimed. They are demanding to see you about it, sir. *Now*, they say. They seem pretty worked up about it, sir."

"Okay, now Audrey, be a good girl now. Do not go and have an asthma attack on us. I know about their claim. I'll see them. Thanks for the heads up," he said crisply and punched the speaker off. He bounced to his feet. "Listen, Maud, I'll go to the conference room. You meet this bunch at the front desk and bring them in, but don't bring along anything from your file with you. I don't want them demanding to see our paperwork."

Maud stood beside the reception desk and listened to the whirr of the motor moving the elevator cables in the shaft. The polished steel doors sprung open, and a huge man moved forward like an advance guard. He was wearing a navy blue nylon jacket that had the letters

F.B.I. printed in white on the back. Maud knew that among Natives, the acronym stood for Full-Blooded Indian and that on the street, many said it really means Fucking Big Indian. He braced one-half of the door open with his back, and a very large hand and arm reached across the opening to the other half-door and held it ajar.

Bernice Spence walked under this arch and over the threshold of the office with brisk steps taken in her black square-toed pumps. She carried a black leather briefcase and wore a determined look. The man, whom Maud estimated stood well above the 6-foot mark and who looked like he weighed about 300 pounds, closely followed her. It was clear he qualified for the street's definition of F.B.I.

Bernice Spence approached the reception desk. She ignored Maud and placed her briefcase on the top of the desk and snapped open the locks and extracted some papers.

"We are the family of Georgia Lee Kay-Stern, formerly, and correctly, known as Rosie McKay. We are here to claim her body for burial. I want to see . . ." She paused to consult her face, though expressionless, showed high colour on her broad cheekbones.

The big man stepped in behind her left shoulder. He doffed the black Stetson he was wearing, leaned down, and in a conciliatory tone said, "I'm Teddy Boy Beardy, and I come along with my cousin, here, Bernice Spence. Like she said, we be the cousins of Rosie McKay, that girl who got killed during the blizzard. We want to take her home and give her a proper burial according to the ways of our people."

Maud greeted the two and asked them to follow her. They entered the boardroom close on her heels, and she swung around and asked them to take seats at the table. Bernice Spence set her briefcase down and opened a file and began to review its contents. She gave no indication that she had ever seen or spoken with Maud before this encounter. She pulled a cell phone out of her purse and keyed in a number.

"All ready to go down there?" she asked. "I'll call after we finish meeting with their chief." She dragged out her last two words in a parody of a politician's concerned tone. She snapped her phone shut and said "It's a go" to Teddy Boy Beardy, who had already settled into one of the leather swivel chairs. He nodded and began picking at his teeth with the silver toothpick that he'd taken out of his shirt pocket. He made a real production of it, daintily flicking his wrist as he worked his way around his mouth and sucking back the morsels he liberated.

Dr. Bekker walked in, and the visitors stood to greet him. He quickly introduced himself and shook their hands. "Now, what is this all about?" he began.

Bernice Spence handed him a business card. "I expect that your assistant" – she indicated Maud, who was standing off to the side – "told you that Mrs. Spence, the girl's grandmother, and I positively identified our Rosie's body for her yesterday afternoon at 3:30 p.m., and I fail to see what is holding up the release of our cousin to the Aboriginal People's Funeral Chapel, as we informed your office that they are the family's choice for Rosie's funeral arrangements.

"I am speaking as the representative of the birth family of Rosie ,McKay, also known by you folks as Georgia Kay-Stern, the name she was given when she was stolen by the white social workers and adopted out of our nation. I also represent the Manitou Repatriation Association, which, as you probably already know, is dedicated to finding the stolen children and bringing them home to our ancestral lands."

Bekker held up his hand to silence her and said, "That's rather strong language, isn't it? Saying she was stolen?"

"It's the truth, and we will keep telling it. How our people, how many of our women, were mistreated and brought to a low end and often a sad death here in your city."

She paused for breath. Bekker, who had been examining the business card she'd handed him, said, "I see that you are a member of the Manitoba Bar." He nodded at her. "Then you must be familiar with the legislation that governs the running of this office and the rights of families of the deceased to claim bodies. And you are aware that there is another family involved. The Kay-Stern family. Do you know them? They also wish to claim this girl." He lowered his voice and enunciated each word. "This girl that they raised from her infancy."

Bernice Spence jumped to her feet as he finished speaking. "So that means we, the members of the Cree nation from Footprint Lake, the birth family of Rosie McKay, cannot look to this government for justice?" she exclaimed. "We gave up too many of our children after our economic defeat under the Burntwood River dam project in the '70s. We are determined to find them all before time runs out." She banged her fist on the oak table. "First Nations repatriation programs have found hundreds of the 3,000 children adopted out and denied their heritage in the twenty-five years of our shame under this racist policy. We will not be denied again." She nodded to Teddy Boy, and he picked up the cell phone and called a number. He said a few sentences in Cree, then turned and nodded to Bernice.

"What you need to know," Dr. Bekker continued calmly, "is that there is, in the legislation, a preferred order of claimants for the deceased. We specified a hierarchy of types of relationships that is stipulated in the law to avoid any unpleasantness at what is always a difficult time. Later this afternoon, we are meeting with the adoptive parents, the Kay-Sterns, about their daughter. I will mention to them that you have contacted us. I request that the two families meet to discuss a solution to this situation. I am reminding you that, as Chief Medical Examiner, I can, under the legislation, impose a solution on the families, but it is always preferable that you come together for the sake of the deceased daughter."

Bernice returned her file to her briefcase without looking at Dr. Bekker. "Don't think you can buy us off with easy promises. It does not work anymore. I will apply to the courts for an injunction to prevent anyone other than her birth family from claiming her."

"Madam," said Bekker with a hint of the courtly demeanour he was known to use to charm the public, "that is your right. May I suggest that before you do, you review the governing legislation."

Bernice Spence ignored him and turned to Teddy. "Are they out there now?" she asked. Her arms were folded over her chest, and she stood her ground like a fierce miniature terrier ready to bark, bark, bark.

Teddy Boy nodded. He moved closer to the large windows that overlooked the street. "I see them. They're out there now," he said.

Bernice Spence, Dr. Bekker, and Maud followed him over to the windows. Down below and directly in front of the Forensic Sciences building, more than a dozen protestors carrying placards walked resolutely up and down from one end of the property to the other. An old man wearing his long, grey hair in a single braid and carrying an eagle feather led the marchers at a slow pace. He was dressed in a plaid shirt, blue jeans, and black cowboy boots. Another older man, who was beating on a round, flat, skin-covered handheld drum, followed him. Behind them walked two young men dressed in pants and shirts made of the blotchy green and brown fabric of Army surplus gear. They carried a sagging white banner that read *Footprint Lake Cree Nation* in large red letters. Behind them walked several women of varying ages and sizes, with two of the younger ones pushing children in strollers.

Bekker read the messages aloud. "'Medical Examiner unfair to Cree Nation.' 'Give us back our children.' 'Medical Examiner guilty of cultural genocide.'"

"First time we've been picketed, isn't it?" said Maud.

"I think their language is too strong, but they can go ahead as long as they do not block the entrance or interfere with the business of this office," he told Maud. He turned to Bernice and Teddy Boy. "Tell them that," he said. "And tell them that if they do interfere, they will all be charged with obstruction under the Fatalities Inquiry Act." He reached behind the drapes and pulled on the cord, closing them over the windows.

"Your group is going to have to meet with the Kay-Sterns, the adoptive parents, and work this out between you. That's the best, the easiest way. You discuss it together and have one spokesman contact me. I won't release her body for burial before then."

The two visitors nodded and walked out of the room. Bernice Spence was in the lead, holding her chin high and marching quickly. Her black high heels tapped a brisk tattoo on the tiled floor. Teddy Boy swaggered after her. He stopped beside the receptionist's desk and banged the flat of his large palm on its surface. "We'll be back," he said in imitation of Arnold Schwarzenegger's trademark retort.

At twenty minutes to 2:00, Maud walked into the boardroom and peeked out the window from behind a corner of the drapes. The marchers were still on the street. There were more of them now. A black pickup truck with the Brotherhood of Manitoba Chiefs logo emblazoned on the side door was parked at the curb, and several of the women were sitting on the tailgate and picnicking on hot dogs bought from a street vendor who had parked his cart across the street. A crew from the CBC newsroom was talking to Bernice Spence and Teddy Boy Beardy.

Dr. Bekker came up behind Maud to look over her shoulder.

"Now they've got the Chiefs involved and our friends from the media." He turned to Maud, who had stepped away from the window. "What time are the girl's parents coming in?"

"In twenty minutes."

"They'll have to walk in past this blockade. We can do nothing about that." He jerked the edge of the drape back over the glass and led the way out of the room.

As they passed the receptionist's desk, she held up fistfuls of pink message slips. "Dr. Bekker," she said wearily, "I've got calls for you from every media outlet in town. And both the Aboriginal Funeral Chapel and that Jewish place." She hesitated. "They're both asking when the girl's body will be released to prepare it for burial on Sunday. Both of them want it before five o'clock today. And the media are all asking the same question: Who is going to get her? Which family is going to bury this child?"

"They will all have to wait. No exceptions, that's my ruling. Nothing gets released on this case until I say so." Bekker shook his right index finger at her for emphasis. "Tell the media people that I have no comment for now. And tell our security guys to make sure the press and the protestors are not blocking our front door." As he walked down the hall to his corner office, he called back over his shoulder, "Get Grand Chief Billy Muswagon on the phone for me, will you. He's got to do a better job of keeping the other chiefs in line."

The cab driver pulled up under the portico, and Ben helped Rona from the car. She wore a scarf over her hair and large oval-framed sunglasses that covered her reddened eyes. She leaned heavily on him with her head bowed. They walked directly to the front door. Neither seemed to notice the protestors.

In the boardroom, Maud seated the Kay-Sterns side-by-side at one end of the large oak table and took a seat opposite them. They looked weary and bewildered. Professor Stern did not react when Maud introduced herself, so she decided not to mention that she was his former student. One of the thousands he'd taught. She began with the customary words of condolence. As she offered them, she thought her remarks seemed rehearsed, and she worried that her acknowledgment of their loss struck a note near false, like a keener's professional lament.

"How can they be so sure it's her?" asked Rona. "I have not seen her body. I would like to be sure. It could be some other girl." She spoke hesitantly and softly as she looked at the photograph Maud had handed to them. "Look at her, Ben. How can they say that this is our little girl?" She reached over to fish Ben's reading glasses out of his jacket pocket, set them on the narrow bridge of her nose and looked closely at the photo.

"This isn't her face," she cried out. "This isn't Georgia Lee. She doesn't look like our daughter. Her hair is long and she doesn't have bangs."

"Rona," said Ben in a gentle tone, "remember that Mark said she cut her hair? And they said she was wearing the yin-yang medallion that Waylon sent her from Japan."

Maud reached across the open file on the wide boardroom table to take the Polaroid photo from Rona's hands. She ignored Rona's last question. "We are sure that it is Georgia Lee," Maud said. "The forensic dentist did a special comparison of dental X-rays from Georgia Lee's orthodontist." She continued in a calm, firm tone. "We know she is your daughter, and we know she died quickly as a result of a blow to her head." She wished she could assure them that it was painless. There was no way of knowing.

Ben put his arm around Rona, pulled her close to his body, and cupped her left shoulder with his wide, square hand. She turned her face in toward him and buried herself against his neck. Her kerchief slid back, revealing wet, uncombed, flattened hair.

Maud tucked the photo back into the file. She had deliberately concealed the official police photos taken at the autopsy under other reports. She looked over at the parents. Ben met her glance and widened his eyes, as if asking for a moment's quiet. The Kay-Sterns' faces were hidden now, turned inward, completing their circle of two.

Maud briefly turned her attention to straightening out the papers in the file. A line from T.S. Eliot, which she had heard her dad recite, came to her: "After such knowledge, what forgiveness?" She heard herself silently ask why and then let that question flit away and moved on, eager to get through the business at hand. Ben looked directly at Maud again, nodding as if to ask her to go on.

"The information related to Georgia Lee's autopsy and the medical examiner's report will be available to you at a later date, if you wish to have a copy," Maud continued. "Remember that for reasons of law, we cannot release the details of these reports to anyone until there is a trial after the police find the person who may be responsible and lay charges. That may take some time. In the meanwhile, this office will assist you with completion of any medical or insurance forms you may have. Let me give you this brochure that describes our work."

Rona had been mute through this recital of bureaucratic policy and procedure. But when Maud pushed the brochure toward them, she snatched it and threw it on the floor. "Don't you understand?" she yelled. "I've got to know who murdered my daughter. Why wasn't anyone watching out for Georgia Lee?" Ben reached out to put his arm around her shoulders, but she angrily pushed him away. "Not even God cared."

"I am sure that the police are doing all they can," said Ben.

"I want to see her." Rona's words escaped like a low moan. "I have to see her."

"It's important that you remember her as she was," Maud said gently. "Your brother, Mark, identified her, and we are satisfied with that and the dental X-ray examination." She searched Ben's face for confirmation that he agreed with her.

"Why? Why do you say that we shouldn't see our daughter?" demanded Rona. "How can you know what a mother needs?"

Maud said gently, "I say that because I know from experience with other families that this is best. Remember her as she was. You will understand in time." As she spoke, she watched Rona's face go slack and pale as these dark notes sounded a moment of cruel lucidity, the death of dreams.

"You may see her at the funeral home," said Maud. "Believe me; it will be for the best." She got up and retrieved the discarded brochure from the floor and placed it on the table next to Ben. She did not say, *I know because I could scarcely bear to look at her myself.*

"Where is she?" Rona asked angrily. "Where have you put my daughter?"

"Her body is here in our morgue, and she will stay there until her funeral arrangements are finalized." Maud stood up. "Dr. Bekker, the Chief Medical Examiner, would like to meet with you for a few minutes. I am going to ask him to join us now." She picked up the file and began to walk out.

"They're never going to find the bastard that did this," Rona sobbed. "His trail's run cold. There's no way. It's been far too long."

Maud had to escape this raw grief. Her head began to throb as she strode down the hallway to summon the boss. Let him break the news about the McKay family's demands for the girl's body. She did not have the heart to deliver that news.

Dr. Bekker entered the boardroom first and introduced himself to the Kay-Sterns. He sat down, opened the file Maud had passed to him, and leafed through the documents and case notes. He bowed his head, pulled off his reading glasses, and rubbed each of his eyes in turn with the heel of his left hand. He looked directly at the parents until both of them met his gaze. He began by offering his condolences to Rona and Ben. "This is awful," he said. "This is very bad, very difficult for you. I can tell you your daughter died quickly. That we know her suffering was brief and there may be some consolation in knowing that although she was assaulted, she was not violated."

Rona exhaled a soft hiss. It seemed his use of formal language had done little to cushion the effect of his words. He did not elaborate on the nature of the assault. This was not the time to speak of bite marks, lethal blows, and semen.

He added that he knew Maud had advised them about the official reports and when these documents would be made available to them. He continued to talk about the girl's death and the wide effect it was having on the larger community. He mentioned the vigil and march that the members of Victims of Violence had conducted. He continued with a number of familiar platitudes about the circle of life and then asked them whether they remembered their daughter's birth family. He mentioned, almost as an aside, that some family members had contacted the office.

Ben nodded as he absorbed this. He had not forgotten the McKays. Yesterday, Mark had whispered to him that the police detectives who had interviewed him had asked questions about Waylon Spence. Ben was planning to try to locate them. He thought he could leave a message at the band office in Footprint Lake. Who was left? Was Granny Spence still alive? Someone at the band office would know. He'd planned to phone up to Footprint Lake. He'd been hoping for a good moment to discuss this with Rona.

Dr. Bekker coughed and continued, "Well, these people, they are taking the view that your daughter is also their daughter and relative and so they also wish to claim her body for burial. According to their custom. Of course."

"Of course," said Rona in a clear and loud voice.

Ben looked quizzically at Dr. Bekker. "We adopted Georgia Lee in a legal adoption when she was days old," Ben said. "And raised her in our home. Surely, we are her parents."

Rona stood up and even more loudly added, "We are, we are. My beautiful daughter was murdered. Now you tell me that those people, who never cared for her, for even one day, want her back." She started for the door, yelling over her shoulder, "Of course not."

Ben gave Maud a bewildered glance. "Excuse us," he said and hurried after Rona. She was in front of the elevator, pounding on the door with both fists. He bundled her into the elevator as soon as it arrived. Downstairs, she broke away from him and rushed out through the front door. He caught up to her on the pavement under the portico and tried again to restrain her in his arms. Some of the Native protestors stood on the sidewalk, doing interviews with news reporters from the CBC, and others milled around them, holding their placards aloft for the cameras. Rona pushed through the crowd of protestors, which parted in her wake. Dozens of pairs of eyes followed her as she sprinted out onto the road. A delivery van screeched to a halt inches from her in the westbound lane. The driver sounded his horn in an angry exclamation. Ben looked left and right and dashed after Rona.

As Ben went past, one of the reporters from the news crew called out, "Professor Stern!" Ben glanced back over his shoulder and made a dismissive motion. He could see Rona ahead, halfway down the block. She turned and looked back at him, then continued, walking more slowly now down the sidewalk along Maryland Street. Ben scurried after her.

Beryl saw Mark as soon as she stepped onto the down escalator at the Winnipeg airport. Her brother stood alone on the edge of the sizeable crowd with expectant upturned faces that waited in a ragged semi-circle at the foot of the escalator in the arrivals area. Mark was leaning on a luggage cart and reading a newspaper that he had balanced on the cart's upper basket. As usual, he'd dressed in a charcoal grey pin-striped suit and his trademark flat-crowned, embroidered hat like the Moroccan Jews favoured, which she knew concealed the guilty secret that he was undergoing hair transplant therapy. He had been trying to keep his treatments a secret, though the change was obvious to all who saw him hatless. His hat was larger than a *kepah,* but he preferred to be seen as observant rather than as a victim of hair loss.

He bore his weight on his left leg, favouring his right, which remained slightly wasted since he'd had polio as an infant. Beryl remembered the small leg brace that she had buckled on each morning over his thin white cotton socks and little high-top oxfords, the cold metal and the dark brown leather harness caging his weak lower leg from ankle to knee, and the sad soft clicking sound the brace had made as he struggled to walk. She used to rock him to sleep after lunch when she was in the first grade while their father worked downstairs in their deli. Mrs. Klymkiw, their housekeeper, could carry on with the laundry and begin the dinner preparations. By then, their mother was a permanent resident of the polio ward at the old Municipal Hospital. *I was the capable one, Rona was the pretty one, and Mark was the son. That's all they had to be. I had to do.*

He looked frail, she thought, thinner than when he had last visited. Was it in November? She hoped Rona wasn't too angry with him. There was no need to blame little Markie for things he had no control over.

Beryl felt Zach slide his arm under her elbow, and she turned to him and smiled. *Thank heavens he's here,* she thought. *My dearest one, squat, broad-bellied but not balding, temperate, and after all our years, a considerate lover.* She was lucky in love, she was.

He returned her smile and, though neither of them spoke, she knew that they were affirming, as they'd discussed before they had left Vancouver, their determination to be kind and loving and supportive to Ben and Rona. "You know how jealous Rona's always been of us," they'd said aloud in the same moment. That's what they expected to see. More emotional outbursts from the family's reigning drama queen. She'd been too distraught to speak on the telephone, so it had been impossible to gauge her state of mind. Ben had said things were very difficult, so Beryl knew that meant Rona was in a bad way. What else could be expected when she'd lost her only child?

It was a good thing that Daniel had to stay back for his exams, since it was pretty unlikely that Rona would be in a mood to forgive him for "ruining everything" by telling Georgia Lee that she was adopted. That had happened six years ago, but it might as well have been yesterday. They'd have to tread carefully.

Barbara and David, the 15-year-old twins, saw their uncle and called out to him. Mark looked up from his reading and waved.

"I've booked you into the Westin," Mark told Zach. "It's across the street from the Assiniboine Apartment Hotel. That's where Rona and Ben are for now. Their tenants are still in Canora Street, and in the this-is-not-for-believing category, their renters are not willing to move out any sooner than planned. Anyway, the hotel is near everything downtown, and there's a deli two doors away. And it will be convenient for Pesach. The first Seder is Wednesday night, and they do a completely kosher deal. You can eat there for the whole eight days, if you want."

"Is that the *plan?*" asked Beryl. Did he really want them to stay that long?

"Who knows what to want these days?" Mark said. "Rona says nothing. Ben is trying to fix everything up for the *levaye.* On Sunday, we hope," he added in response to Barbara's confused look. "It's Jewish for a funeral, remember?" He shook his head. "*Oy vey is mir.*"

Beryl nodded. She hoped that they would get to leave for home by Tuesday. What was it about Winnipeg that made her want to leave as soon as she arrived? She didn't feel trapped here now – pegged, that is – by that smothering feeling that everyone thought they had your number.

She remembered driving away from Winnipeg in Zach's beat-up old MG. They had left right after graduation, with the back seat crammed with their clothes and newly framed degrees. Driving away from rain-swollen rivers, canker worms, mosquitoes, ice-cold winters, and all the smallsville irritants that rankled. The car had limped all the way over the prairie miles and had to be coaxed over the mountains and down into Vancouver, but Beryl had cheered every mile of highway that passed under their wheels. They were free.

"Uncle Mark, we flew over the flood," said Barbara excitedly as she took her uncle's hand. "It's awesome. It's like a massive lake that goes right down to the States. The pilot let us look out the cockpit windows for a while. We couldn't see the end of it. The water meets the sky like one great big sea that you can't come to the end of. We even saw the floating houses and stuff."

"Those houses weren't floating." David sounded exasperated by his sister's poor grasp of the sights they'd viewed. "They're surrounded by, like, dikes." He bulged out his eyes at her and said "duh" loudly.

"Have you seen it, Uncle Mark?" asked Barbara. She turned her back to David.

"Only on TV, Babs," Mark answered, "and that's more than enough for me. Next week on Passover, all the *goyim* will be singing *dayenu* along with us. Enough. The whole city is saying it's enough already."

Winnipeg   **April 19, 1997**

Beryl watched as Rona began to pull at her hair and twist a hank of it round and round her fingers. "I am so tired. So tired of trying to think," said Rona. "Who would want to hurt her? She never did a thing to deserve this. Who could hurt my little doll?" She began tugging vigorously on the entwined hair, pulling it away from her scalp. Her long face was as immobile, expressionless as any of Modigliani's women. "You know how I love her. I've loved her every single day of her life. Now everyone knows what she looked like when she died. It's been in all the papers. And now the Indians want to take her back."

Beryl reached over and took Rona's hand, unwound the tangled hair from her fingers, and gently rubbed her sister's scalp. There was no use in attempting to discuss this. Beryl remembered that when Georgia Lee had visited her birth family and gone into her lamented Indian phase, Rona had showed a distinct coolness toward her. Ben had enlisted Beryl and Zach and friends to try to reason with Rona, but she had taken it very personally, and it made her bitter. Everything had changed then.

Beryl wished she had known more about Georgia Lee. Who that lovely girl really was. She could have made a larger effort to understand her niece, but on the infrequent occasions when their small family gathered in Vancouver or Winnipeg for a *bar mitzvah* or some other *simcha,* they never seemed to have time to really talk. Or they didn't want to risk the possibility of talking about it. *It* being the fact that it was her Daniel's fault that

Georgia Lee had even found out that she was adopted. And half Native. This topic was off limits. Rona blamed Daniel and Beryl. She insisted that the revelation had ruined her life. Their lives. Beryl lamented that she'd told her children about the adoption. Rona had planned to make some grand announcement when Georgia Lee turned 21.

Rona had claimed that her motherly love was being mocked and insulted by her daughter's interest in her other family and Native culture. Rona preferred that it not have any important part in their lives. It was not like being Jewish, she'd said, where the mother's identity determines the child's. She had made Georgia Lee contribute a part of her allowance to pay for her jingle dance dress. All of her Native stuff had to be kept in her bedroom.

Rona had begun to act, in Georgia Lee's words, "like a wicked stepmother." That accusation had hit home. It was mean to try to keep Georgia Lee from her birth family. Worse, it was wrong. Unkind. A word that should never be coupled with the word *mother*.

Rona was 5 when their mother died, and her memories of being mothered had faded out like photos printed in sepia tones, growing fainter with each year. After Mama died, she'd had their daily, Mrs. Mary, humming away in the kitchen, and bossy big sister Beryl. Rona wished she could stop herself from thinking about these things, but thoughts and memories buzzed around her head like bluebottles that landed to give her a few moments of quiet and then began buzzing again, and she knew in her heart that all that had happened to Georgia Lee was her fault. For her refusal to love, love Georgia Lee for all she was. To love her completely. She couldn't tell anyone about that.

The sisters were in Rona and Ben's hotel room, sitting side by side, on the edge of the second queen-size bed. On the floor beside them a jumble of clothing, clean and discarded, spilled out of two open suitcases. Rona was not dressed. She wore the faded red Folk Festival volunteer t-shirt and black lace panties that she had slept in. Her long, tanned legs hung down the side of the bed, and she restlessly banged her heels on the floor. She had not showered or combed her hair. She didn't respond to Beryl's suggestion that she hurry up about it and get dressed. They were to go over to Georgia Lee's apartment as soon as Ben returned from eating brunch with Mark, Zach, and the twins. Rona and Beryl had taken some tea and leftover Danish earlier. All Rona wanted to eat were sweets. When she ate anything at all. Her cheeks were hollow, and dark reddish grey circles marred the skin under her eyes. Her eyes were black pools, like night in a distant galaxy.

Beryl didn't know what to think. On the one hand, she tried not to imagine what had actually happened to her niece. On the other, she was trying to figure out how her shy, sweet niece's life could have ended so brutally. Was she so naïve that she'd gone with a stranger? She must have been forced. That was the only explanation. She had been murdered but not raped. For this they were to be grateful. Beryl had heard the raw anger in Rona's voice again as she had confided this detail. "That's what he told us," Rona had said of their meeting with the medical examiner. "Am I supposed to feel good about that? He said she was not violated. Murdered, but what good luck – not raped. We never should have gone away and left her."

"Rona, don't dwell on it."

"I can't help it," said Rona. She curled up on the bed again. "My poor baby. Who would hurt her like that? He must be a monster. She is good, she is good, a good girl. Everything is gone now. I can't understand how this is. Why won't those awful people let us back into our house? It's our house, for heaven's sake. It's unbelievable. Cold, cold Brits. It's unforgiveable."

Rona stopped talking and stared off into space. The sound on the TV was muted as the newscast showed yesterday's footage of the flood engulfing Grand Forks, North Dakota, and the fire in that city's old downtown centre. Rona turned her head to look at the TV screen and the images of the drowned city with its fiery heart on the newscast. Would the flood put out the fire? The words *water, water everywhere and nary a drop to drink* floated through her mind like the ephemeral images on the television news. She couldn't make sense of them. She rolled over on her back and stared up at the clean white ceiling.

Beryl got up and went around to the opposite side of the bed. She went through the heaps of Rona's clothes, folding the clean ones and stuffing the soiled ones into the plastic laundry bag the hotel had provided, looking for some suitable combination for Rona to wear to the funeral. She sorted and folded silently. She thought about how they'd divided up the tasks connected with making a funeral for her niece. Ben wanted to have it as soon as possible. There would be no *shiva* – or better say, only a private *shiva*.

Ben and Zach had an appointment to see Rabbi Berman in the afternoon. He was Zach's Uncle Louie's rabbi and had agreed to help the family, who had no affiliation with any congregation. They hoped to make arrangements for a simple graveside service on Sunday morning. They decided to put a brief notice in the newspapers on that morning. The only family members in town were Uncle Louie and two ancient cousins, Malka and Pearl, who were too ill to attend. Friends and colleagues from the university had been calling Ben and were asked to check for the details in the Sunday papers. No more was said about the McKay family's request.

Was that sensible? Would this plan make a problem with the Medical Examiner? Beryl pushed that thought away. Not her problem.

She and Zach hoped to leave on the earliest flight on Tuesday so they could sit at their own table for the first Seder. She was planning to call home to the deli at 41st Street and Oak after the noon hour to place a large order. It wouldn't be like their usual holiday dinners. She usually took three or four days off work to do the cooking and prepare the house for the holiday. At least she had roasted and frozen a good-sized brisket last week. Daniel would be home from university in Victoria, and they would be together.

Her table would be complete. Beryl was daydreaming about the pleasure of setting the table: fresh linen, a floral centrepiece, setting out shining silver and stemware. As she smoothed and folded her sister's clothes, she began humming the melody that Barbara and David would sing as they asked the Four Questions. So far, she had not found anything suitable for Rona to wear to the funeral. Beryl wished she had brought along something extra, because even if it were a size large, it would be fine. Rona had always been smaller than Beryl. That meant Rona had never had to wear hand-me-down clothes when they were girls.

Beryl put the folded stacks of her sister's casual holiday clothes into the drawers of the hotel's armoire. Rona could wear her white linen skirt and blouse and borrow her sister's navy raincoat to go over top, Beryl decided. That will be fine. She pressed these and hung them in the closet by the door.

"There is no word for it." Rona's voice sounded soft but clear. She had been lying so still with her eyes closed that Beryl had thought she was sleeping.

"No word for what?" asked Beryl.

"When a husband dies, it makes a widow. When parents die, it makes orphans. When a child dies, we have no word for it. No word for the survivors. There is no word to describe who I am now."

It is certainly the greatest of all sorrows, thought Beryl. She refused to contemplate the thought of losing any one of her children. It was not natural, to have a child die before you. Before their time. *That's why they call it untimely death.* She took such pleasure in her twins and Daniel. In their growing bodies and developing minds. She recalled the sweet intoxication of their individual scents and the delight she took in caring for them, especially when they'd been babies and she had known every fold of their skins. How she'd nearly swooned with the physical pleasures of their dear sturdy bodies. The gurgles, the smiles, the drool, the fat little thighs and baby jowls that were only a few things from the list of pleasures she enumerated like a besotted lover. The embodiment of the love between Zach and her.

"She is still my daughter." Rona sat up on the bed, pushed her back up against the padded headboard. "She's my daughter. Why didn't I know? I should have called her. I can't forgive myself. I should have warned her." She was playing with the hem of the bedsheet as she spoke, folding it widely into a white fan of pleats.

"Rona, listen to me. She is your daughter. But you have to find the strength to go ahead. Do it, for Ben's sake. For your own sake. You have to go on." She wanted Rona to forget the ugly details of Georgia Lee's death. She wanted Rona to do as she was trying to do. Dismiss the details and allow the mind's natural inclination toward serenity and contentment restore her psyche. How else could she live?

"What are you talking about?" Rona's words cracked through the air like a lash. "What are you talking about? Go on with what? With life, with shopping, with dinners, with laundry? And from here?" She gestured around the rented suite and its ugly furniture. "What are you talking about? Have you ever spent the whole night without sleeping while you are begging for someone to take these thoughts away? It's too confusing. Painful. Like when you are dreaming and then open your eyes to bright light and see how horrible it all is."

Rona shook her head to silence Beryl, who was waiting to respond.

"Do not say a single word. You have your three healthy children." She enunciated each syllable carefully. "No, not one word about Georgia Lee." She lowered her head. "My little girl, my little darling – Georgia Lee – Georgia Lee, all that I loved is gone now." She began to rock back and forth and moan.

Beryl put her arms around Rona and pulled her head down onto her shoulder. She began to stroke Rona's hair with a soft touch, as if she were a small girl.

"Sweetheart, try not to think about all of that now. All we need to do is to get through today and that's enough. The family will be back from breakfast any minute now. You need to get ready. You go shower and I'll find you something clean to wear." She took Rona by the hand and led her to the bathroom. She turned on the shower and handed her sister a fresh bar of soap. She smiled at Rona, but that did not elicit any response. She placed a hand over each of those sunken cheeks and looked deeply into Rona's dulled eyes. She pulled her close and hugged her tightly. Rona trembled and then backed away. Beryl reached out and pulled her sister's t-shirt off over her head, as if Rona were 5 years old, not 50. Rona turned away from her, shucked her panties off, and stepped into the running shower.

"Don't forget to brush your teeth," Beryl added as she closed the door behind her sister. She walked over to windows that looked out on the busy downtown street. Relieved that Rona would not hear her voice over the sound of running water, she called Zach on his cell. He said they were leaving the restaurant and would drop Barbara and David off at the Eaton's Centre, then pick up the sisters.

Rona was calmer after her shower. She looked younger, fresher, in that that temporary right-out-of-the-spa kind of way. She let Beryl comb and tie her hair back. She pulled on the clothes Beryl had set out for her: a pair of tan cotton slacks and a white sweatshirt with the university's crest printed in red on the front.

Beryl held up the clothes that she had chosen and pressed for the funeral.

"I can't be bothered looking," said Rona. "It's all right. Whatever you pick is fine." Rona waved them away and sank down on the edge of the bed. "I can't be bothered to get up in the morning." Her face again softened in grief, the flesh of her cheeks only barely suggesting the incipient jowls that the years would bring.

This alarmed Beryl. It was so unlike Rona, who was famously vain about her face and rigorous in maintaining her figure, which even now had a degree of slenderness and tone that hinted at youth.

Rona and Beryl. Two sisters and yes, Beryl said to herself, as she had many times before, *I was the older one. I was the dutiful child. Our mama, Lily, died of polio when we were 5 and 8 years old. And Mark was 3. A baby practically. Our father, Chaim, lived a quiet widower's life. Poppa put me in charge of Rona and our younger brother, Mark, and the house. Poppa never had much time to play with us; he came home from the store, exhausted every night, smelling of herring, of pickles, of wurst.* Poor guy, his only recreation had been his Saturday nights of card playing at the Tre Monte club downtown. He had never looked for another wife. He'd had enough on his head.

Ben paused outside Georgia Lee's door. He examined the brass hasp the police had installed at eye level over the door and jamb and what remained of the paper seal that they had glued over this lock. He made out a scrawl of initials and the date written as 97/04/17.

He remembered that the guy he had hired from the janitorial service recommended by the detective had been there yesterday to do a clean-up. Although the police had assured him that the crime had not taken place in Georgia Lee's suite, the detective had seemed concerned about what they might see.

Ben opened the padlock with the small key the police had given him and opened the door. Rona brushed by him, sliding under his arm and into the foyer. She stopped a few feet inside the doorway and looked around expectantly. "Let's look for her," she said. She began walking down the long, narrow corridor toward the living room.

Beryl, Mark, and Zach stood fast. Ben looked at them. Suffering had refashioned his heavy features into a solemn mask. Beryl felt his eyes gazing deeply into hers. For a second, after Rona spoke, she saw an expression of sorrow so open, so unguarded, that she gasped out a small sound, something like *oh*.

Ben shrugged, bowed his head slightly as if in apology, turned, and started after his wife. The others followed in single file, their steps echoing on the bare hardwood.

The narrow, outmoded, inefficient kitchen was clean and in good order. There was nothing sitting out on the countertops, and the large, old white porcelain sink and taps sparkled clean. The fifties-style round cornered fridge hummed a bass tune. Beryl read a handwritten recipe for bannock bread that was stuck to its door with a flat yellow-and-black magnet that advertised the video rental place on Osborne. The recipe was similar to tea biscuits, she noted.

Georgia Lee's living room looked bare and miserable with its cast-off furniture. The maple floors creaked loudly with each footstep. Maybe if she'd had a carpet to warm it up. *What's the difference? The dumb things you think of.* Beryl recognized the old red sofa as one item from their mother's last attempt to refurbish the three-bedroom apartment over the family store: transformation with cut red velvet. Considered very elegant after the War. Possibly an antique now. Dangling springs and all. Where had Rona stashed it for all those years?

The brass stand that Nikolai Gadol's cage usually hung from was in front of the bay window overlooking the river. During their childhood, it had stood next to the glass-doored bookcase that held the twenty-four brown volumes of the encyclopedia set. The Britannica. *Look up the Britannica,* Papa would say. His answer to any question. She remembered the door-to-door salesman, red-faced and panting like an old hound as he climbed their stairs carrying the deluxe edition. She ran her fingers from the stand's tarnished brass curves and its graceful arc to the small hook that could secure the dangling cage. She had been given the task of polishing it twice yearly, before the New Year in the fall and Passover each spring. She had not thought of that for years.

Every Sunday afternoon until the week after Beryl's 8th birthday, when her mother's death brought an end to her childhood, she and Poppa had made the drive south through the city to the old Municipal hospital set among the tall elm trees on the riverbank. The cleats on her stiff patent leather Mary Janes had echoed on the worn white marble stairs as she and Poppa climbed in their best clothes. And Poppa was always smiling wide at the nurses, showing his cigar-stained, old-country teeth jostling for space at the front of his mouth. Every year he brought each of the nurses the biggest box of rich chocolates he could buy for their Christmas.

The hospital smells had greeted them with the reliability of old friends: boiled potatoes, applesauce, dark medicines to drink, and richly vile body odours. It was like visiting a foreign country with a population of one. Her mother's pale, shiny face: that was all they could see of her. Her body encased within the tan metal carapace of her iron lung. Throughout the day's long hours, Mama looked way up at the high ceilings and waited for the white uniformed nurses to come and go.

On Sundays, Poppa sat in the blue velvet-covered armchair with the white lace antimacassar their newlywed Mama had crocheted. With the matron's permission, he'd had the chair trucked into the hospital from home. He would pull the chair up close to her head, and they would whisper the afternoon away.

Beryl no longer remembered how her mother's arms felt. Now, there was only her low, husky voice and the scent of Arpegé, the French perfume that Poppa had dabbed on her temples with a lace-edged hanky. Beryl would smile at Mama and kiss her scented temple. Then, Nikolai Gadol's cage had stood over by the wide, deep-silled hospital window. Beryl would carefully close the door to the hospital corridor and open the small door in the side of the cage. Nikolai would fly over and perch on the top of the iron lung and peer down at his caged mistress. After Beryl relined the cage floor with clean paper from the funny pages, she would station herself beside it, chirping to him and threading her thin fingers through his bars to feel his hard beak carefully explore them.

Polio was the name of the spell that had held her mother captive. Baby brother Mark had it, too; it gave him a limp. *Polio, paralysis, Pesach* – any word that began with the letter *p* could make Beryl stutter. It was worse if she thought about it. Then it might expand to *n*. *N-N-Nikolai want a cracker?*

Rona went directly into Georgia Lee's bedroom. She opened the closet and paged through the clothing hanging there. Almost every garment was dark coloured: black or grey or navy. Where were all her daughter's pretty things? There were many items she did not recognize, and this confused her. Did Georgia Lee have a roommate? She was not supposed to. That was not part of the arrangements she and Ben made with their daughter last September.

Everything else in the room seemed right. Rona was pleased to see that Georgia Lee's clothes were neatly folded instead of tossed over the back of the old brown velvet armchair. Georgia Lee was taking responsibility for her life, as they'd planned together. The bed was made, too, and Rona looked at it, trying to make out the soft oval indentation her daughter's head left on the pillow. The last place her daughter had rested her head.

Rona lay down on top of the blue denim comforter, stretched her legs out, and pulled the pillow over her face, hoping to find a trace of Georgia Lee's sweet natural scent. The pillowcase did not smell fresh. There was no trace of Georgia Lee's favourite herbal shampoo in its weave. Rona looked up at the dreamcatcher hanging on the wall over her head. What frightening dreams had it trapped for her daughter?

Ben found his wife rolled up in the comforter, her cheeks wet with fresh tears. He sat beside her and tenderly stroked her hair.

"It doesn't smell like her in here anymore," she said. "You remember how she liked to use that lemon-scented soap, don't you? I loved giving her hugs. I can't find her, Ben. Do you think she could have gone back to that awful reserve?"

"No," said Ben. "I doubt that very much."

A rectangle of butterscotch sunlight poured through Maud's kitchen window and warmed her back. Sunday morning sunshine. After she and Jake had showered, she'd gone straight to the kitchen in her robe to cook their eggs just the way Jake liked them. Two poached eggs each, perched on English muffins with a drizzle of her homemade Hollandaise and three rashers on the side. A thermal carafe of freshly brewed Columbian coffee waited on the table between them. Jake had quickly dressed in jeans and a blue work shirt and had tucked into the business of his breakfast as if he was in some kind of rush to get started on his day.

"I feel so sorry for the Kay-Stern family," said Maud. The front page of the newspaper she'd just set aside had an article on the dissention between the birth family and the adoptive family over the frozen girl's remains. "I took first-year Anthropology from Professor Stern. He made it really so interesting that I almost changed my major. He's a really nice guy."

Jake said nothing but nodded briefly to show Maud he was listening.

"They've had so much heartache, and now there's this ugly squabble with the Natives over their daughter's body, her funeral. Don't you think it seems unfair that her birth family is coming out of the wood-work now?" She showed him a large photo of Teddy Boy Beardy and Bernice Spence on the front page.

"There's been little contact for years," said Maud. "The chief – and I mean Dr. Bekker – does not want to get in between them and the Kay-Sterns, or so he says. I don't know how they're going to resolve the problem."

Jake nodded again.

"It's curious, isn't it, how everyone is so eager to give her a funeral? As if they believe that burying a body or catching the killer will actually mark the end of the pain. It's only the beginning of the next stage." And again Maud was there, kneeling on the icy frozen leaves beside the body, recalling how her weight had crushed them and how a faint version of their sour rot had risen like the devil's incense. *That's it,* she'd thought, *what can happen to a girl when that old rough god goes riding.* "It takes much longer to get over a murder than even a suicide." She looked intently at Jake over the rim of her coffee mug. "I think so. I am sure of it. There's no cure for either one. I don't think you can get over it. You may get used to the pain.

"I know they need these rituals, these ceremonies. I guess we all do. It's human nature. But on days like today," Maud added, "I don't like my job much. I hate the thought of these lowlife murdering slime and the damage they do. You can see that mother will never be the same again. Everybody knows there's no cure for it. You have to move on, you accept the everlasting sadness. I think I've seen enough." She set down her cup and leaned forward on her elbows, massaging her temples with the heel of each hand. "Had enough. I mean it. Don't you ever feel like that? That you don't want another miserable case?"

Jake gave her a puzzled look. He found her questions unwelcome, though she spoke in a softened voice. *Work is work,* he thought. *It's simple as that.* Work was what he wanted. Not her questions.

"Not often," he said. "It's my job."

No. He did not want to go there. That was slippery slope stuff, and he needed to hold steady.

"Yes, I know," continued Maud. "I know. It's only that some days I feel these things more acutely. And you know" – she looked right into his eyes as she spoke, enunciating each syllable crisply – "every savage little bite life takes out of you leaves its own ache."

"The grief of others," Jake said and slowly shook his head, denying that burden.

Maud watched as Jake drained his cup of coffee. He reached behind him for the navy blue windbreaker that he had slung over the kitchen chair when they'd come in from the late movie the previous night. "Say babe, I've got to get going." He stood, checked his watch, and leaned across the table to plant a quick, soft kiss on her lips. "I told Mom and Dad that I'd drive out and give them a hand today. They've taken in a family of five from near Letelier, along with their cattle and horses, and they've got a lot of extra work to do. I'm taking some extra groceries and supplies out to them."

"I remember you mentioned that," said Maud. "Will I see you later?" While she spoke, she was thinking that if he said no, she'd leave the bed unmade, their sheets unchanged, so that if he did not come back, she'd have his, their mingled scents to lull her to sleep later. She would still feel the weight of his body, have his taste going bitter in her throat.

"Are you going to your mother's?" he asked.

"Yes. She has gone all twitchy since Grand Forks was flooded. The Kingston Row residents have been told to increase the height of their dikes by 2 feet, and she's going to have another squad of volunteers to boss around today. I told her I would donate my Sunday and help out." She smiled. "You know, she didn't ask for your help this time. I think she doesn't trust us to behave together after that last episode in my old bedroom." She reached for the belt of her robe as if to pull the bow loose. "And, by the way, you should know, it wasn't the sex she objected to. It was our timing."

Jake ignored her bold look and waved her away from his side of the table. He didn't want to get trapped in another discussion about their relationship. He knew she wanted marriage. He did, too. Sort of. Why was he walking away from what he always said he wanted? No answer. But he thought that they had begun to bore one another, or maybe it was only the effect of this stalemate over their future. He didn't have time for this now. He stood up.

"Don't move, I'll be back." With a small frown, he continued. "But I don't know when. When I'll be back from my parents, I mean, so I think I'll plan to stay at my place tonight. We've got an early strategy meeting downtown. The sergeant wants everyone to be on deck, and we'll see if the wisdom of the tribe can move this thing." He shook his head. "We've had every fucking slimeball and cock-sucking perv we know of in for a talk, but it's going sideways on us."

He'd already decided to spend some time away from Maud. He deliberately used this coarse language to put her off. It helped him focus on what was important now: seeing a way into this case.

"So you've got nothing new," said Maud. She sat down and poured herself another cup of coffee.

"Wish there was. We've interviewed everyone she knew or went to school with. It's surprising, but she didn't mix with the Native students at the university. Didn't join their clubs or anything. Rob D. and I made two trips out to Headingley jail to talk to the Indian Posse dudes and Warriors, and if they do know anything, they won't say. Our informants don't know. Nobody knew that girl. We checked everyone she worked with. The whole family, both of her families, for Christ sakes, including that weakling uncle of hers. The lawyer. There's something off about him.

"The Ident and tech guys have been all over her computer, and there's nothing new. There's not much there. Her online journal is pretty basic girl stuff, 'This world is not the world we want' kind of thing. She mentions how she feels more Native" – he waggled his fingers in the air to indicate his last word was in quotation marks – "that she feels more identifiably Native the moment she goes into the core, north of Portage Avenue. But she was nervous. I think that she didn't want to be taken for Native. The graffiti and gang tags that the Posse and Warriors and the Deuce sprayed on those boarded-up houses near her grandmother's apartment on Pacific Avenue frightened her. In families like hers, the Kay-Sterns, you lock your car doors as soon as you leave the South end. She goes on with the usual stuff. 'Don't say peace is impossible. We may be young, but our ideas are not. There is an undercurrent, we all feel it. I won't give up. I'll use theatre.'" He snorted loudly in disdain.

"It's all so painfully naïve. Her little friend, that blonde space cadet from the video store, told us that she thought there was someone in the girl's apartment the night of the blizzard. She went over to find out why the girl didn't show for work. Lights were on. Knocked but no one answered. Thought she might have been with a guy. We know that someone was there. They, well, a *he* probably, peed in the kitchen sink. We've got a sample of that. Jesus! She said the girl talked like she was in with the drama school crowd. They did improv stuff on the weekends. The street gang unit has run the names of every kid she knew. No hits. That cousin, Waylon Spence, is nowhere to be found. Hasn't been seen in Winnipeg in months. From what the family says, he's supposed to be something of a pro wrestler or martial arts expert. They claim he went to Japan for training. He may be there now.

"She was ripe fruit for some perv to pick off. We got the saliva and semen and dental imprints from her body. We've got dental imprints from the cheese at her apartment and some stray hair samples but nothing to match them to. Except her. Maybe. Rob's got the lab looking to match up the DNA on blood and saliva and semen from her body to the exhibits from her apartment and the piss from her kitchen sink. We checked out the grounds of the old monastery that she mentioned she wanted to go to in her last journal entry. There was nothing to see. Or we were too late. The other thing I've got to work from is a print of his boots. So, I'm looking all over this city for a guy who wears a Western style boot that's been re-soled. It's driving me crazy. We know a little bit about a lot of things, but we don't know enough about her.

"Children. They are nothing but trouble with a capital *t*. I don't have a right feeling about her. I'm so pissed about the stupid choices she made. I don't understand why, and that's getting in the way. There's got to be something we aren't seeing, and I've got to get away to think about that. I haven't had a case with so little to move on in years. We're running on fumes here."

Maud locked the door behind him. She stood there, staring at it, then stepped forward and pressed her forehead on its smooth, cream-coloured surface, whispering, "He's gone, he's gone, he's gone."

On Friday evening, the air had been crisp, with an ivory crescent of moon. Maud had decided to go to the art gallery after work. She'd thought that looking at something beautiful would loosen the grip the day's miseries had on her. It hadn't worked. The big show at the gallery was a Mary Pratt retrospective. *Nature morte*. It was full of technically excellent, cold, painterly pictures of raw eviscerated chickens and gutted fish, along with two portraits of the artist's husband's lover, Donna. She was nude, her dark hair chin-length. In both portraits, the lover's eyes looked sunken, haloed by dark shadows.

Maud had immediately pictured Miriam, whom she hadn't thought of in ages. Miriam, with her dark shadowed eyes, was the neglected wife of Dr. James Salter, Maud's sometime lover. What a fool she'd been. It was classic. For two off-and-on years, Maud had loved that man and believed he loved her. He had in his own way. He, such a charming cheater; she, so willing to believe that he really would leave Miriam to marry her. Maud had picked out a gorgeous dress; they'd composed their vows while lying naked in their afterglow. She'd almost told her mother. He had told enough of those old white lies to frost a wedding cake, and then he had flown back to his nest, well-feathered with Miriam's family money.

Maud had been bare-hearted, the cold wind of abandonment blowing through her chest. She had conducted an exorcism of her bedroom and shredded all his loving notes. That was the end of June, and in the summer, on many evenings when the sun had set, she would drive round and round the city on the Perimeter Highway – cruising and singing the blues along with Billy and Joni and Aretha – thinking about, waiting for the man from dream city. Then along came Jake, who was not quite right, either.

In the vast Tyndall stone lobby, an Art and Jazz evening for single art lovers was in progress. Boisterous laughter punched up through the conversational buzz generated by the eager-to-please crowd. A lanky, handsome young pianist twinkled his way through Gershwin's "I Can't Get Started with You." It was intolerable.

Maud drove home, then dined on orange juice and popcorn while playing along with *Jeopardy!* She lost 2,000 dollars in the final round but retained her championship. "I hate my life," she said aloud. She drank a large scotch and did part of the daily paper's cryptic crossword before falling asleep while Mozart's final incomplete horn concerto serenaded her.

Out on the road leading south, the top down on his red 1968 Mustang convertible, with Winnipeg in his rear-view mirror, Jake felt relaxed for the first time in days. He was happy to be exchanging the cityscape for the sight of wide skies and open prairie horizon. That – and nothing else – in his windshield. Driving away from that urban island of trouble and contradictions.

The sky was overcast, a cheerless pale grey that rose up from the dun-coloured earth. He could feel the heat of the spring sun through the low cloud ceiling, warming his face, and he began to sing the old familiar words along with the Gospel singers on his CD player. This was his secret vice – that was, if singing aloud (but only when you were alone) was considered a vice. Maybe it was merely an indulgence. He had admitted this to Maud, who'd said she was convinced it was a vice, but then she had never heard him sing.

He thought of it as a vice because of the pride he took in his singing voice, a clear tenor. The physical act of singing gave him an intense feeling of relaxation and comforted him in a strange way he could not describe. Maud would be surprised if she could hear him. He told her he only sang when he was happy. "So," she'd said, "that means you've never been happy with me." It had sounded as if she was teasing. "Well, I, uh . . . I have to be alone," he had growled.

He admitted grudgingly, but only to himself, that he had doubts about his capacity for loving. It was not right, was it? That he never felt as content with others, even Maud, as he did sometimes when alone.

He turned off the highway at Morris and continued west and south on secondary roads towards the farm. Near Rosenfeld, he saw a freshly ploughed field and at the sight of the deep lush furrows of dark earth, he pulled off the road. He walked to the fence line and stood there for several minutes, taking deliberately deep breaths. The air was rich with the scent of organic decay. "It's the smell of promise," his father liked to say. "Mother Nature's perfume, and no farmer can resist it."

While Alma Friesen measured out flour for yet another pan of her cinnamon buns, she took a sidelong glance at her Jake's profile. He sat in his customary place at the family table. She recognized that he was troubled and that he would not speak of it. It was their long-standing custom, to leave the details of his police work within the perimeter highway. She would ask no questions about the cause of the deepening furrows that scored his tanned face, bracketing his smiles.

The grandmother clock ticked away politely in its walnut case while she explained that his father and his brother, Peter, and the others had already gone out with some neighbours who were helping to move cattle to higher ground. The men had set out for a farm south of Morris after their second breakfast. Peter's wife and their three young sons and the flood evacuees were helping out in the community kitchen at the arena in town. Since yesterday, when Grand Forks had been inundated, the danger had been inching closer with every hour, and everyone was working in a fever against the flood.

The watch on the mighty Red River was an anxious springtime ritual, and Alma knew that this year Mother Nature seemed determined to turn the tables on them. She had lived in the valley all her life and believed the promise the Lord had made to Noah that never again would all be destroyed by water. She felt a strange, low hum vibrating from deep within the earth. It came up through the soles of her dainty feet and quickened her step. In her dreams, the flood waters rose, lapping at the edges of her dreaming mind, the soft slapping sound a warning sign of the great angry sea of water that was hurrying its way north toward their farm and the city.

"How is Maud?" she asked. Were they still going out? They were still together, he said. End of that story.

Alma wondered what kind of romance it was. Over two years now, and the time for the announcement of an engagement and wedding plans was long past. Jacob had not had much luck with marrying so far. She sighed as she thought of that first short one to Bettina Harms – that girl pregnant, so all was hurried up and hushed and they went to the city. Then it came out after the baby died in its crib that it was from an uncle. Everyone supposedly knew the story. About the uncle, and there was talk of her other men. Jake had divorced her, and she had moved somewhere to the east. He hadn't heard anything of her after. And there was no more talk of weddings. Alma wondered if someone had given him a charm against love.

She and Armin thought that Maud was a lovely young woman whose visits to their home in the past had been easy. Her family had Christian roots, and they appeared to be fine, educated people. Mrs. Fallon had not yet accepted an invitation to visit along with the young people, nor had she extended one to the Friesens. Alma did not want to make too much of her apparent reluctance to be acquainted with them. People are full of mysteries. No need to take offence.

She watched as her son continued to sit in silence. He bowed his blond head, and he drummed his fingertips on the white, hand-embroidered

Sunday tablecloth so softly that there was no sound. She smiled at her recollection that it was this habit of drumming his fingers that had alerted them to his musical ability. Armin had noticed it first and remarked to her that their two-year-old boy was keeping time while she and her pupils laboured over the Royal Conservatory scores.

"Why don't you go and play a little, Jacob?" she suggested. "The piano was tuned last month. It needs playing." She wanted to say, *Why you don't give up that work? It is making you unhappy. You could have been a musician, a professor.*

He looked up at her and quickly brushed his hands over the tablecloth, as if he were sweeping the musical notes away like breadcrumbs. "Later, maybe. I want to go see if Pa left me any work in the barn. There are always chores to see to." He smiled at her and stood up. "Do you have any of my old boots around?"

"Give a look in the back hall cupboard." Alma was thinking about his smile, how it retained a boyish sweetness. "You should smile more," she said. "You have a good smile." She meant that he had the kind of playful smile that gave others heart. He smiled again to please her and headed for the back door.

Nothing was out of order in the barn. The stalls had been mucked out, and fresh straw put down. Everything was neat and clean in accordance with good order or, in the local parlance, heaven's first law. Jake walked through the lower level, his boot heels sounding hard on the clean cement floor. He walked outside and around by the pasture behind the kitchen garden. He saw that there were more than three dozen unfamiliar Holstein cattle, including spring calves, and a bay mare and her foal grazing there on the hay flakes that had been scattered for them. The foal was a lovely thing, its tawny back level with the darker-toned stifle of its mother's hind leg. The foal's only marking was a white blaze on its forehead. It ducked its head under the mare's belly and began to suckle.

This is what I needed, Jake thought. *To see that this beautifully simple way of life continues.* Though he had always loved it, he knew he wanted more, needed more – a hard direct tussle with the world and the pleasure of justice's occasional triumphs. And he got it all, along with the mean streets, the evil badass people, the unfortunate, the desperately stupid, and the nonstop river of lies that poured out of mouths and filled every minute of the job with annoying background noise. Like the constant squawk of static on the squad car radio, it was in the back of your head for your whole shift.

Jake walked back to the house and called to his mother through the screen door. "Things are looking fine around the place, Ma. Thought I might take the rototiller to your garden here by the back. What do you say?"

She came out to stand beside him then. "That would be a help, Jacob. You know where to find it, down by the side of the car, out in the garage. That's the only job your Pa hasn't got to yet."

Jake got the machine revved up and began turning the ground over. He worked from west to east through the soil that had produced the family's vegetables and greens since they had settled this land. Purplish green spears were already above ground in the asparagus patch next to the tightly curled glossy rhubarb leaves emerging on ruby red stalks. He made a mental list of all the other varieties of delicious vegetables he recalled his mother serving, including his midsummer favourite, sweet corn. He was content; perhaps he would admit to being happy, in this task of preparing the ground to receive the seeds. Every variety had its place in the grid marked off in orderly green rows.

This was the earliest map that he remembered drawing. The map of their Garden of Eden, as Ma called it. He loved maps and had devoted hours to drawing and redrawing the ones assigned in grade school. He liked to get every detail, every feature correct, especially on his favourite, the map of South America. The romantic and exotic-sounding names of its countries and cities had felt rich in his mouth like a thick guacamole, a tasty pozole: Argentina, Brazil, Paraguay and Uruguay, Quito, Cartagena and Caracas, Montevideo, Asunción, and Buenos Aires.

His mother's beloved twin brothers, Abram and Daniel, had gone there, immigrants willing to scratch out any possible living, and they had found work as musicians: Abram on piano, Daniel on guitar. They had wandered from dancehall to dancehall, Bahia to Tierra del Fuego. Dark-haired, dark-eyed, lean and tanned, they were identical in every physical way and dressed themselves out of one closet. His uncles had written about all these magical cities, describing their travels in letters on thin, light blue stationary. He and Peter had taken turns saving the beautiful foreign stamps in glassine holders in their albums. Jake had dreamed of joining that far-off, never-seen branch of the family, perhaps living the life of a gaucho, riding his horse far out over the pampas, free and happy.

In the kitchen, the cinnamon buns were cooling on the counter. Alma was playing the piano in the front room. Today it was J.S. Bach, the beautiful measured cadences of the Master. Jake sat on the piano bench beside her. She was playing Sonata 966 in C Major. She broke off when he leaned over to turn the page for her.

"You're going? Won't you stay to eat with us?" she asked, though she saw a look of farewell already set on him.

"Sorry. I can't, Ma. There's too much for me to do in the city."

"Do you ever play these days?" Alma ran her fingers up a scale and thought regretfully of the hours of practicing and the lovely touch he had.

"No, I don't. I have no piano. But I'd play often if I had you, my favourite duet partner to work with." He smiled.

"Your father is going to be disappointed that he missed your visit." This was as close as she would come to nagging or trying to make him feel guilty about his infrequent visits.

"Tell him that I'm sorry I missed the chance to go with him today." He smiled again and kissed her soft cheek.

On the car radio, the announcer was giving an extensive list of rural road closures. Highway 75, the main corridor to the States, was closed south of Morris, along with various other provincial roads from the border to as far north as Swan River. Jake was relieved that he knew this part of the province and alternate routes so well. The program continued with special bulletins on flood facts and a quiz show that tested local celebrities's knowledge of Manitoba's history. The story of Duff's Ditch and construction of that floodway was reviewed in minute detail; it was mentioned that there had been over 2,000 workers on site at the height of the project in 1965 and that it had been a bigger project than both the St. Lawrence Seaway and the Panama Canal.

They all missed what Jake believed was the most interesting fact about the project: that it had been visible to the crews of the Apollo space missions. Jake had been thrilled by the idea that Neil Armstrong and Buzz Aldrin could see their floodway and, he hoped, perhaps even his parents's farm – perhaps even him – from their spacecraft.

He'd spent many nights of the summer of 1969 out on the prairie with his telescope watching the moon. He would go to bed at 9:00 as his Ma directed. Then she would wake him when she was ready to retire and the sky had fully darkened into night. He would pull on his jeans and a t-shirt and walk out under the midnight sky to his special place beside his mother's rose garden, behind the house. He loved to feel the sun's warmth radiating back to him from the earth through his bare feet on those balmy nights and to breathe in deeply the sweet scents of the garden filling the air around him. He'd liked to think he was watching over the moonlanders and they, over him. He would wave to them and use his Cub Scout's sema-phore to send them coded messages about the weather on earth and his exact location. They were standing on the moon's ancient seabed, the Sea of Tranquillity, and he was on the earth's ancient seabed of Lake Agassiz.

What wouldn't he give now to see his dreams as clearly and as simply as they'd been then in the moonlit dark through his first telescope? (Was it clear and simple, though? The moon had a dark side. So did people. Everyone had a dark side, like the moon, that no one ever saw.)

As he passed close to Brunkild, Jake saw the evening sky was illu-minated by the bright, hot white glare of the flares being dropped by the Air Force as the crews worked round the clock to finish the Z-dike. Time was running out, and the Red River would soon widen into the Red Sea. In a matter of days, the massive gates to the floodway would be opened for the eighteenth time. The floodwaters would flow over the earthen dam and into the diversion channel, and Winnipeg's "Gates of Salvation" would save the city from the rampaging Red River again.

The tantalizing aroma of fresh cinnamon buns filled the car and reminded Jake that the autopsy report had stated that the girl's stomach contents had consisted of coffee and undigested cinnamon bun. These simple facts led him to believe that she must have met her killer at a coffee shop or very soon afterward. *That's what I'm looking for. I'm on the trail of the cinnamon buns and a dude in heeled boots.* He turned his cell phone back on as he crossed over the Perimeter highway.

***

Rabbi Sol Berman's pager vibrated angrily in his breast pocket. He checked the LED display. It was his wife Aviva. Again. When would that dear woman learn to be patient? He switched it off and stepped out of the elevator on the sixteenth floor of the Assiniboine Apartment Hotel. Yes, it was their thirty-first wedding anniversary, but she would have to wait, he decided as he stood outside the door to suite 1608. He would call home as soon as he finished his meeting. He used both hands to reach up under the brim of his black fedora and pat down his fringe of greying hair. He adjusted the knot of his blue-striped tie and brushed over the lapels of his black suit in case of crumbs or flakes of dandruff. He cleared his throat and pinched the fleshy bulb on the tip of his schnozzle to halt a sneeze before he knocked firmly on the door.

The teenage boy who answered rushed out a hello, then turned his head to call out, "Dad, I think the rabbi's here" as he opened the door wide. The seven people in the sitting room of the suite paused as if in mid-flight. The father came forward to welcome him and made the introductions.

The rabbi began his meeting with the Kay-Stern family with his usual remarks. He said unexpected death means a forced parting. This is one of the difficult lessons of being human. Every sudden death causes the predictable emotions of shock, grief, anger, and guilt. They should not be distressed by the fact that they were experiencing confusing, angry feelings. It was to be expected. It would take time for the healing to begin.

They all listened carefully to what he said. He could see that no one wanted to upset his applecart – Zach's Uncle Louie's rabbi who was doing them a favour. They were like orphans, these secular Jews, in their hour of need.

"What about forgiveness?" asked Beryl. "Do we have to forgive someone who does a terrible thing like this?" She was the first to speak, and she zeroed in on the question they no doubt all silently asked. Who could forgive this crime?

"Does your faith rest on it? Is that what you are asking me?" Rabbi Berman hesitated and took a careful sip from the cup of clear Earl Grey tea that had been cooling on the table beside his left elbow. "Forgiveness is difficult. It must be complete, or it is not forgiveness." Six of the seven mourners nodded their heads in acceptance. Only the mother sat staring into deep space, so he moved on to practical details.

It was decided that the graveside service would take place at the Hebrew Workman's Benevolent Cemetery early on Tuesday morning. Rabbi Berman agreed to officiate. This would give enough time for all to be in order before the Passover holiday began at sunset on Wednesday.

Beryl registered this decision with satisfaction. It was what she'd hoped for. They would be able to leave and make their noon-hour flight on Tuesday and, with the time-zone change in their favour, gain a further two hours by the time they'd arrived in Vancouver.

It was the same thing all over again. She couldn't get out of this town soon enough. She decided she wouldn't let herself feel altogether too guilty about leaving Rona and Mark behind. Ben would take over, that was a given. He was a mensch, and Rona was a lucky woman. Beryl looked across the room at Rona, who sat immobile on the ugly purple couch, her head lowered and her eyes closed as if in prayer. Beryl was fairly certain that her sister was tuned out. Not praying. Not Rona.

When Mark picked up his calls, Bev Cunningham had told him that Teddy Boy Beardy had dropped into the office, trying to see Mark after lunch on the previous Friday. "Said he's a cousin to your poor little niece. He wants to set up a meeting," she'd said. "He said that the McKay family wants to take Georgia Lee back. Claims the white folks have had her for long enough. Says that she was stolen from them by some white social workers. They say her name is Rosie McKay. He showed me that they had an obituary printed in the paper under that name. Did you see it? There is no mention of Rona and Ben Kay-Stern. Or of you, for that matter. He says the McKay family wants her to be buried from the Aboriginal Funeral Chapel. Said the adoptive family is to be invited to the wake in Winnipeg. The McKay family wants to take her home to Footprint Lake to be buried beside her mother. That's what he said. Can you believe it?"

Mark had told Ben and Zach about the other family's request, and the men had agreed to set up the meeting with Teddy Boy on Sunday afternoon, after they saw the rabbi. They were to convene at the downtown Tim Horton's on Notre Dame near the Exchange district. That was the spot Teddy Boy had insisted on for a pow wow to talk about Rosie's funeral.

Mark saw that the balance of power seemed to have shifted now that the press and public were watching, waiting for the family's decision. Everyone and their uncle were mixing in. He didn't much like the guy. Teddy Boy seemed to be baiting him with expressions like "pow wow" and "stolen children." *Who knows how they talk about us among themselves?*

After the funeral arrangements were set and Rabbi Berman left, the three men walked the few short blocks from the hotel and crossed to the north side of Portage Avenue under cloudless blue skies. While they sat at Tim's, lingering over their coffee and donuts, Zach addressed the obvious by asking, "What is our answer going to be? That we already have an arrangement with Rabbi Berman, so that's that?"

Ben did not answer. He reached for a discarded newspaper that lay on the next table. On the front page was a large photo of the Native protesters with their banner and placards outside the Medical Examiner's office. An elderly couple led the marchers. The man had a rough deerskin cloak draped over his shoulders and carried an eagle feather. The frail-looking woman who was being pushed in a wheelchair was Granny Edna Spence, though Ben did not recognize her at first. The accompanying story was about their demands that Georgia Lee's body be returned to her birth family and the injunction they were seeking to counter the Kay-Stern family's claim. In this photo, the protestors were accompanied by several tough-looking young Native men dressed in camouflage gear with black bandannas tied around their heads, covering their foreheads right down to their eyes. Though they were identified as members of the elder's honour guard, and one of them was pushing Granny Spence's chair, Ben thought that they looked more like members of the Indian Posse or the Warriors, the ruthless gangs that ran the drug trade in the Winnipeg's core area.

A longer, in-depth article outlining the history of cross-cultural adoptions had been printed in the Lifestyles section. The story of the controversy over Georgia Lee's funeral had been covered on every radio and television newscast. There were unconfirmed reports that she had applied to Indian Affairs to get her treaty status. In on-air polls, listeners voted 65 to 34 per cent that she should have a traditional funeral service. Many agreed that she should be considered Native because if you have any Native blood in you, that's how you'll be seen in this town anyway. Set aside all inflammatory talk of cultural genocide, and accept the fact our human nature sees race in the face. Callers to "talk back" shows were highly emotional, regardless of their views.

Teddy Boy walked in through the front door of the restaurant exactly twenty-three minutes late for their appointment. His large belly led the way, shadowing his dainty steps in highly shined black cowboy boots. He swivelled his big head around, checking out each table until he stopped at theirs. His denim-clad body was cut in half by a wide black leather belt cinched with a grizzly-bear-shaped hammered silver buckle. He nodded at them and went up to the counter. He returned with a large double-double in a take-out cup and a dutchie. He sat down but did not remove his dark mirrored sunglasses. For a few minutes, he gave his full attention to his donut and coffee while the other men watched.

"I'm here on behalf of the McKay and Spence family," he finally said as he wiped his hands with his napkin, and then he lowered his voice as he proposed that the two families agree to a traditional aboriginal service with a sweet grass and smudging ceremony. One of the Cree elders would speak, and Ben could, too, if he wanted. Or they could get their minister to do it, his people had no problem with that idea. Then he and the family of Rosie McKay wanted to take her remains home to Footprint Lake for a traditional burial. Indian Affairs would pay her burial costs. No problemo. She had begun her application for her status and treaty rights in February. They would ask for it to be made retroactive. "Footprint Lake is her place on this earth. She doesn't belong to your people."

"She doesn't belong to anyone," said Mark. "And," he added, "it's the rabbi. We have a rabbi, not a minister. And anyway, how can you say she is more a Native than white?"

Ben turned away at these words. How had it all come down to this? A political squabble. *They don't know our Georgia Lee. It's not her they want.*

There was silence at the table for a full minute or more while they waited for Ben to speak. He was thinking of Georgia Lee's journal entry about the Teddy Boy.

Cousin Teddy Boy, well he really wants me to get the status card. And Waylon, you said to watch out cause Teddy Boy, he's slick. Look at his hair dyed as dark as fresh two-lane blacktop, cell phone on his hip. He's got political ambitions. You don't know this yet but his latest thing is he's in the tourist business. His company's called Sacred Places Tours Inc. He takes these German people from the Berlin who like to play dress-up Indians to stay in a tipi out on the land and he puts on pow wows for them. He's says he's a cultural heritage promoter. Ben said he's a big *macher* in trade with the Indians. It's a living. I guess.

"I agree," said Ben. "She doesn't belong to anyone. We, too, have been thinking of how to honour her spirit. Her mother and I have spoken with Rabbi Sol Berman from Temple Israel. He has agreed to do a graveside service on Tuesday, at 8:30 in the morning. Remember, Mark, we arranged to bury her beside your mother and father in the Hebrew Workman's Benevolent Cemetery."

Teddy Boy swivelled his bulk around in the cramped molded plastic chair and whipped off his sunglasses. He couldn't believe his ears. These white men didn't understand a thing. They don't hear the heartbeat of Mother Earth. They didn't hear anything important.

"Just a minute now," he said. "Is that really a good idea?" He cleared his throat lustily. "You do not want to do that. It is not fair to Rosie or her people. You whites stole her from us. You've had her for 18 years. Now is the time for her to come home." He shifted in his seat and pushed his sunglasses back on the bridge of his nose. He could feel damn little beads of sweat forming along his hairline and starting to itch him.

Cousin Bernice Spence had given him no room to manoeuvre in these negotiations. That was the only way she would agree to let him handle the matter, and she was not the kind of woman he wanted to disappoint. She was up on the legal ins and outs of everything on account of she got herself a law degree and she said that education was "our buffalo now." He knew he was too old to hunt that meat; he wanted her to make him her assistant and take him under her strong wing to the Assembly of Chiefs meeting in Ottawa come June. She could make or break your chances in politics. She talked 100 miles an hour with gusts up to 150, and she whispered in the ears of many powerful people.

With her, it was all about numbers, priorities, like first, second, third, and such. "You . . ." And she'd poked him in the chest with a sharp fingernail. "You take control of the negotiations." That was the top one with her. He thought he'd done that when he sat down. He silently reviewed the talking points she'd given him.

Mark blurted, "Think about it, Ben. Maybe Rona will agree with us that this is the best way. After all, we are not planning to sit *shiva* for Georgia Lee." The thinness of this response shamed him. *All roads lead to Rona* – that was a familiar fact. If Ben could get her to agree to a shared ceremony, their nightmare would soon be over.

Ben leaned back in his chair and spoke softly and directly to Teddy Boy. "When we adopted Georgia Lee, we did it with the best possible intentions. No one from your family was interested in her then. She never knew her mother or even who her father was. We gave her a good and loving home. She was happy with us. I know that. I brought her to be with her other family when she asked. As often as she wanted. Did any one of your people come to see her?" He hesitated. "Other than Waylon. He was the only Spence she really knew. The only one who seemed to care. You know that is the truth."

He wanted some acknowledgment of the years of love and care that they had given their daughter. He refused to have the right to call her *daughter* taken from them. *We gave her advantages she would never have had otherwise,* he reminded himself. How she had ended up murdered he did not comprehend. He refused to allow her death, which belonged to her alone, be taken over and turned into an opportunity to advance any political view. He did support the halting of the adoption program per se. His faith in that grand idea had run down, run out.

It did not matter what was considered correct now. He was not about to bow to the false god of political correctness. He and Rona had acted in good faith, according to what was being done then. The 1970s seemed a long way in the past. You could not wipe out that past, and trying to explain how things were then so that they made sense now was like searching for the words to describe a kingdom that no longer existed.

"Doesn't matter if that is all true." Teddy Boy held up both hands and turned palms outward, then showed their backs to the three other men. "It's a question of blood and bone but mostly skin. *Indians, redskins, Natives, breeds,* that's what we have been called. And they treated us like children. Took our rights. And that's called racism."

Ben focused his gaze like a spotlight on Teddy Boy, who looked away as if checking for the nearest exit.

"Don't talk to me about racism," Ben said. "I'm only a Jew, but I know something of it. My whole family was murdered in Hitler's gas chambers." Leaning forward with his elbows on the table, he calmly

191

held his right hand up, palm facing Teddy Boy. He said in his distinctly professorial manner, as if uttering the final words on this particular topic, "My wife loved Georgia as any mother loves her child. We are her family. We are her parents. She had no others."

Teddy Boy turned back to face Ben. He placed both of his hands palms up on the table between them.

"Only her granny's left now. You know Granny Edna Spence. Her diabetes got worse now. She had to move down to the city to get her kidney dialysis last summer. She got a little apartment – one room is all, over on Pacific Avenue, and Rosie's been visiting her a lot since then and making her bannock and such. Guess you didn't know that, eh?" He leaned forward in his seat and set his features firmly in a scowl as his cell phone rang loudly. He checked the display and pocketed it without answering.

"Cops have been around to her asking about Waylon. He's a cousin of ours and, you remember, he was the one Rosie ran to when she left you people. When was that? Say, about three years back? He's one of Granny's Spence's other sister's daughter's boys. We don't know anything about where he is these days. He usually phones Granny on her birthday. But that's not coming up 'til into the fall time. Could be he's down in the States or out on the West Coast." He shrugged and reached up to take off his black Stetson. "I can't say about that. Can't say for sure where Waylon is now. He was in Japan for a time. He's fallen out of touch.

"Granny Spence wants little Rosie to be buried at home beside her mother – I mean beside Ruby. She still mourns for her daughter that the city took. It's worse for Granny Spence now that she had to come and live here. She feels it more. It's harder to survive here in the city. 'It's a harsher wilderness than our grandfathers and grandmothers knew,' she says. 'Let the daughters be together now,' she says, 'since they couldn't be together in this life. Let those whose lives were taken be together.'"

"I thought that Ruby died of exposure," said Mark with the quick response of a lawyer correcting an error of fact.

"Yeah, she died of exposure," said Teddy Boy angrily. "Exposure to the white man. The elders, they say that the world is as sharp as a knife. Some children don't know that, and they slip."

At this, Ben cleared his throat. He looked at Teddy Boy steadily for about ten seconds. He found it difficult to accept Teddy Boy's truculent attitude, though he could see through this pose to the hurt beneath and felt he had to agree with him that Georgia Lee, that Rosie, had embraced her birth family and they, her.

It made sense that both families share the weight of sorrow. He was sure that was what his daughter would want. What she had written in her journal confirmed this. That she wanted to be at peace, to feel that she was part of both families.

"One thing we want is that her funeral does not become a media circus," said Ben. He tapped the table right beside Teddy Boy's empty cup. "It must be private. Absolutely no media people can attend. I will talk to Rona and let you know our decision first thing in the morning."

"And let the tears fall where they may," said Zach. He had been silent throughout the discussion. He had nothing to offer in these deliberations and, though he agreed with Teddy Boy's view, he did not want to take that side publicly. He wanted to get through Georgia Lee's funeral without causing more grief between his wife and her sister. Like a flea in his ear, Beryl kept whispering, "Be supportive but don't get mixed in." *Be like Switzerland,* he thought, *a quivering neutralist. Never thought that day would come, did you, you non-aligned coward?*

"And let the tears fall where they may," repeated Teddy Boy as he got up to leave. "I'm okay with that." He handed one of his Sacred

Places Tours business cards to Ben and said, "You can get me on my cell when your mind's made up. I'll be listening."

Ben delayed talking with Rona until late in the evening. He found that his interest in the solution Teddy Boy had proposed grew as each hour passed, and by nightfall he had decided that making a shared funeral with the Spences and McKays was the right thing. Rona needed all his attention now, and that demand made it easier for him to agree to let Georgia Lee be taken back to Footprint Lake.

Rona had fallen into a deep sleep about 5:00 p.m. He heard her stirring when he turned the radio off after the evening news. She was lying flat on her back in the centre of the bed, soft eyed, in a half sleep, caught in a web of dreams. He sat beside her, took her hand, and leaned over to kiss her lightly on her dry lips.

"Hello, my sleeping bride," he whispered. "Did you have a good rest?"

She nodded.

"Can I interest you in an omelette, darling?" he asked, then lifted her warm hand to his lips and grazed her fingers with them.

She nodded again.

"Let's say an omelette with a small green salad, rye bread and cheese, a glass of Muscadet? It is nicely cool now."

She nodded again.

"You say yes to all, then." He kissed her again, turned back the bedcovers, and held out his arms. She sat up and embraced him, and they held each other like that: lightly, warmly, gratefully, for a minute or two.

"Why don't you freshen up, and I'll get going in the kitchen?" Ben stood now and held out his arm. She stood and took it, and they walked over to the bathroom.

"Do you want mushrooms in the omelette or your salad?"

"In the salad, please, and with some of that good balsamic on the side." She kissed his cheek then and went in to shower.

As he whisked the eggs, Ben thought that in some queer way, their separation from Georgia Lee during the sabbatical year almost made his decision easier. This was not to say that they had broken with her, or she with them. She had been leading her own life, and that changed the balance. He continued to gently whisk the rich saffron-coloured yolks into the frothy whites and poured them into the foaming butter. He knew that he and Rona would always be her parents and she, their daughter. Nothing could tarnish that truth.

Only after they had eaten and their tea was poured did Ben begin to talk about the new plan to make a funeral with Georgia Lee's other family and to let the McKay and Spence families bury her at Footprint Lake. Rona listened uneasily, sitting upright in her chair. She frowned at her reflection in the bowl of her unused teaspoon as she polished it on the sleeve of her worn blue terrycloth robe.

"If we let them take her way up there, I'll never see her grave. It will always be covered in snow." She said this even though she knew it was not true, did not have to be true. "I wish we could sit *shiva* for her and have a memorial and an unveiling for her. That's what we do. Ben, darling, you know that's what we are required to do. I really wanted to do it. What about our plans with Rabbi Berman? We love her and she loves us, and that is more important than any facts about whose flesh and blood she is. She is ours. She always will be." Rona got up and walked over to the big window overlooking the bustle and the lights at Portage and Main. She stood still, staring out as her breath fogged her reflection in the glass.

"That reserve is such a faraway place in the middle of dark green forest. There's nothing around there. You've seen it. That small pink rectangle labelled IR on the government map."

"I know it is far, Rona, but Georgia always will be our daughter no matter where her bones rest. Sweetheart, please. Trust me to do what is best for us. I will speak with the rabbi. We can ask him if instead of the graveside service, he would say Kaddish at the other place." He took her hand and led her to the couch, where they sat, facing each other. He hoped they could fashion for Georgia's story an ending in reconciliation. Forgiveness. Friendship. Love. These words glowed like beacons for him.

Ben wanted to tell her that the police had given him a copy of the journal they had discovered on her computer, but he hesitated. He knew she would want to read it immediately, and that was impossible. Georgia Lee had been keeping notes for or writing a sort of letter to Waylon, and in them she'd written that she wanted to find her own way and go beyond the racial divide. "Which is better?" she had written. "Native or white? Why does one have to be better than the rest? Whatever you chose, you lose."

Sometimes I look at men on the street and wonder: Are you my father? I never look at Native men. I see them at the Portage mall or on the street but I never think one of them could be. I look at white guys that are around 40 years old. I guess that's about right. I'm eighteen now and that's supposed to be a lucky number because 18 is the same as *chai*– that's life in Hebrew. Ruby would be thirty-nine if she were alive. Maybe this year I'll find him. The Unknown Father. I have a feeling that somehow I'll recognize myself in his face.

I thought I was Jewish until I was 12. I believed that lie until my doofus "cousin" Daniel accidentally told me that you have to have a Jewish mother to be Jewish. So. The truth was out. I was adopted. Rona and Ben Kay-Stern are with me in all our photo albums but my only parents aren't my real parents. That's a fact just like my crooked little toe. I am not the daughter of a professor of political science and a beautiful potter. I am not who I always believed I was. I keep thinking about everything I thought was true. Everybody – well, not you – said knowing didn't change anything but they were wrong. It changed everything. It orphaned me.

It wasn't the same for any of us. I wasn't their daughter in the same way. I thought I had to be an Indian. Full time. I wanted to. I got Ben to take me up north to the rez at Footprint Lake so I could meet the family. I wanted to honour my birth. That's what the elders say to do.

Rona cried for a month. Every time she looked at me, tears started. One day I felt so close to her, then, overnight she was like a stranger. Instead of the truth, I guess she wanted to pretend that she found me like Miriam found Moses floating in the bulrushes. Too bad. I am a half-breed. That's the beautiful truth about me. I'm half half.

She says that was my teenage rebellion. ME trying to find out who I am. Believe it.

My lucky life was over. Sounds dramatic don't it? Yeah, but that's how it felt. Poof! The earth opened under my feet, tearing me away from my roots. My mind went all grey with storm clouds.

I had that same dream so many times that first year where I fall into a deep crevice in a glacier. I could see light way up at the top of the steep walls of milky bluish ice but I couldn't climb back up. My fingers were burning from trying to grab onto the ice. I'd wake up crying. Ben would sit in the rocking chair and hold me, wrapped in my quilt until I got warm.

First, they said I was one of the Chosen People, then, our cousin, Bernice Spence said I was a stolen child. That's the way activists talk. I speak good French, some Hebrew, some Yiddish but only a few Cree words. Who was I supposed to talk to???? Are you listening Waylon? Rona didn't. She acted like it was all a game of pretend I was playing. That I'd get tired of it. Anything you tell her that she doesn't want to hear, she ignores. She'll act as if you are not there, if you offend her. That can go on for days but I always check the weather in her eyes.

Remember my real Indian phase? Turtle Island middle school for grade 7 and 8. Quit ballet and learned traditional dances. (OK, I wanted a jingle dance dress.) Had my hair in long braids and tried to speak Cree. That lasted until I was fifteen, when I got into trouble for running away from Rona. REMEMBER? I was sleeping on that lumpy old street couch at your place on Qu'Appelle when the cops busted us. I hated the way they looked at us. If I was sixteen then, they couldn't stop me. I had to go home. I couldn't let you go on sleeping on that hard wooden floor, could I, Waylon? You had to get up so early for your carpenter helper's job.

You called Ben and talked. I stayed on the couch with the blanket pulled up over my ears.

You told me their love was something I shouldn't forget. And I should go home. Rona was a real bitch about it. You know what she can be like. Like a wicked stepmother. She made me feel ashamed for nothing because she decided we had sex!!! I almost had to see the doctor for a freaking examination but Ben said no. And I had to promise not to run again. Then I couldn't even open my mouth to tell you what she said.

Everybody kept saying I was having a difficult time. She's a little mixed up. She doesn't know if she wants to eat challah or bannock. So many therapists, so many ideas of what was wrong with me, what was good for me. I was disappointed. I wanted to live in a better world where I wouldn't have to choose my one family over the other. In a better world they all could get along.

Instead of showing Rona the journal, Ben explained again that Georgia Lee was 18, over the age of majority. They must remember that she chose not to have a *bas mitzvah,* not to be a Jew, many years ago. "Let her be free now," he said. "Yes, she's our daughter. Now we must let her be free. Her love for us was a reflection of ours. Yours and mine. Deep and true. Constant. She was with us for almost all the time she had here in this world and that seems a short time to us, but don't think now of all the time that might have been because you had no guarantee of it. It doesn't matter where her bones are. She was with us for her whole life."

"*Was, was, was.* How I hate that word," Rona said. "Every baby I loved died. Our own two baby boys and now Georgia Lee. I'll never be a grandmother now." She was shaking, crying soundlessly. Ben took her cold hands and sandwiched them in his.

"We have to let her go. Rona dear, you know we have to. She would have wanted that from us, she was struggling to be who she wanted to be. She's more than our little girl now. We need to honour who she was, not what we wished her to be." He was so weary of the attention that the public was paying to them, of trying to keep his composure when called on for comments by the press. It was like trying to discuss a private matter with a circle of strangers staring at them and listening to every word.

Rona nodded in agreement. Ben was willing to decide for them, and she would let him. She knew that what he said about Georgia Lee's feelings was true. She looked at him with a steady gaze, with a kind of grave, trusting joy that signalled another one of the countless bargains, large and small, they had made and kept.

"I don't know. I don't know," she said, her voice muffled now as she turned her head and snuggled against his chest.

"What don't you know?" His lips were grazing her right temple as he held her, all he loved, close.

"I don't know which is greater. The happiness I had or the unhappiness I have now."

"Think of all the happiness," Ben said. "Think of your last best memory." He rocked her gently and hummed that little lullaby about a mockingbird. *Hush, little baby. Don't say a word.*

Hand in hand with Zach, Beryl walked up the cracked concrete sidewalk leading to the front door of the Aboriginal People's Funeral Home. A gust of wind danced a whirl of paper scraps, crushed and discarded Styrofoam cups, and varicoloured tattered plastic grocery store bags before their feet. The curb side and sidewalks were gritty underfoot with the winter's accumulation of sand because city road crews, seconded to the flood preparations, were too busy to begin the annual post-winter sweep up of road sand.

Both looked straight ahead, ignoring the cameras and microphones that the TV news people thrust out to catch any stray words, like panhandlers begging for coins. They paused outside the heavy wooden double doors decorated with carvings of thunderbirds flying over dense coniferous forests. Suddenly the darkly stained doors were pushed wide open, and Teddy Boy stepped out. He was wearing a blue work shirt and black denim jeans and held a lit cigarette in his free hand. No mirrored sunglasses tonight. His small, dark-brown eyes were red-rimmed and set closer than one would expect. He moved to the side to let Beryl and Zach pass into the foyer.

As they stepped over the threshold, Beryl looked back over her shoulder and saw that Ben was paying a cabbie. Rona stood beside him, and Beryl noticed how slight and frail she looked. She knew that she had been unfair to her sister. Beryl had been trying to avoid feeling anything, trying to distance herself from their misery, trying to delay mourning her niece. Her intuition was that this was necessary in order to avoid being swept up in their flood of grief or contaminated by their misfortune. *A murdered child.* Nothing like this was supposed to happen to them. She remembered how Zach's mother used to spit on the ground and mumble some now-forgotten words in Yiddish to ward off the evil eye. Beryl was relieved that Georgia Lee was being buried far away, that her people wanted to reclaim her. Let them take the *tsouris* back with her and let peace come to all of us.

A circle of straight-backed wooden chairs lined the pale rose-coloured walls of the parlour, and almost all of the chairs were occupied. As Beryl looked around the room, she slowly became aware that she, Zach, Ben, and Rona were in the minority at this gathering. Their pale Jewish faces were highly visible. Many pairs of eyes turned their way and just as quickly turned away. A crescendo of talk, laughter, and spiky energy rose in the warm, overcrowded room full of men, women, and children from babes to teens.

Ben had his arm around Rona's slender hunched shoulders and propelled her toward the open doors. As they passed Teddy Boy, Rona stumbled over the threshold and lurched toward him. He leaned down and slipped his hand under her left elbow. Together, the men helped her walk across the room.

Teddy Boy smiled at Ben and gave Rona's forearm a soft squeeze. He was pleased that these white people had agreed to his demands. Anybody could see it was working out good for all now, and Cousin Bernice seemed impressed with him and she was acting a lot more friendly. She hadn't asked him to be a delegate to the Chief's conference yet. That was still two months away. He was working on that.

It was part of his big plan to get on the committee that was going to negotiate for an urban reserve. But tonight was for the family.

Beryl saw that the coffin was at the centre of the east wall and banked by floral arrangements. Roses and carnations and lilies and mums scented the air. The Kay-Stern family had not sent a wreath. Perhaps they should have – perhaps it was expected. How could they know? They hadn't thought of it because, for them, for Jews, it was not done. No flowers, no music, no viewing.

Caroline and Charles Nash, now known as the tenants from hell, had their names on a showy funeral wreath and a condolence note that were at the centre of the display. Did they imagine that this gesture could make up for their refusal to vacate their rental agreement? That woman had the *chutzpah* to have stationery printed for her stay at the Kay-Sterns address on Canora Street. People would expect Ben and Rona to use their home address. That's where condolence cards would be sent.

Georgia Lee's coffin was made of a highly polished oak, and Beryl realized that in all the years of her adult life, she had never seen a body laid out in this fashion. She had always viewed this *goyische* custom as peculiar and even ghoulish. She felt uneasy and anxious about what else they might see. She had fleeting recollections of a long ago Anthropology course and images of inexplicable, fascinating, and bizarre tribal rites involving feathers, fire, dirges, and lamentations. Beryl was worried about Rona's reaction to the aboriginal customs. They had been told that the ceremony would be holistic and low key. Not a particularly descriptive response.

Beryl remembered from their father's burial that by their custom, the coffin was to be made from thin pinewood, and it should be opened briefly at the cemetery. Then you were to look. They were accustomed to their private way, the silent mourning, the heart stirring words of the *Kaddish* and then the *shiva* and the comfort of friends and familiar foods. She usually made a sour cream coffee cake to take to the sitters. Not this time, though. Without consulting anyone, Ben had announced there would be no *shiva*. All they had done was a token rending of their garments. Mark had brought each of them a limp strip of black cloth, already ripped by someone in the Jewish funeral industry (whose job could this be?) that they pinned on their lapels without making the blessing for *Keriah*, since none of them recalled the correct words.

There was a *prie dieu* in front of the bier, and a steady stream of mourners approached to pay their respects. Georgia Lee was laid out in pale blue girlish dress with a white collar that looked new and cheap. The mortician had done a careful job and dressed her hair so she looked as sweet and lovely as she had ever been. An 8-by-10 photo of a smiling Georgia Lee in cap and gown on her high-school graduation day, and a single red rose in a crystal vase, sat beside the Visitors's Book on a white-draped table next to the bier.

Old Granny Spence was seated on the right hand side of the table, and Bernice Spence was beside her. Granny sat perfectly still, rooted like an aged tree that had been harmed but had not succumbed to its history of long droughts and extreme winters. Her nearly spent body, her heavy lidded eyes, her tired bones all told the story of her years.

A murmur sang around the room as Rona's escorts led her into the assembly. Granny whispered to Bernice, who got up and approached Ben. He followed her back to Granny's chair and bent down low to hear her speak. He beckoned to Rona and Teddy Boy. As they approached, at a signal from Bernice, five young women who were seated along the row to Granny's right got up and moved to empty chairs on the opposite side of the room.

Beryl watched Rona walk. Her shoulders were slumped, and she was leaning so far forward it seemed that crossing the room was taking every last bit of her strength. Ben reached out his arm to steady her when she stopped in front of Granny.

"You remember Mrs. Spence, don't you Rona?" he said.

She stood, staring, and then almost collapsed as her knees buckled. Ben and Bernice helped her onto the chair beside Granny.

Granny reached up and touched Rona's cheek. "That's good," she said. "Sit here, beside me. Let the mothers sit together. Let us sit together and pray." She patted the open page of a worn brown leather-covered Bible on her lap with her knobbly fingers and bowed her head.

Rona covered her face with her hands. She was crying silently now, and her shoulders shook with her ragged breathing. Ben sat beside her and stroked her hair and leaned forward to whisper in her ear. He took the scarf from her hair and used it to dry her cheeks. All in the room were silent, and then Rona gave a deep sigh, an exhalation that sounded like the release of some sorrowful energy. The mourners seemed to understand that it was a moment of both an ending and a beginning. Granny murmured a few words in Cree. Her twisted empty hands moved restlessly in her lap like two small birds pecking at the black words in her book.

Zach took another of the vacant chairs and motioned to Beryl to take the seat beside Ben. None of the Kay-Sterns went near the coffin. He saw that others were crying, too. It was as if Rona's tears had started a flood of salt water that filled the room. He thought a funeral without tears was cruel and meaningless, yet his own eyes remained dry.

Zach heard sounds of a commotion at the front door and watched as Teddy Boy hurried to attend to it. He led an elderly Indian man into the room, and a crowd of men and women, young and old, and children surged forward around him. Now there was only room for standing. No one paid the slightest attention to the strangers in their midst.

The elder was dressed in fringed leggings and a long tunic and carried an eagle feather. He wore a flat neckpiece made of bones and silver disks and coloured beads. His lean face was as creased and lined as the bottom of a dry slough, and his long grey hair hung down his back in a single braid. He walked over to Georgia Lee's coffin and waved the feather over her length about 6 inches above her body.

Bernice Spence and two other women slowly approached. Bernice carried a low, shallow bowl that held tobacco, cedar, sweet grass, and sage. She turned to the now-silent mourners and said, "We burn tobacco to show the unity of life. Sage is for healing, cedar for strength, and sweet grass stands for our love." The offerings smouldered, filling the air with an agreeable pungent fragrance.

"*Wa hey heya hey,*" the old man sang in a low voice that held the weary majesty of deposed royalty. Granny bobbed her head along with his rhythm as he danced slowly in his hide moccasins. Others in the crowd began to sing along with the elder, and the insistent beat of a ceremonial drum drove the voices round and round in a circle of prayer.

The rest of Kay-Stern family, including the twins, Barbara and David, arrived with Mark and Rabbi Berman. They crowded into the back of the room. Ben and Zach and Mark and David and the rabbi put on *yarmulkes* and *tallit* over their suits. The four of them stood in silence as the elder continued to sing his farewell song to Georgia Lee's spirit.

No one, except 15-year-old Barbara, noticed the extremely pale and slender young woman with inch-long spiked platinum blonde hair who edged her way into the room and leaned her black leather-clad frame up against the wall. Chick Fontaine was one-eighth Native through her mother's side; but that blood was so diluted it had receded into her bones. In the inside pocket of her biker style jacket, she had a white envelope that contained some of the photos she and Georgie had taken at the booth in the mall after Georgie had gotten her hair cut short and dyed black. Chick planned to offer them to Georgie's parents.

She was still dreaming of Georgie at night. Dreaming of what had happened to her, and in the dream, as Chick watched the faceless man whack Georgie over the head with a long black rod, as the rod hit her head, it became Chick's own head. She had woken so many nights at this point, with her heart thumping wildly and hot vomit scalding her throat. She tried to think of the words to the Beatles song her mom had sung to chase childhood nightmares away. *Once there was a way to get back homeward. Once there was a way to get back home.*

Not now, though. These nights, no golden slumbers filled Chick's eyes, so she was trying to limit her sleep. She'd begun taking only the late shift at the video store and sitting up and delaying going to bed until 5:00 in the morning, until her eyes were burning and every one of her bones ached. If the dream came then, she would wake to daylight. That was easier because the dream faded faster, and she could push it behind a dark cloud in her head and the cloud kept the dream at bay.

Chick edged her way forward to the short queue near the coffin and waited her turn to stand in front of Georgie's body. Georgie was the only dead person Chick had ever seen this close. Somebody had put her in an old-fashioned blue dress that was not stylie at all, and with her hair combed flat and her bangs smoothed, she looked a lot younger. Only about 13 or so. She looked sweet and lovely as anybody's little sister.

Chick reached out and touched Georgie's cheek. Chick's bitten nails with their dabs of green polish made a strange contrast against her friend's smooth tan cheek. It was cold as ice. A shiver travelled up Chick's arm and into her chest where it stopped. She pulled back and bowed her head. She tried to think of a prayer, but all she thought of to say was *Sorry, Georgie. Sorry it was you.*

The lingering smoke from the burnt offerings and the warmth of the crowded room began to make Zach feel wheezy. He decided to get some air before his breathing worsened, so he made his way to the vestibule, where he happened to see the homicide detectives approach the funeral director. He watched as the blond detective handed over a parcel wrapped in brown paper to the funeral director. He was called Friesen, wasn't he? Yes, he was. Friesen and Dunblane. They had been very polite when they had interviewed him. There had been little Zach could tell them about his niece.

He overheard Friesen tell the undertaker to be sure to put the parcel in the coffin with the body. The man nodded, and Zach heard him say he would do as the family wished. The custom of burying a victim of a murder with the clothing the deceased had been killed in had been unknown to Zach. The package of blood-spattered clothing was going to be placed in the coffin; this was done in a special effort to seek mercy from the Lord.

This burial custom had been news to the rest of Kay-Stern family, too. The Reform rabbi had suggested it, and as soon as Rona had heard his explanation, she had insisted that it be done. She was full of anger now, righteous anger, her demand for an explanation from the heavens unanswered. In this case, though, the girl was dressed not in the traditional clean white winding sheet but in the new blue dress supplied by her birth family. Only her black sweater and skirt were in the brown paper parcel. That was all the police had agreed to part with at this stage of the investigation.

Zach had agreed and convinced Ben to go along with Rona's wishes, ignoring lightly veiled sarcastic comments from Mark and his own reservations about the nature of this deferral to primitive, magical thinking. He thought about the nature of history, his subject: what we choose to remember and record. *We believe in the preservation of those stories whose lessons must be carried forward.* As he told his students, *it's all about how we assign value.* He thought about the great change that came about when humans began to bury their own, at that seminal moment when Man tenderly laid his fellow to rest in the earth. To put love into the grave as the dead one was buried with what were seen as the necessities for the afterlife. *The heavens do not weep. That is left to us.*

The funeral director was not aware that Rona had wanted to put old Mr. Mischief, the battered toy monkey that Georgia Lee had slept with every night, into the coffin as well. Ben and Zach had gone back to her empty suite to look for him, but the brown velvet monkey dressed in a red plaid vest and black bow tie was missing. Rona was devastated that Mr. Mischief was gone. It was bizarre. Ben had tried to comfort her, but there was no substitute. Would the monkey have been a useful object in the afterlife? Zach did not want to think about that. Life after Georgia Lee, life without her.

Zach continued to stand in the doorway, watching the crowd in the viewing room. He saw a thin blonde girl dressed in a motorcycle jacket sidle up to the bier and give it a hasty sideways glance. She nodded to Barbara, and his daughter approached her. He could see their lips moving but couldn't read their words. There was an exchange of hesitant smiles. They walked over to Rona. The blonde leaned down and spoke to her. Rona put her arm around the girl's neck and pulled her cheek down close to her own tear-stained one. The blonde girl crouched down in front of Rona and took her hands in her own. Ben leaned over to speak to her, and he smiled warmly at her and squeezed her shoulder. She and Barbara moved aside and sat down on nearby vacant chairs to continue their conversation. The blonde girl gave Barbara a white envelope and then abruptly stood and hurried out of the crowded room.

Chick stopped for a few moments outside the chapel, leaned against the closed doors, and pulled out and lit up a cigarette. She took several deep puffs before throwing the half-smoked fag on the ground and ran to the corner to catch the #18 bus southbound.

Rabbi Berman didn't know where to look. He stood with his hands at his sides as he waited for the elder to finish his song. He was eager to say *Kaddish* and call it a night. When the graveside service the family had requested was abruptly cancelled, he had found that they'd remained in his thoughts all day. He was not entirely comfortable with agreeing to be part of this ceremony. After all, the family had admitted that the girl did not want to be considered a Jew. Refused to become *bat mitzvah*. And looking around the room now, he could see that they did not have a *minyan*.

The family had said they were non-observant, yet clearly this was very important to them. He did not recall ever meeting any of them, or perhaps only the brother, a face slightly familiar from the High Holiday services. And as his old mother often said, "You, maybe, from chicken soup, a borscht can make, but from borscht a chicken soup – never."

It was no good to run to the Temple only when you needed a rabbi in a crisis. He'd agreed to do the service because he had hoped it would ease the mother's suffering. He had told her that there was no simple way to understand why these terrible things happen to the innocent. Life can only be clearly understood when it has passed, yet we must live our lives now, in the present tense.

After the drums and chanting stopped, the rabbi stepped forward and began to sing the *Kaddish* softly and clearly, as if he were trying to explain something difficult to the mourners. All listened quietly and carefully as the plaintive melody filled the air.

None of those in attendance were aware that the Floodway gates had been thrown open that afternoon by the elderly retired politician who had commissioned the diversion project thirty years earlier. None knew that the hospitals in St. Pierre, Emerson, Rosenort, St. Adolph, and Morris had been evacuated that day. Nor that the city's total sandbag production had gone over the 3-million mark. Or that a thief, robbing a Safeway food market, had assaulted the store's security guard by hitting him in the face with a steak.

Maud was sitting comfortably in front of her wide living room windows with a cool glass of Chablis, watching the light fade from her view of northern sky. She loved to watch as the sky slowly, slowly darkened, deepened through peacock blue to ultramarine and then to indigo behind the black crisscross of bare elm branches. She was in a state of perfect melancholy. At this time of day, she could not see the soft green budding leaves. During this cool, late April, it was more a winter's sky than a spring one.

She had taken the day off work and would have another free day tomorrow. That made for a long weekend, and she was ready for it. She was planning to catch up on her missed sleep. She had avoided staying on for dinner with her mother, saying that she had made plans with Jake. An excuse made to spare telling her the unpleasant truth: that a whole day and evening in her company would be overdoing it. That Maud's own frivolous life called to her. And trivial as it might seem compared with others, with her crises, infrequent triumphs, way too much wine and too little love – and no matter how inconsequential her mother might judge it – it was hers. She needed all of it, including her reluctant lover. It was true, Jake had agreed to call and perhaps go out to eat if he was free. Her phone could ring any time now.

Georgia Lee's graduation photo had been on the front page of the morning paper, a wallet-sized one in the bottom right hand corner. The caption read "Returned to Footprint Lake. Details on page 7." Maud did not bother to look for the article. She had read the girl's journal in all its heart-breaking detail. She was sure there was nothing more to learn about the girl. The only essential fact that remained unknown was the murderer's identity. He had also murdered sleep, hers and that of many others. If only the dark would yield its secrets and whisper some comfort in her ear, wide open at 5:00 in the morning, listening to the thud and brawny grinding of trains shunting in the C.P.R. yards and struggling up from her dream.

She dreamt Jake was there on the riverbank. It was evening, and the sky was her favourite shade of ultramarine. She swam happily with a strong stroke. She saw his profile against the night sky. The river widened, and an ocean liner ablaze with light passed between them, between her and the shore, in the gulf where love was meant to be. She began to panic, to lose her rhythm. It was that childhood terror of swimming in water over her head. She waved at Jake; he did not see her. Why was she swimming out so far? She knew she was out too far.

Maud had kept her promise and given her mother a hand going through the many boxes of her father's papers that now crowded her old bedroom. There was time for this now that her ever over-organized mother had stripped everything out of the basement and first floor ahead of the encroaching floodwaters. Maud had sat on the hardwood floor with the pale sun streaming in behind her and warming her back as she leafed through the manuscript for Michael Fallon's last book on W.B. Yeats. She saw her father's pencilled final edits in his familiar clear hand. He had died when she was 23, and she dearly missed him in her world.

At the time, she had not clearly understood what it meant for her mother. Her parents had lived the fullest part of their lives within a magic circle that had excluded their children. Their private life had been their masterpiece. Endearments and their most private thoughts had been expressed in the old country tongue. *Mo chroidhe dhil* – she'd heard such mysterious snatches of Gaelic floating up at night through the hot air registers. She could make out her father's deep bass and the trilling of her mother's soprano, their duet, and its recurring phrases central to the composition of their private magic, and Maud had felt their conversation was important. If only she could understand it, she would gain something profound.

Maud knew the many-times-told story of the whirlwind Dublin courtship of Michael and Delia. He was only a scholarship student to Trinity, but what had distinguished him, made him acceptable to her family, was his great love of the word. His raw west coast Gaelic. His character. Steady. Steady, he was. In this censored version, Maud had not understood the true source of their faithful love. They were, after all, her parents, and their private talk was a wide river that more than any other thing separated their world from hers.

Maud wanted to believe that Jake would marry her. She'd told her mother as much.

"But my dear, has he proposed?" Delia had hesitated and continued in a softer, more intimate tone. "Marriage requires making the adjustment of holding all things in common. To my mind, you and Jake hold little in common but this crime business. Does he want a home and family? I know that you do. You say that you are sure he is the right one for you, but then where is he? Even now as you struggle with this difficult and emotionally painful work that you insist you love, where is he?"

Delia had looked directly into Maud's eyes and then quickly away to show that she was not going to press the question when they both knew Maud's answer would not please.

Maud had never told her mother about Jake's early marriage. It had been a brief one, to a girl from his hometown, who had said she was pregnant and he, the father. He could have been, though there were others, other men, he'd said with a shrug.. They had left quietly after dark and were hush-up married in a hasty ceremony by a Justice of the Peace in Winnipeg. He had later been surprised to find that he was not the father. Her uncle was. The infant son had died in his third month, a crib death, and the 20-year-old wife had left for Toronto the following week. Jake had no idea of or any interest in her whereabouts.

He did not return to Altona. He was not shunned; he saw there was no place for him. He had taken responsibility for a sin he'd committed and one he had not. He'd wanted to do more, to correct the imbalances he saw in the world. He wanted a world where principles as sound as the law of gravity ruled. He had answered a want ad for police work. The idea of keeping order, of keeping watch over the city and restoring balance, even harmony, claimed him with a voice insistent as any call to duty, promising grace in exchange for fidelity.

Once bitten, twice shy he was – and, Maud told herself, in need of understanding on the issue of commitment. Jake had told her that he could not, would not imagine a life that she was not part of, and she had believed him and felt reassured that, given time, he would want more than they had now. She had told her mother that, definitely, it was a given, she did want a husband and children, but not yet. ("Not yet?" Her uncle Thad had questioned her closely, and she could hear his disbelief all the long-distance way from Sligo. "Not yet," he'd repeated, "not yet. There's something wrong with a man who can resist you.")

She was mostly certain that Jake was the one. Undomesticated, he was. They rarely spoke of it. She would make no demands on him. She wanted him to come to her freely or not at all.

In the beginning, she'd been attracted to Jake partly because of a purity of purpose she had seen in his dedication to his work. Was that stupid or what? Romantic? She knew he'd seen many tragic and brutal deaths, and these had taken a heavy toll. Their love was barely a close second to his interest in the murky matters of crime, and she resented that he chose that life over what they could have together.

They'd been together for nearly two years now. Time enough. He was 37. She was 33; there was time. Maybe she needed a younger man. She should break it off with Jake now while it might end without bitterness. She had been on the verge of that final conversation a few times, but he had seemed to sense her intent, her deliberate coolness, and fluent in the language of caresses, he'd persuaded her to stay in his arms.

She thought about the lovely small brown mole on Jake's left cheek. How she'd watched it move when Jake, deep in thought, had been stroking his chin.

He'd withdraw, and how this absence made him seem vulnerable. She was drawn to this side of him. She wanted to restore him. She was certain that if he truly loved her, he would let her.

"If Jake does not want marriage . . ." Delia had hesitated, shrugged her shoulders before going on. "And my guess is that, for whatever his reasons, he does not, you should break it off." She'd set aside her black marking pen and list and looked directly at her daughter. Her gaze was warm and love was concentrated there, and she thought of how much Maud's green eyes were like her father's and how this had always pleased her. Delia reached out a slim manicured hand and brushed Maud's hair back behind her right ear.

"You'll find love with someone who wants you and knows it. And don't be too fussy. You are getting older, being too particular. I am concerned that your concept of an ideal romantic love may prevent you from recognizing a true lover. Take care that does not become your story."

As soon as the words were out of her mouth, Delia fell silent. She only wanted the best for Maud. Still, she wished she had not spoken. Not been so hard on Jake. He wasn't a bad fellow. When she saw them together, though, there was no sign of that special sense of coupledness about them.

I cannot be blamed for wanting the best for my children, Delia thought. *Now that I am old, I have come to understand that the only world worth having is the world of love. Your lover should be the one who brings out the best in you. Michael and I, we had that. The Quakers say that great pain or great joy can open the gates of the soul. I want Maud to know this joy. Goodness makes too small a sound in this world. There is no point in agonizing over the eternal questions to which we have no answers – the nature of God, the suffering of the innocent, the problem of pain. It is more edifying to concern oneself with learning to love well, to work well, and try to be good. If I start up with that, though,* Delia thought, *when we've never talked about such things, she'll think I've gone soft. I wish that Michael were here to talk it all over. I believe that there is an afterlife. And I believe that in that life we will be with those we love, truly love, even though it is said to be foolish and damaging to be in love with the dead.*

She looked over at Maud, who was leafing through an album of old photos.

Maud raised her eyes and smiled contentedly. "Will you look at Dad in this one?" she said.

***

Paul Boudreau saw the girl's photo on page 1 of that morning's paper. It was a short article. That was good, he thought. The fuckin' flood was all anybody could talk about here. They were getting too busy to worry about her. The paper had printed her high-school graduation picture, so she didn't look much like the girl he'd offed. Not like the other picture he'd seen, before they'd found out who she was. That was good because seeing that picture with her dead face really pissed him off.

The report said that both of the families had agreed to have her buried on her home reserve up near Norway House. He read the story over, saying *yeah, yeah, yeah* to himself. So what? She deserved what she'd got. He was feeling good about it again pretty well down to the last paragraph, where it said that sandbagging crews working on the flood preparations along the Seine River had reported seeing the police combing the grounds at the ruins of the old monastery south of the city. A police spokesperson had refused to comment on the ongoing investigation.

Those assholes wouldn't be able to smell him out there at those ruins. Paul was sure of that. He knew the snow was gone now, and so would any kinda tracks he mighta made. Still, it was a fuck ass piece of bad luck, and he hated to think of his luck going south – where *he* should be by now. He'd been thinking about hitching out the Number 1 east to where he'd dumped his car to see what it looked like now. Probably crawling with maggots and flies. Like this city, crawling with police and the army and who the fuck else, he didn't know. He wanted to make a move out of town, but it was fuckin' impossible to head south now. The highway heading south was closed. Under flood waters. The Red River had turned into the Red Sea, and Moses wasn't around to part the waters for him.

He was sick of being Julian Russell. What a stupid, cocksucking name. He had to get his life back on track, because everything that had happened to him since he'd got to this town had been wrong.

He remembered the disgust he'd felt as he'd pulled her body out onto the snowy field. He hadn't wanted her messing up the inside of his car. He'd gotten out of the back seat and walked around to the other rear door. He'd grabbed her under her armpits and tugged her out. She had been warm, and she'd gurgled like she was still alive. He'd tried to think of how to do the first aid thing. Was she breathing? For a minute he'd even thought so, but her eyes had been dead looking. He'd pulled harder and dumped her on the ground, on the snow beside the car. Her head had rolled to the side, and he'd seen blood running out of her right ear. He'd got busy then, cleaning out the back seat as best he could. He'd dug some yellow plastic rope and Charlie's old blue camping tarp out of the trunk and spread it on the ground. He'd figured to wrap her up in it and dump her off somewhere she wouldn't get found for a few days. Buy him the time he needed to get the fuck out of here. He'd planned to be in Mexico by now. Go south through the farmland, and over the border on a back road where he wouldn't be noticed. A perfect plan.

He hadn't seen it until he'd gone to move her onto the tarp. How her blood had spread out around her head like a fiery crown on the snow. He'd scuffed some fresh snow over it. The rest would wash away with the spring melt.

"You are a wicked man."

Two days later, and Paul still heard a voice, maybe his own voice, echoing these words like a final judgment.

Padre Martin Kroeker at the New Path ministry was tough on sin. His Sunday sermon was meant to instil fear in the hearts of the unrepentant. He spoke of the message delivered by the floodwaters threatening the city and of Noah's ark. How the world was flooded in ancient times to punish the wicked. Man is weak, he said, weak and wicked. It could happen again, he thundered, and continued on about the evils of the pornographic world flooding the Internet.

The dark mood of Sunday's sermon was giving Paul a headache like a morning-after hangover. He wanted to move on, leave the New Path residence, but the deal was too sweet for now. Besides, he had very little cash left. He had to put out 40 bucks for his new boots, and they were second-hand. The bachelor suite he was renting from the ministry took over half of his issue, and he had to buy food sometimes when he couldn't steal it. Or get it off the food bank. And smokes. He had to have smokes. Listening to the sermons was part of the price. The price of his safe cover act.

Julian Russell – that's who he was now. An ex-junkie from Vancouver Island. Nothing like the real Julian Russell, who'd died when he was 2 years old. It had amused him to start this game, stealing a new identity.

Answering to Julian or to James. He told people his name was James. He liked that more. He was undercover like Bond. James Bond. He kept to himself. Took off for the day labour office every morning. Hanging to the back of the line. Half the time, there was no work left when his turn came.

It had been okay in the beginning, making up a new life story, but some days he got pissed with the deal. He'd end up back at the mission, and the padre always had some unpaid work for his idle hands. Martha Wiebe, the secretary, offered to teach him to run the Internet, but he'd turned her ugly butt down. Told her he didn't type. He didn't want to be close to a skanky witch like her. She'd never let him look at any porno sites anyways.

He was nursing a large root beer in the food court at the Portage Avenue Mall. He finished his burger and fries but was pissed because he still had a headache. There was no day work this morning, and he was supposed to be on his way to a join a volunteer sandbagging crew in Elmwood, but he'd wanted some food that didn't come out of a soup kitchen. So he snuck into the mall and sat watching the action. He perched on a stool at a counter with his backside to a floor-to-ceiling wall of glass that ran the length of the food court. It was quarter to 12, and the lunchtime rush was in full swing. There were lots of shoppers, loafers, and students.

He had his eye on four young giggling bitches a few tables away. He liked the little blonde fox with the blue striped sweater stretched over her really big tits. He could see her nipples pressing through her sheer bra. Down the road she'd be all hanging low like any old cow, but now she was sweet. She was leaning forward on one elbow over the table and held her forearm over her chest like she was trying to hide it and sucking on a straw with dark red lipsticked lips. He'd be dammed if he was gonna give up his freakin' seat one minute before he was ready. Place was full and he didn't give a shit. Bitch looked over at him like she was going to ask a question. Then she looked away all scared after he gave her a hard look.

He turned his back to the crowd and noise and looked out over the street. The sun was bright, and cars and people passed in his view. Lots of people busy with their tiny lives. Everyone free to run around shopping and screwing each other while he was caged with the heavy-duty Christians in their rundown boring flat city.

The old Native guy in the seat next to him left, and a young one took his place. He was wearing a lot of lemony aftershave. Smelled like a goddam fuck-ass fag. His black shoulder-length hair was tied down under a black-and-white doo rag, kinda like the Arab dudes got. Paul watched him out of the corner of his eye. The guy was big with monster pecs but stupid looking. He was chowing down on some kind of Chinese-looking food and paging through the morning paper.

Buddy started yammering as soon as he caught Paul's eye. "Look at this," he said, pointing to an aerial photo of 4-foot waves on the lake that the media had dubbed the Red Sea. "This is *biblical,*" he said, stretching the word out to its full reach of syllables.

When Paul did not reply, the guy said "biblical" again but softer this time, making it difficult to hear. But Paul heard him.

The guy looked down at the newspaper again and said, "So the guys in Ottawa decided we're going to have an election. Waste of time. Nothing's going to change." He pushed his empty Styrofoam plate aside and spread the tabloid out on the counter. He pointed to an article captioned "HE'S ALL WET, SAY SANDBAGGERS." There was a photo of Prime Minister Chrétien out on the campaign trail, tossing a sandbag up on a dike on Scotia Street.

Paul grunted in reply and looked away. He didn't like being next to this guy. He gave off a feeling of being a real shitkicker. Paul took the lid off and upended his super-sized drink to suck up the dregs and ice.

"Don't make no difference to me, either. Fucking politicians can't tell me they really give a shit." The guy kept turning the pages of his newspaper. He stopped at an article on page 7. The heading read "RCMP Find Abandoned Car." He leaned forward over the paper and ran his index finger along the printed text under each word like a child.

Paul watched him out of the corner of his eye.

"Interesting," the guy said, "very interesting. See this?" he asked, pointing to the article. "Now lookee here." He pointed to the photo of Charlie Hardwick's Dodge. "The RCMP find a car with a blood-stained back seat at a gravel pit out in the country off the Trans Canada going east. This is good. See, there are no plates on it. It was dumped. These kids" – he pointed to the other photo, one of three young teens leaning on their dirt bikes – "they're the ones who found it and got it going and drove it into a tree." He glanced at Paul. "I bet it belonged to the guy who did that girl they found in a snow bank under the railway bridge. You heard about it?" He carefully traced the border of the photo of the car with his index finger. "You musta heard about it. Happened about three weeks ago."

Paul didn't answer any of these questions. He was angry at the picture of his blue Dodge with its grill all smashed up. It gave him a steely evil monster's grin. He stood up quickly, knocking his stool over. He startled at the noise as it hit the tile floor and looked around to see if anyone was watching. He bent over and straightened the stool. He set a dead-eyed look on his face and turned back to the guy and said, "Fuck off. I don't give a shit."

Next thing, the guy was on his feet and had his face in Paul's. "Don't give a shit, you asshole? I don't know how long you've been on the street, but it ain't gonna last." He nodded. "Yeah, you're the kind of asshole makes a good lifer. I know you. Yeah, you're a little kinda man thinks he's big."

His breath warmed Paul's face, and the smell of the guy's lunch that he'd drenched in soy sauce instantly made Paul feel like he had to puke. He stepped back and drew a big breath. He looked at the other guy, taking deadly aim with his mind so all his hate was blazing out from his eyes. The guy didn't blink.

"I see your kind all the time, asshole," the guy said. "You get all bulked up in the joint 'cause ya got nothing else to do but pump iron. You come on to me, but you don't know who you're dealing with. You weren't in Headingley last summer, were you? I was there, man. For the riot. And you know us. We Skins made it hot. The Warriors and the IP. I'm a professional fighter. Got my black belt. I ain't never been beat. If I want, I can break a guy's neck in two seconds." He snapped his fingers twice, quickly, a loud, hard sound. "Anyone's. Yours." His eyes were black, flat, cold. He took a step back from Paul and made a downward brush over his chest with the back of his hand, like he was swatting away a mosquito, and turned his back.

Paul stepped off, and as soon as he saw the back of the guy's head, he turned on his heel and began threading his way out through the crowded tables of the food court. He glanced back toward the window and saw the guy hadn't moved. As he turned toward the exit, he saw a huge Indian guy in a black cowboy hat. The guy made a fast slashing movement across his throat and gestured toward Paul. Instinctively, Paul jerked his head back slightly, and as the guy started coming for him, he scuttled to the closest exit. He slowed a bit as he passed in front of the security guard, and once he was clear, he bent down to get his blade out of his boot and hustled along the street, making good time east on Portage toward the river.

He hated this fucking city. Pissed him off that he went to the fuck-ass mall. Everybody said it was the biggest reserve in the province. That guy was just another fucking Indian from the Portage reserve. Yeah. Like he knew anything.

Paul was thinking about the licence plates he'd taken off the Dodge. He'd tossed them in the ditch while he was walking in that fucking blizzard toward the gas bar where he'd hitched a ride. That was stupid. Now the snow was gone and anybody could find them. Charlie's car could be traced through them, though Paul had the registration. Was there anything else in the glove box? He had no fucking idea. Did the old bitch Patsy report it stolen? Probably, but so what? The car could be traced to Paul Boudreau but not Julian Russell. That pussy Julian Russell was clean.

He wanted to go back to his crib and get rid of his parole papers and the other shit he'd stashed in his toolbox. He'd have to kill time until tonight. Couldn't go back earlier, or the padre would be on his case. Paul knew he'd done wrong of the worst kind and he deserved to be punished for it. He thought about taking off for Mexico. But he couldn't. Fucking flood was messing things up for him. He thought of how it came down to what his bunkie Pedro had said. Pedro used to tell him that life isn't like a bowl of cherries. It's more like a jar of jalapeños. What you eat today might burn your ass tomorrow. And when you're guilty, don't expect nothin' but shit.

Overnight, Rona looked older and wearier. She was adrift, her face lined by worry and pain. Only two weeks ago she'd been in balmy Costa Rica, in that distant, carefree world of sunny days, warm breezes, and the bright holiday mood she'd had there seemed less real than a dream. Her posture had gone slack, and she seemed immobilized from within, responding slowly when spoken to. A simple task like dressing could take hours.

She sat, almost mute, in the furnished suite they were renting in a downtown apartment-hotel. The rooms were decorated in grey and pink tones, and she found this décor aggressively ugly. The glass-topped tables and soft, overstuffed furnishings were cheap goods, chosen from one of those stores that advertised on TV – *Decorate every room in your house for only $999.00! Buy your dreams, a dollar down.*

There was nothing here to bring her comfort. Although the building was linked by an enclosed walkway system to many of the city's core area facilities, she never went out. She saw no one. Her world was reduced to this parched territory whose borders she refused to cross. Her head ached as if the wind had sucked everything out, and she could feel the exact shape of the bones of her skull.

Ben kept searching for a way to reach her. He tried to coax her out into the streets to see the city coming alive. The days were warm, and the whole city, the whole province, was on the move. Everywhere there was bustle and energy. Twenty-four hours a day, the whine and grunt and roar and clang of heavy machinery rang out over the Red River Valley, the bellow and uproar of men and machines racing against the rising water.

The spring light was dazzling, glistening on the dew on the budding leaves, warming the bareheaded. Ben took his wife to an old favourite café of theirs on the edge of the Wolseley, where she enjoyed a bowl of fresh borscht with caraway-seeded rye bread but began to shiver uncontrollably when he suggested a walk through the familiar streets. Ben hid his disappointment. He'd hoped that this lunch – a weekly ritual they'd liked to linger over with second cups of coffee and the fat Saturday newspapers – he'd hoped that repeating one of their usual diversions would bring some consolation. The consolations of the ordinary. Wasn't that what Rabbi Berman had suggested?

Ben had rearranged his schedule and their affairs so that Rona was alone as little as possible. He worried about her sanity, her safety.

Ben didn't know that Rona spent each day reviewing their daughter's life. The life she could have had, the one Rona had wanted for her. Rona recalled little of the funeral: Granny Spence's bright, dark eyes and the dry heat radiating from the thin, muscular hand that had stroked her cool one. Those laughing photo booth pictures of Georgia Lee and her blonde friend – what became of them?

At night, awake in the circle of Ben's arms, Rona berated herself, asking, *Why didn't I know?* He told her that she should not, that she could not, expect to know everything that happened to Georgia Lee. He avoided responding to anything she said about a mother's intuition. She needed to mourn the idea she'd had that there was a singular bond between them; the belief she clung to that she and Georgia Lee had shared a psychic connection that linked them forever like a vestigial umbilical cord.

Ben did not try to make love to her now, though they had always spoken to each other through their fingertips, their lips, following intimate Braille patterns they'd written on each other's skin. *Be with me now* was his silent wish. In bed, he nestled with her, his chest against her back. Siamese twins whose bond was sorrow.

He reached for her left hand and slowly turned her heavy gold wedding band around between his thumb and first two fingers. Their rings were identical. He felt the uneven surface of the incised Hebrew letters that stood for a few words from the text of Psalm 137: "If I forget you, O Jerusalem, Let my right hand whither! Let my tongue cleave to the roof of my mouth, if I do not remember you, if I do not set Jerusalem above my highest joy."

You are my Jerusalem was his silent vow to her each day.

On their wedding day, her face had been radiant as she'd walked the seven slow circles around him under the *chupah*. He was still happy he'd decided to set aside his opposition to ritual and agreed to be married by a rabbi. It pleased him to please his bride.

When they'd met, Rona had been a partner in a catering business, strictly for small affairs, in private homes or businesses. She and Ruthie Hirsch had made a specialty of parties and events with themes, and they were very successful. Ben first saw Rona at a fundraising dinner that she and Ruthie had catered for the *Shalom Achshavniks,* and from that moment on, Ben and Rona only had eyes for each other. It was the end of catering and the beginning of life with Ben. The twelve-year difference in their ages was irrelevant.

He had fallen in love with the sound of her voice. Its honeyed undertone. Her whispering laugh. Her manner had been languorous;

nothing could encourage her to rush. He loved to watch her brush her long, dark hair. She'd tuck it behind the shell-pink whorls of her pretty ears with such delicacy; it was as if his watching eyes caressed her as she caressed herself. Now that dreamy beauty of hers had changed to a graver kind, the wounded beauty of sadness. He saw her whole life in her eyes and found himself more in love with her than ever.

We are beginning our descent. Ben had heard those words again in the creamy Southern tones of the stewardess on the flight from Texas to Toronto. That had been the beginning. He was distressed by their fall from grace. He accepted condolences with deep gratitude. On his behalf and Rona's.

He had always believed he could bear his burdens. Take whatever life dished out. He had plenty of experience, didn't he? He wanted to carry the weight for both their sakes. Until she was able. Would she ever be? He was not sure. Privately, he was deeply, coldly angry in a way that was foreign to him and he had no language for. He wanted to cry aloud for their mistakes but knew this truth: the world doesn't need any more of that sound.

He understood her anger, her bitterness at Mark's lack of attention to Georgia Lee, her regret at their decision to go away, to dismantle their safe world and push their little girl out into the real world with its attendant cruelties. Things fell apart.

Rona believed she had failed her daughter, that because there was no shared blood between them, her mothering was fraudulent. Some mornings she believed it had never been good enough, though she knew she loved every bit of Georgia Lee, right down to her flat little feet. All Rona's stirrings and striving had been part of this secret history of her wish to make this daughter her own.

Rona was not moving on, though everyone was encouraging her to. She did not want to hear about the stages of grief. About closure, the *c* word, all of that fraudulent New Age crapola. Theories didn't interest her. *I should follow a schedule?* she asked. *Why?* She felt no need to forgive anyone. Not her brother Mark, not the man who had murdered her daughter. People spoke to her of forgiveness and healing and a time to move on. *Count your blessings. Remember the good times.* These words did not make any sense to her.

The past was her place now. She was comforted only by the coming of evening; she became calmer then as she went to sleep with her hand over her heart, waiting for the tides of night to come in. With the help of Dr. Murray Fine's excellent sleeping pills, she slept deep and long, lingering on into the morning. A traveller with her net cast out below the surface of night to draw in the shape of another day.

She knew that, each day, she would learn again the hard fact that Georgia Lee was dead. It smouldered darkly, its power undiminished. A fire rekindled every morning when she woke to the hard blue prairie sky, the sun full on this saved town, the hours before her. Georgia Lee was dead, and her murderer was free. It was unbearable to know this was permitted. He was breathing, eating, drinking, shaving, shitting, walking the city, even working, wishing, making love. Rona denied him every breath.

Winnipeg   **April 30, 1997**

Without asking Rona, Mark brought Rabbi Sol Berman over to see her. The good rabbi found that there was little he could offer. As he spoke, Rona sat quietly examining her fingernails and twice reached out to make little adjustments to the arrangement of pink roses and white freesia on the coffee table and did not respond to his overtures of consolation. When she did speak, she looked at Mark with a hard, unwavering glare.

"You tell me that Georgia Lee gave me pain and joy," she said. "So very true. That I shouldn't try to balance those accounts. You cannot expect me to get over this. *This* is not something you get over. I don't want to forgive any of us. I do not want closure. I want revenge. I want justice."

"Anger is a strong emotion," the rabbi replied. "You may find that you can use that power to help yourself if you are careful." He took another sip of his tea. "We live in an imperfect world. What is chiefly visible to you now is a great darkness. The Torah can be a source of solace. Yes, believe me, another door will open. With sorrow, with loss, an opportunity for a change is given, for something new to enter through the opening in your life. You and your family will travel on a path of discomfort to reach a state of peace. Each of you walks a singular path and can hope to arrive at the same place. Try to help each other. Try to forgive."

"I am not going to forgive him." Hot words, hot tears would flow out of her, burning, burning anyone close. She was not about to forgive

God for allowing this to happen. At last she understood Ben's refusal to pray; now her anger balanced her grief.

"Rona." Mark took her hand. "You sit and sift the ashes. Where does it get you? Life is hard." He gently rubbed her hand between his as if trying to warm it. "It is hard, and what can we do? We must live. People need to forget their troubles. If you keep remembering, you can't live."

Rona pulled her hand free so sharply the movement resounded like a slap. "I like remembering. I like remembering it all. Every sweet moment of Georgia Lee's life. I like living in the past," Rona insisted. "I feel at home there. She is gone from this world, and I wish I were too."

Dead means gone, and Georgia was as gone as she could be. Ben had acknowledged this hard fact when he'd walked into Georgia Lee's apartment to pack up her things. Mark had agreed to store her furniture and packing boxes in the locker room at his condo until their Canora Street tenants left. Ben had arranged for a moving van to meet him and haul her furniture there. Georgia Lee's things would be safe until Rona was able to go through them once they get back home.

Ben began by boxing up her books and papers. He opened one of her binders and paged through her notes for her first-year Psychology course. Her precise handwriting with its rounded loops brought tears to his eyes. He brought the page close to his lips. Every letter dear to him. These next few years at university, they would have been the best years of her life. He had so looked forward to advising her through her years of study. She was a bright one, and there'd been no reason for her not to do well. The same as his two Israeli sons. Both Avi and Lior had excelled in their studies. He didn't think he knew them, loved them, half as well as his little girl. Why had they all the luck and she none?

Had he loved her well enough? He thought he had. He was sure that he and Rona had given their daughter every advantage within their reach. He was grateful for all the countless moments of happiness she had brought them.

They'd believed she was safe here with loving eyes keeping watch on her and everything she needed close by. It did not make any sense. Why was he in her empty apartment bagging her clothes for the Goodwill?

He planned to leave the old TV for the next tenant. Her Canadiana pine rocker would go back to Canora Street. He stripped her bedding and bundled it into one of the green trash bags. Her body's sweet mild citrus scent was faintly, cruelly, present on her bathrobe, and he cursed and crushed it roughly into the plastic bag with the rest of her clothes. It felt as if a sinister cosmic force had taken hold of his life and a displeased and wrathful god was shaking him hard. He was fully awake to it, and he was angry with her. Why had she put herself in harm's way? She'd known the rules. They'd told her often enough. From the day she could understand. Don't go with strangers. He stared at her black boots, worn favourites, empty forever.

Did she? Go with a stranger?

It was hard to believe that she'd chosen to put herself in harm's way. But what other explanation was possible? The police had no suspects. They said they had searched the city. They had questioned all who knew her. They'd found no one to punish. The thought of his daughter's last moments came to him, of the beautiful head of his shy, sweet girl, the crack of her bones, the surprise, the look of surprise, lasting seconds.

He did not like to think of her caught between her two worlds and unable to feel at peace in either. Her need to balance the two halves of her self was reflected in the family photo album he found in her desk. Rona had put it together for her before they'd left on sabbatical. Georgia Lee had rearranged the leaves and added new ones that held photos he had never seen. There were two group photos of her northern cousins. He recognized only Waylon Spence. She had also stuck in photos of the reserve and people at pow wows and a sketch of Granny Spence and a drawing of her family tree. He and Rona were grafted on beside Ruby, and a question mark stood for her unknown father.

Inside the back cover of the photo album, he found some loose hand-written pages she must have torn out of an old diary. He remembered that it was after the summer she'd turned 15 that Georgia Lee had refused to spend any more holiday time on the reserve. Then she had written, "It's like it's not even part of a civilized country. There's nothing for me to do. I don't want to make bannock every day with Granny." She'd written about what he had forgotten: how he had cried when he'd seen the rickety plywood houses there. "I saw Ruby's home on the rez. In the broken-promise land. It's not the end of the world, but you can see it from there."

Ben sensed that the monotonous life on the reserve did not match any remembered landscape she had carried within her. That landscape was urban, organized, and full of colour and promise. She hadn't known know exactly how to express this. She had wanted to feel love for her birth family. She should, shouldn't she? She had been confused by all of their earnest declarations of love. She had wished she could love them, but her feelings had been all mixed up.

Granny Edna's wrinkled face was kind, Georgia Lee had written, but she had a strange old lady smell, like fruit going bad, that had made Georgia Lee choke when her grandmother drew her close to her bony chest. That family had wanted Georgia Lee to answer to a different name. Little Rosie, they called her.

She'd written about how they had wanted her to answer to a Cree name, too. But her tongue had gotten tangled up in that long string of letters every time. Uncle Archie McKay had been firm about calling her by her Cree name. He had seemed angry that she could not pronounce it properly. He had tried to be patient with her lazy tongue and had told her not to look him straight in the eye. What pleased one family displeased the other. Her gaze had kept returning to his scarred brown hands. Two fingers were gone from the right one and the tip of the middle left one.

And she'd written how her Daddy Ben had said nothing, only smiled a not-quite-happy smile, and walked all around their place, looking, measuring, and filing everything away in his smart professor's brain. Auntie Florence had watched him look at everything. She'd given them bannock and moose stew and tea and canned pineapple from the Northern Store at five o'clock in the afternoon. Granny Edna had gotten medicine in a needle with hers.

Georgie had said that Waylon Spence was the only person she liked there and the only one she laughed with. The others all seemed to want something from her that she didn't understand. She had been upset by the talking to she'd gotten from angry Cousin Bernice from the Spence clan, who had been the gold-medal winner in Native studies and politics at the university in Winnipeg. She had been the most insistent that Rosie belonged to them. They had wanted her to choose them, be like them.

That summer, Georgia Lee and Waylon had been together every spare minute of her two-week stay. He had taken her out on the land to show her where he put his traps in winter. He'd said that the previous year, he'd gotten twenty-seven marten, eleven red fox, and four lynx. He was through with that residential school, he'd said. Can't learn anything there. "All I got was a dose of religion, and I quit that too."

Ben read that even then Waylon had dreamed of being a wrestling star. Waylon had heard that the World Wrestling Federation had a training school in Las Vegas and he wanted to get there. "Someday, I'm going to be a superstar and you can say you know me. I have to have my act worked out," he'd told her. He'd studied the WWF matches on satellite TV at

Uncle Archie's house. "I am going to be big. B-I-G. Bigger than the Hulk," Waylon had said. "I'm going to be the Red Devil. I got the moves down now. Wear a little bit of cloth over my dink and a lot of war paint like a real warrior. I'll be more famous than Geronimo."

He had showed Georgia the eagle feather Cousin Bernice had brought him from a pow wow in South Dakota. He had taken Georgia out to his secret gym in the bush. "This is where I train," he'd said, and showed her the tree he did chin-ups on and the lean-to where he kept the barbells he'd made from a discarded broomstick and two tomato juice tins filled with stones. They had sat nearby on a tussock of sweet summer grasses with the sun warm on them. He had handed her the eagle feather and watched as she ruffled, then smoothed, the barbs along its vane.

"How much you think they weigh?" he had asked, pointing to his barbells. "Go on. Try to lift it." Georgia Lee wrote that she had gotten the contraption about 3 or 4 inches off the ground. She had grunted and swung dizzily around as she struggled to raise it higher. The bar had slipped out of her grasp and crashed on his bare feet. She'd dropped to her knees and rubbed his feet softly. "I'm sorry, I'm so sorry," she had repeated.

"It's okay. It's okay. You didn't kill me or nothing," he'd said. Waylon had put his hands on her flushed cheeks and leaned over and kissed each closed lid. Little starry eyes, he had whispered.

She had opened her eyes then and jumped to her feet.

"You can be my spotter,' he had promised. "And, if you come to Vegas with me, I'll buy you a beautiful pink evening dress to wear to the ring." He had stood up. "You'll be like the Lady Elizabeth." He had snapped his fingers. "We'll get a new name for you. I think I like the sound of Princess Esmeralda Rose. That will be good. We'll make up a good story for ourselves, and when I win the big belt with all the jewels. I'll give it to you to wear."

Ben smiled as he read of these sweet dreams of success the cousins had had. At 15, it all seemed possible. She'd written that she wished for it, for success for Waylon, but that in this land, which was supposed to be familiar, she had felt like a stranger. None of their stories about tribal memory had changed that fact. The territory of Footprint Lake Cree Nation near Norway House had been foreign to her. As foreign as Winnipeg had been to her mother twenty years earlier. A door had opened and let the uncertain future in. Both of her lives had felt counterfeit, although life in Winnipeg with the Kay-Sterns was the more familiar.

Ben recalled that he and Rona had agreed that she need not go back to visit the reserve. She must write to her grandmother to explain. She did, though Granny Edna could not read English and heard only what Uncle Archie decided to tell her.

Georgia Lee had given on going to pow wows. Hung up her dancing dress with its jangling rolled-up strips cut from pop tins. Pop tins instead of hollow bird bones. They used white man's junk, and no one seemed to care that it was ugly. Nothing they had was even close to the old ways. She had given up on her efforts to study the Cree language and traditional culture. "They go over and over the same things, show a lot of movies," she'd said. She had transferred from the new Aboriginal high school in the north end to the Collegiate at the university downtown. Ended three years's worth of Saturday mornings taking classes from activists and elders with other urban Native kids. "At the Turtle Mountain Centre at the old train station, they talk a lot about Aboriginal Pride," she had told Ben, "telling us to walk on this earth like we own it. But I see how they put the proud face away as soon as they step out on the street."

"When people ask me why I turned away from my roots," she had written, "I tell them I woke up. I stopped dreaming."

Ben went into the bathroom and removed the framed photo of himself and Rona with 12-year-old Georgia Lee standing between them in her pow wow dancing dress. She looked so sweet and happy. In his memory, they all were happy then. They believed she would dance her dream between her two worlds.

So this is what it is like: the ninth day after your daughter's funeral. How quickly Georgia Lee's short life became a memory. His hot tears were falling now. If only he'd had another chance to hold her in his arms. Flesh and blood. He tried to recall the last time they had hugged each other. He should have been able to describe her face and see its exact replica in his mind's eye.

He remembered her bitter disappointment in learning she was adopted. "I'm a lost member of a lost tribe," she'd said. What comfort could he offer her other than to put his arms around her and give her a tender embrace? He wished that they had seen a way to have a proper Jewish funeral for her in the city with the customary stipulated periods of mourning. After the seven days of *shiva,* there would be an end to the tears. They would lift their heads and go on.

"*Yitgadal v' yitkadash sh'emei raba,*" he said aloud. The old words with their melody of comfort were suddenly on his lips. He, the unbeliever, repeated them. And meant them, despite his inability to believe. Comfort and blessing were needed. Was there any other faith for him to turn to?

In the end, there were eleven cardboard boxes and eight trash bags to be moved over to Mark's. The sum of her 18 years on earth. How could it be so little when they had lost so much?

Mark and Nikolai Gadol were alone in his condo overlooking the river when Beryl made her weekly call from Vancouver. She liked to call him to get his impression of Rona and Ben's situation before she contacted them. As soon as he heard the double long distance ring, he knew who it was. It was five o'clock and the sun was slanting gold down the river. He listened to his sister spout off the list of her family's weekly activities. "I can't talk to Rona about any of this," she said. "Rona has always been resentful of my children and me, and this whole situation has made it worse, much worse." She had been thinking about her niece and the trouble she'd got into. She went on and on, droning in his ear with her long spiel of concerns. *Maybe* this, *maybe* that, *maybe* if he had taken more time with Georgie. Implying that maybe if he wasn't such a selfish bastard.

"What do you mean I didn't do anything nice for her?" he interjected. "I offered to take her out for Chinese, but she turned me down. Yes, I still go for Chinese every Sunday night. And, yes, I have the same routine. Monday, it's ribs. Tuesday, it's pizza. Greek on Wednesdays, and yada, yada, yada. I've got it programmed – that's how I like it. And every night at 6:30, the cab pulls up and I get dinner from wherever. And I get good service because they know I tip big. I invited Georgia Lee every week. She had a standing invitation to join me. She knew that. I'm only about four blocks from her. But she always had an excuse. She had things to do. Studying, papers, tests. Nearly broke my heart, but I'm only the uncle. Beryl, I couldn't make her want to have dinner with me. She didn't come often. Not even on *erev* Christmas for Pete's sake. I'll swear by the truth I know. I tried with her.'"

He didn't need Beryl's accusations to feel guilty: he knew he'd been wrong not to insist that Georgia Lee meet with him as they'd promised. He didn't need Beryl to tell him he'd failed. Why did she, in the middle of his worst suffering, think that this was the best possible time to remind him of his shortcomings? Why did she tell him all this when he was least able to make a case for himself? Not every question had an answer.

Mark longed to hang up. His weak leg was aching as he dragged himself across the room and stretched out on his tan suede couch. He pulled a soft black silk cushion under his head and tucked the portable phone under his right ear as he thought how good a nap would be – as soon as Beryl stopped talking.

A look from Rona was enough. Rona and Mark, who used to be on the phone each morning, had spoken only once since the funeral. Frankly, he was afraid to call her. He would have to tell the truth about him and Georgia Lee – Rona always knew when he tried to lie. He wanted to say *I'm sorry* to her. "We all wish we had done things differently. My sorrow is silent like my love."

It made him weary to think of his sisters. Mark was always at the mercy of one or the other of those capable, superior women. He was determined to take his share of this bitterness. How can one know? – one cannot know – which day is to be the last.

The whole month of April had been a write-off. It had begun with the unseasonable blizzard that had marked Georgia Lee's disappearance, followed by the discovery of her body, by the sad evening of her strange funeral, by the ongoing police investigation, and by the nightmare of the media attention, plus the unwelcome public curiosity. He had the feeling that he'd been onstage the whole time and being blamed by everyone in town for not looking out for his niece, clobbered in the court of public opinion.

He should have done more for her. In his dreams, she called out. She was in trouble, and he couldn't get to her. She was on the other side of a sheet of thick glass.

He wished he could leave Winnipeg, but he didn't know where he could go. He made and discarded plans for trips. He was not in the mood for a holiday. He avoided the corner of Osborne and Roslyn Road on his way home, detoured down Broadway to Maryland and over the Assiniboine by the bridge near the synagogue. He doubled back along the Crescent and stopped to go into the *shul* and say the mourner's *Kaddish* for her. It wasn't much, but it was something. When is her *yartzheit*? They cannot be sure. He liked saying that prayer. It seemed a kind of blues for Jews, and the singing itself like a deliverance from sorrow. He often stood there for a further ten minutes or more, thinking about the family, about Georgie, awaiting some sort of message, to be dismissed, forgiven.

They had not celebrated Passover this year. Beryl and Zach and the twins had taken off for Vancouver the morning after the funeral, and Mark didn't blame them. There was no *shiva* and no *Seder*. Nothing. Not a bite of *matzo*. No celebration, not even in their usual non-conforming way. Other years, there were at least a dozen of their friends sitting around the long communal *Seder* table at Rona and Ben's house. The favoured guests who every year came to read the service aloud and eat their weight in traditional foods. In other years they rejoiced in their freedom, in other years Georgia Lee asked the Four Questions, in other years they talked and sang *zimmerot* until the late hours. This year, you could say it and really mean that this night was different from all the others. They had the flood, and they had the slaying of their first-born. Rona had said she had tasted enough bitterness to last the rest of her life. She would not taste *maror* this year.

Mark walked over to Nikolai Gadol's cage, which was set up beside the orchid-laden credenza under the south-facing window. He lifted the cover off and chirped at Nikolai a couple of times. He tapped on the door of the cage. The bird looked lethargic. He must be depressed, too.

"I know. I know. I don't feel like singing either, little bird."

Mark stepped out on his balcony and stood there in the fresh, cool air, looking over the banks of the Assiniboine River. It looked as if spring had arrived when he looked straight out over the trees. The old elms were leafing out full and green. Below, the river, swollen, dun-coloured and turbid with debris, continued to flow backward, pushed by the floodwaters of the mighty Red.

Chick Fontaine arrived on time for her second appointment with the homicide detectives. She was stopped by the desk sergeant at the front entrance to the cops's concrete fortress, but when she showed the business card that Detective Friesen had given her after her other interview, the cop who was on guard phoned upstairs. The same two cops appeared, Friesen and the dark-haired partner. Then she wasn't so afraid. They'd been okay to talk to before.

She followed them into the same bare interview room as the last time. The heavier, dark-haired one with the bushy moustache sat down behind the desk. He said he was Detective Dunblane and he thanked her for coming. "What's on your mind today, Sandra?" he asked.

She looked at him like *what's with the gay question?* She didn't forget for a minute that they were the ones who had called her to meet them. So why was he acting like she did the call? She'd never asked for a freakin' appointment. He didn't know her name was Chick now. She had given them her full name – Sandra Louise Fontaine – that other time 'cause like it was for legal reasons and all. And that was a major freakin' rule with her: don't lie to the cops.

She said she was wondering if they had found out anything about who killed Georgie. "Not sure yet," they said. "But we are all working on it."

"Did you think of anything else?" he asked. "Tell us everything you know or remember from the beginning, Sandra. All the details, even if it doesn't seem important. Don't worry about what you said last time. Begin again."

The other time they'd interrogated her, she had told them about going over to Georgie's apartment during the storm and how there was a light on and she thought she was there, but Georgie didn't come to the door. It was like when someone pretends to be asleep but you know they're faking it. She had been sure Georgie was in her apartment then. The cops didn't seem too interested, even though it was after the time they said she was already dead.

Chick was thinking hard, leaning forward with her thin, black-clad legs twisted up like pretzels. She picked at the frayed denim cuff of her right sleeve with severely chewed nails painted with silver glitter. She wanted to begin, but her stomach was all stirred up and she couldn't think right. And she thought, *If only I could go away to the far side of the earth.*

Dunblane asked, "Did you meet Georgie when she started working at the video store?" They already knew that Chick had been working there for over a year. They had come into the store and talked to Bruce, her boss, about her and Georgie.

Chick started at the beginning. "I had to train her on the system at work," she said, "and like the boss is really a maniac about it, but we had some laughs. We were always going back and forth for videos or coffee, so we became friends. After, we didn't always work the same shifts, but we'd cover for each other sometimes."

Chick told them again that Georgie had talked about wanting to go out and see the ruins of the old Trappist monastery. It was on the La Salle River south of the city in St. Norbert. They did Shakespeare plays there in the summertime, and Georgie had gone there with her parents to see *Hamlet* and she had said it was awesome. Beautiful. She also went with some kids she knew at the university that were doing some improv games. "It's something like acting, but you make up your own character and story." Georgie had told her that she thought they might do one of their plays out there. So she wanted to check it out. She wanted to be an actor. And she could've. She could've tried. She was really smart and pretty.

Chick told them, "She said she was supposed to maybe get a ride from a guy she met when he came in for coffee at the place she goes to in the Village opposite the video store. Or she'd take the bus. I went, like, 'Who is he?' And she shrugged, like, 'Never mind,' so I went, like, 'Take the bus.' I asked her to 'chill until Sunday, and I'll go with you.' I don't think she'd try to hitch out there, but maybe she did. Like, if the guy didn't show up or whatever. But I never found out if she did it. I mean if she went there. 'Cause, like, that was it. That was right before the blizzard, and I never saw Georgie again. I told you guys all this before. I thought you already searched out there. I can't think of anything else." Her blue eyes were bright with unshed tears.

Later that afternoon, after their interview with Chick, Jake Friesen and Rob Dunblane decided to once again make the drive out past the perimeter highway to the Trappist monastery. To see if there was anything to see, as Dunblane put it. "Sometimes at a crime scene, you get a feel for the killer," he insisted. "For the way it went down." They had searched the ruins during the first week of the investigation after they had read about the girl's plan to visit the site in her journal, but it was worth a second look. They had run down every lead and every avenue and so far had nothing, absolutely fucking nothing, to show for it. Twenty-four days of solid nothing. Everything was cold. Checked and rechecked.

At the entry to Rue des Trappistes, they were stopped at a roadblock manned by volunteers from the local Neighbourhood Watch group. The 42-hundred residents of Ste. Norbert had been evacuated. The detectives had to talk their way past a stout volunteer guard dressed in a hardhat and bright orange vest with an X in fluorescent yellow stitched on the front and back. Like a modern major general in the Gilbert and Sullivan mode, he instructed them that he would permit their entry but would make a report to his coordinator. They should be aware that, strictly speaking, they were city police and outside their jurisdiction. He could not guarantee their personal safety. The river was dangerously high, and flooding was expected at Grande Pointe late that same day. No unnecessary traffic was to be allowed. He wrote their names and particulars down on his clipboard before allowing them to proceed.

The grounds of the old monastery were quiet under the great blue dome of sky. The men left the car in the public parking lot and strolled around the manicured lawns. There was no one in sight as they walked around through the footprint of the beautiful ruined limestone building. The grounds had been rained on and heavily trampled in recent weeks by crews of volunteer flood fighters. The sniffer dogs had not found a trace during the earlier search. The detectives had learned nothing of interest on that visit.

They could see down the bank to the swollen La Salle River. A 4-foot dike of sandbags lined the riverbank. The monks's original residence, now converted to an arts centre was also encircled by a sandbag barrier.

They found the manager in his office. He sat in front of a computer screen and stared at a busy-looking flow sheet. He held up a finger to signal one minute to them, and they halted in the doorway. He tapped away at the keys, a frown of concentration furrowing his heavy brows.

He took a sip from a mug of tea and stood up abruptly and corrected his posture as if unexpectedly called to attention. He was thin and pale, and his egg-shaped head seemed precariously balanced between his narrow sloped shoulders. He was 6 and a half feet tall, but the length was all in his torso, and with his thin, short arms and legs, he looked like a child's drawing. Or Charles De Gaulle without that nose.

"I'm sorry," the manager said, gesturing toward his computer screen. "This flood has played havoc with our spring season here at the arts centre." He stuck out a hand in greeting. "Andre Ricard. May I assist you gentlemen in some way?"

While Dunblane explained their errand, Jake surveyed the many posters for arts events that decorated the white-walled office. Maud had attended many of them, and he'd gone with her once or twice. He did not like going to the theatre. Somehow he always felt restless and edgy. Impatient with the actors. He wanted to stop the action, inter-rogate them, and get at the truth behind their words.

"I wish I could help you. Very sad." Ricard shook his head. "*Murder* – such a dark word. I read about the girl in the paper. The violence in the world makes me sad and weary. It must be terribly difficult for her family, her parents." He paused. "Grief fills the room of my absent child, Lies in his bed, walks up and down with me."

The detectives looked steadily at him, listening for more.

"That's from Shakespeare's *King John*. We are not doing it this year, but it came to mind. I have been following the girl's story in the news. Here's the other thing I've been thinking about: *aqua et igni interdictus*."

The phrase hung in the air like a pronouncement from an Old Testament prophet.

"And that means?" prompted Jake.

"Perhaps the old ways are best. It's the early Roman proscription for the criminal. They were physically removed from the community, and it was forbidden to furnish them with water and fire. Outlawed. You may think my attitude obdurate, but I'd like to see that happen to the criminals of today. I believe we have erred on the side of mercy. It is getting harder than ever to believe in a Providence that oversees all when you're moving downstream on this century's dark river."

"Right," said Jake. He was eager to leave now. It was a wasted afternoon. Empty theatrics. There was no way of knowing if the dead girl had even come out here. The spaced-out looking punk girl thought so, but she could be wrong. No one at the coffee shop remembered seeing the dead girl there with any guy.

"Forgive my editorialising and the unfortunate water imagery. I guess I am somewhat carried away by the current local conditions."

"No problem. First, we have to find the responsible party," agreed Dunblane. "Then we'll put him out of the community. Or at least away from our women for a while."

Dunblane was silent as they drove down the long, dusty road out of the monastery's grounds.

"One blind alley after another," Jake said. "No one from the video store or at the coffee shop remembers anything helpful. No one from the railway police or the Forks Market staff saw anything out of the ordinary. The girl disappeared around the time of that last blizzard. That was twenty-nine days ago. All the snow has melted, and there's been a shitload of traffic and skiers and snowmobilers through the Ruins and La Barriere Park with the dike building and all the volunteers. We're getting nowhere fast, and I'm getting pissed off at the media. They give every loudmouth Native a soapbox to make accusations that we're racist, we don't care about their people. That we aren't trying to solve the case. Well, I say they have to start caring about themselves. That uncle, the lawyer, calls every other day for the family, and even Maud is on my case about it. That girl had every chance to make something of herself, and she blew it."

"Why are you taking such a harsh stance on this?" asked Dunblane. "She was on her own, a young girl of 18, not sure about herself, knocking on all the doors she saw, trying to find her way in. She was dreaming of a world where categories and blood don't matter. That's how kids think." He rolled down his window and waved to the guard at the roadblock. "There's a lot of moving parts to this story. We'll have to keep on working it." He turned the car north and headed back up the Pembina Highway into the city.

Winnipeg

Paul woke early again. It was only 4:24 a.m. He shivered, cold under the covers. He wanted to shake it off. Shake off that fucking dream: For the fifth night in a row, he was in a hallway, like right outside the door here, but it was really dark. Was he trying to get his keys out? He couldn't remember, but he could feel the men, the two big Indian guys from the mall, coming toward him in the darkened hallway. He felt them closing in, inches away, all hard muscle and anger in the darkness. He didn't hear their footsteps, but that was right, wasn't it? Indians walked that way in the forest, so quiet you never heard them coming. He was trying to get his keys out, they were on either side of him, and he felt their breath on both of his cheeks. They didn't speak. They were pulling the warmth out of him, and he was cold, very cold, he was turning to stone.

He'd woken up sweating like a pig, with his dick and nuts shrivelled up to nothing. He laughed silently when he thought of that. No fucking wonder.

He checked the time again on the clock radio the preacher had lent him. 4:27 a.m. There was some faint light coming in through the brown striped curtains. His crib was on the backside of the building with the lane running behind. He liked that. There was an exit door leading to the fire escape from the end of the hallway. That felt okay. Mostly he did like it there 'cause he had the place all to himself. He kept it clean. Never had to come and smell the stink of some other guy. No way he'd ever do time again. *I'm never gonna bend over for nobody again. No cop'll get the cuffs on me,* he promised himself. *No fuckin' way.* He'd rather be dead.

Fucking early. Four fuckin' thirty. He hated this, waking up early when he had nothing to do but think. He reached for the girl's belly ring, which he'd hidden under the clock radio. He put it in his mouth and sucked on it – put his tongue through it, feeling the rough edges of the pink stone. He felt good for a while. Like right after he did that little bitch. He was really relaxed. But it wore off like everything does. Every time.

He'd started thieving when he was a kid. Maybe 5 or 6. At first, he'd taken things and hidden them. Like if he was mad at one of his foster moms, he took something in her house and hid it. He had liked the way they walked around all freaked out, looking for it. Even something dumb like her lipstick or her watch. Later, he'd taken things and thrown them in the garbage. He had taken things from every house they had put him in but Charlie Hardwick's. He hadn't wanted to piss Charlie off when he was alive. By then, he had been working lots of jobs. He liked to get into people's cribs when they weren't home. Looking through cupboards and drawers for secrets. Grabbing up pieces of their lives and selling them. That's how he'd started off.

Birds were starting to call, and he could hear the pigeons cooing and the rustle of lots of wings. Some stupid bird got in between where the old window in the room used to be and the new wall. It was bricked over because of renovations or fire regulations or some other dickhead thing. The bird was trapped now. Like he was. He'd told that guy, Kroeker, about the bird, but he said he couldn't do nothing. Kroeker had thought it was dead, 'cause he didn't hear it yesterday. Stupid thing made Paul's skin crawl. He turned on the radio to drown it out. All that was on the radio was news about the flood. Talk, talk, talk about the fucking river.

"The crest is expected to reach Winnipeg by May 6th," the announcer said. "That's today. The Red River now spans an incredible 18 miles instead of its normal width of 200 yards. Overnight, 60-kilometre-an-hour winds whipped the Red 'sea' into a fury of 4-foot waves. Twenty-five percent of the dikes have already failed. All of Ste. Agathe was drowned, and half of the homes at Grande Point are under water. At Brunkild, the dike workers are at it all night long under the glare of 2 million candlepower flares dropped by the Air Force. Rumour has it that those guys don't get bathroom breaks. They pee into a plastic pop bottle and keep on truckin'. Gotta make up for the time lost during those rainy days last week. That's something, isn't it? I like the way they are using all those broken-down buses and cars as the foundation for the dam. And work has started on an L-shaped dike to save St. Norbert. So if you can get out there and lend a hand, folks, I know it will be deeply appreciated. Remember, to help is human, to sandbag, divine. That's the city's new motto. It's a good one, because the stores are all sold out of backup plumbing valves. Flood forecasters predict that the concourse at Portage and Main will be spared. My bookie isn't giving odds, folks," the announcer added. "All bets are off when Ma Nature is on the rampage. And if you're fed up with flood news, remember the Stanley Cup playoffs begin tonight. I am going to go public now, folks. This is it. I like Detroit and I believe they are going all the way this time. And the way things are going in this long, drawn out post season, my friends, looks like we'll be watching the finals in our shorts with the barbecue on."

Paul didn't care about the hockey. Didn't know who was playing. He couldn't figure out why he'd started dreaming all of a sudden. He never had dreams. The psychologist at prison had said that he must have, everybody does, that you go crazy without them. What a shithead he was. He had it backasswards. It was the dreams that made you feel crazy, low down crazy. Paul had no memories, neither. No good ones. Talking about them, he didn't go for that, didn't bother with it the way some of the guys on the range did – taking them out and polishing them up, smoothing out the rough edges.

He did keep thinking about how he'd hucked the plates off that old Dodge into the ditch near the truck stop. What if someone found them? If they did, they'd be coming for him soon enough. He couldn't get it out of his head. It wasn't supposed to go like this: he was as good as in prison, as good as in prison for life. And like he had to share his cell with that girl's ghost. That was freaking him out. He couldn't stop thinking about her frightened face.

His stupid life of mistakes was shit, and that sunny life he was supposed to have in old Mexico was lost. He was never going to get one of those little rat dogs. A Chihuahua he'd wanted to call Mickey. All he had for a pet was the girl's little stuffed monkey. That was a stupid thing to take.

Now it didn't matter what happened. Nobody was gonna visit his grave. It was like he was choking, like he was the city that couldn't escape the rising water.

Other than the obvious deep furrow on the neck caused by the ligature, there wasn't a mark on the body. The young man had on a pair of worn blue jeans belted with a brown leather belt. A silver hoop earring with a pink stone dangled from the belt buckle. He was shirtless, and his head and face were completely shaved except for a fingertip-sized triangle of beard on his chin. His face and swollen bare feet were the ruddy blue of ripe Lombardy plums. His noose had been fashioned from a widely available brand of hard, bright yellow acrylic rope.

He was suspended from the pneumatic hinge on the inside of the door to his bachelor suite. It was clear that he had stepped backwards off the grey metal folding chair that now stood about 2 feet inside the room. The back of the chair faced the centre of the room, and a metal toolbox was on the seat.

The room was in perfect order. A single badly scarred maple bedstead was made up with a faded blue-and-green-striped spread. A small chrome-legged table with a dark-red arborite top stood under the bricked-up window. Next to it was a roughly made plywood counter painted park-bench green with a single pink porcelain sink and a hot plate. The countertop and sink were wiped clean. The cream-coloured walls were bare of decoration except for a coloured picture of Jesus (with his heart on fire) surrounded by little children and framed in silver-coloured metal. It was a room without a single aspect that could be described as cosy. No comfort available under the irritating buzz of the greenish fluorescent light.

Constable Tim Petrie was setting up his kit on the floor near the makeshift kitchen in the alcove when Jake Friesen arrived on the scene.

"Meet Julian Russell." Petrie nodded in the direction of the deceased.

Jake walked up close to the body and looked at the face. The tongue protruded slightly and looked dark and dry. There were small linear abrasions on the neck around the rope that signified the deceased had had a momentary change of heart. His shoulders and hips were rotated inwards, giving him a pathetic and weak, slightly pigeon-toed appearance. Jake turned away from the body, disgusted and annoyed.

"There was no note," said Petrie.

Jake was glad. He didn't like reading those last words: blaming, angry, or begging, beseeching. I love you. I hate you.

"He doesn't look so bad, Jake," Petrie continued. "You should have been with me last week. Went to see a poor bastard who got smucked between two sets of boxcars down at the old CPR yard. That was gross. Stuff that's supposed to be on the inside of the body was on the outside. I tell ya, I could never have been a doctor."

Petrie crouched on the bare wooden floor with his long legs creased up around his ears. He bent over the aluminium suitcase that held his kit and changed lenses on his camera and kept on talking. "Did you meet the minister on the way in? He says the guy's been living here about a month. And that the guy's story is that he's a construction worker who got into trouble on the Downtown Eastside in Vancouver and he was a druggie and booze hound and he came here to get away from that scene. The pastor says he is reported as clean and sober now. Says the guy has been taking Double A meetings almost every evening and helping sandbagging crews in the daytime.

"Guy is a drifter. Works construction, whatever he can find in day labour. Not afraid of work, apparently. The minister . . ." He paused and called to the uniform standing guard at the door. "Hey, Maddin, what's the name of that minister?"

Petrie knew he was much better on faces than names. He had given the padre a good look. He was short, maybe 5 foot 6 on a good day, and casually dressed for a man of the cloth, in an old brown corduroy jacket over a blue work shirt and jeans. No tie. A thin face with a full beard and longish brown hair. Looked like he was trying too hard with the Jesus-clone thing. The guy was actually crying over this doofus kid and calling him a Prodigal Son.

"Martin Kroeker," answered Maddin. He was chewing the last mouthful of his takeout hamburger and nearly choked on it in his attempt to stuff it into his cheeks and answer quickly.

"Right," said Petrie. "Pastor Martin Kroeker. Now go ahead, son, finish your fries."

"I guess it's true," said Jake. "A hungry cop will eat anything. Anywhere. Anytime. Can't you give this rookie a lunch break, Petrie?" asked Jake. He wanted a break too. ASAP. This scene was so sad, he could hardly wait for it to be over so he could go for a drink.

"Could. But we're in a hurry. No time for frills. He said takeout from Junior's Burger Pit was good enough. Listen, you know it'll be payday in fifteen minutes. And my vacation starts tonight." He smiled with a lopsided full-toothed grin. "I am going to be golfing in Arizona for two sunny weeks. Primo, man. That's primo. First things first."

Petrie set up his whiteboard on which he had written the name of the deceased, date, and police incident number. He was ready to take the first shot on his fresh roll of film. "Anyhow," he continued, "the word is that the guy has no family or anybody locally. His wallet's over there on the bureau. The only thing that's weird is Pastor Kroeker says the guy shaved off all his head hair. Pastor said up until yesterday, he had a full head of hair and now all's left is one of those tiny beardlike thingies – you know. Soul patch, I think they call it." He took his opening shot of the signboard and continued to snap the body from all angles.

Jake pulled on a pair of latex gloves and picked up the wallet. It was worn brown leather with a zipper closing. There was a birth certificate in it for a Julian Russell, registered in British Columbia. Born September 17, 1970. Also a Social Insurance card. There were twenty-three dollars in bills and another eight in coins. No photos, no driver's licence, no credit cards. No photo ID. Jake walked over to the closet and pawed through the contents. There was a thin well-worn black leather jacket and a Calgary Flames ball cap on one hanger, a pair of new-looking black motorcycle boots, another pair of jeans, and two old shirts, one made in a faded red plaid and the other out of denim.

Jake heaved the toolbox off the folding chair. It seemed the guy had used it to weigh down the chair when he'd stepped off and stretched out his noose. Jake opened the toolbox. A steel claw hammer lay on the top tray. Underneath, Jake found a selection of old tools: wood-handled screwdrivers, a crescent wrench, a brace and bit, rasps, files, a square blade awl, various pliers, and odd washers, ring nuts, bolts, screws, and nails. There was a sliver of dried-out greyish bar soap and a few torn bits of old, white flannel sheeting. It made for a depressing inventory that equalled the sum of another poor jerk's worldly goods.

"What'd ya think, Jake?" asked Petrie.

"Not much to say," he answered. "Looks like a routine case." He wondered what drove a guy to it, in this clean, bare room, the few broken-down possessions left behind from a broken-down life. He hated these calls, where his only job at the scene was to rule out foul play. There was nothing out of the ordinary here. Nothing to distinguish this hanging from dozens of others he'd seen except for the fact that the guy, for his own wacko reason, had shaved his head and beard and then left a very small triangle of beard unshaven. It was directly below his mouth. Jake had seen this style on other dudes. Thought it looked like he was trying too hard. A soul patch. The guy had plenty of attitude. Didn't do him any good.

"Funny, isn't it," said Petrie, "that we call these guys swingers? And look how he decided to take his little pal along with him into the great whatever." He pointed to the stuffed brown-velvet monkey that was dangling immediately above and to the left of the deceased's head. The monkey was suspended from a separate short piece of the same yellow rope. His stitched-on red-yarn grin was firmly in place.

Petrie moved in for a close-up of the monkey and his miniature noose. "As far as we know, the guy wasn't Italian, not an organ grinder. I'm sure that hanging this little guy up beside him has deep psychological significance, but what the hell it could be . . . we'll never know what this guy was thinking. I guess he must have felt lonely. Didn't wanna die alone.

"The other peculiar thing is this here." He used the end of his ballpoint pen to lift up a dime-sized silver hoop set with a piece of rose quartz that was fastened to the guy's belt buckle. "Guy doesn't appear to have a single piercing on his body. Well, not on any of the obvious parts, anyway."

Jake shrugged his shoulders, and Petrie mirrored him.

"There's no telling with guys these days," said Petrie. "I'm not checking any further. I figure you gotta leave some surprises for the autopsy crew or the undertaker."

"Was the suite secure when he was found?" asked Jake.

"Yup. Pastor found him. He opened the door with the master key. Guy hadn't been seen all day and missed an appointment with Kroeker. An appointment he had requested for spiritual counselling. Figure he must have done it early morning. There's the obvious lividity in the feet, and he's still got about two plus rigor. I'd guess it'd be coming on to twelve hours anyway."

Jake shook his head and pulled off his gloves, balling them up and tossing them into the brown paper waste bag Petrie had set up beside his camera case. Jake looked around again at the bare walls. There was no attempt at decoration, and the bleak atmosphere of the humble room and the few personal belongings were unremarkable. It seemed the guy had little to offer the world, too little to be missed. This was all he had to show for his 26 years on the planet. Another mean and squalid life fully revealed. His reasons for doing it were not recorded and could only be guessed at. What one person can bear, another can't.

"I can tell that I'm not needed here," Jake said.

"It's a routine call-out. Just going by the book," said Petrie. "I wonder why he did it today. The river's going to crest by this evening, and then everything will settle down. He might've gotten over whatever was bothering him. No way of telling what's going on in a guy's mind, is there?"

"Medical Examiner's office been called?" asked Jake.

"Yeah, but they're too busy to attend. Strategy session for handling cases during the flood, they said. The St. Boniface Hospital is being evacuated, and they're all busy planning with the emergency services crew. The Chief told me to send the case in for a post under his name."

"Seems unnecessary. The cause of death is pretty obvious. But I know, all suicides should be autopsied."

"Irregardless, that's the Medical Examiner's policy. The old cover-your-ass protocol. And it gives a chance for young rookies like Constable Maddin to see his first autopsy. As you know, it's all part of the training." He grinned. "I can tell you I don't know when I've seen a guy so eager."

"You can cut him down now." Jake brushed his hands lightly down the lapels of his camel hair overcoat as if ridding himself of some invisible contaminant. He nodded at the rookie. "Be careful of the noose. Leave at least a foot of the rope above the knot so the doctor can see the intact knot."

"Go on," answered Petrie. "You know we always do it that way. Don't look so glum, Jake. Maddin here, he'll tell you his new joke. He's thinking he might go in for stand-up comedy if being on the Job doesn't work out."

Maddin looked a little unsure but began anyway. "This story is about a miracle. A Mennonite boy and his father are visiting a mall. They are amazed by everything they see, especially two shiny, silver walls that could move apart and then slide back together again. The boy asks, 'What is this, father?' The father, who has never seen an elevator, says he does not know. While the boy and his father watch in amazement, a fat old woman in a wheelchair rolls up to the moving walls and pushes a button. The walls open and the lady rolls between them into a miniature room. The front walls close, and the boy and his father watch as each of the numbers above the walls lights up, one right after another. They continue to watch as the light reaches the last number and begins to move back through the numbers in reverse order. Finally, the walls open up again and a gorgeous, sexy young woman steps out. The father, not taking his eyes from the young woman, says quietly to his son, 'Go get your mother.'"

Jake gave a weak chuckle and signed thumbs-up to the rookie. He didn't like the humour, but it was a necessary indulgence, like tipping your barber or the towel girl at the health club. It was money in the bank.

"'Go get your mother,'" repeated Petrie, "I like that."

"Are you going to print him?" asked Jake.

"I ran the name, and he's not in the system. Never been. Nothing on CPIC. His name is clean." Petrie shrugged. "Seems like he was a full-time nobody. Got no prints for comparison. He's not military. Got no scars or tattoos. No dental records local. But don't you worry. I've taken his prints for the record, and we'll have a toxicology screen and a DNA sample after the autopsy. You know right well that we'll be lucky to have those results by Christmas, given the backups at the lab. That should be good enough for posterity. And if it looks like I'm in a hurry today, I told you, I am. I'm nearly on vacation.

"By the way, speaking of results on outstanding cases, none of the prints from the Kay-Stern girl's apartment or her body matches to that Waylon Spence dude. So he's no longer a person of interest. I mean, like I said, he never was a real contender. It was just to be sure that we checked out the family's story about him being out of town when it happened."

"Okay," said Jake. "And notification to this one's family?"

"The pastor says they don't believe he had any. Illegitimate, fostered out, never adopted. They are going to do some checking back in BC. The New Path ministry is willing to bury him. They'll even buy him a new suit of clothes."

"Good enough for me," said Jake.

"I'd say so, too. It's good enough for the girls we go with," answered Petrie. "It's a lot more care than some get."

Jake was relieved that the pastor would look for and tell the family if there was anyone. It was always difficult to deliver news of a suicide. He had known family members who refused to accept the truth. They wailed and cried and argued that it was not possible, that their loved one had so much to live for, that some mistake had been made, that they had spoken to the deceased that very morning and made plans together. All he knew was that there was no way of telling what a suicide was thinking in those last days, hours, and minutes.

Winnipeg   May 14, 1997

"Operation Noah = A Success!" That news was splashed all over the front pages of the morning papers. The troops were leaving, and a gala send-off was organized. Everyone from the Premier on down was thanking the 8,500 members of the armed forces who had saved Winnipeg from the rampaging Red. Crowds of celebrating citizens, four to five people deep, lined the parade route along Portage Avenue and up Main Street to the review stand in front of City Hall.

Mark Kay couldn't see the parade route from his tenth-floor office windows, but he was close enough to the action to hear the cacophony of brass band and honking horns. He wondered if he was the only one who was full up with the flood story. He leafed through the front section to see if there was any other news worth reading. On page two, in the Crime Stoppers column, there was a reprint of the photo of the old Dodge car that three 14-year-old boys had discovered out near Richer at the end of April. They'd been riding their dirt bikes, exploring the system of roads running through the wide highway median. They had managed to hotwire the car and get it running and cruised around until they'd ploughed into a tree. The young, unlicensed driver, who had not been wearing a seat belt, had suffered a broken leg. The others had escaped with minor injuries. None of them could be named, as their identities were protected under the Young Offenders

Act. A forensic examination of the vehicle was ongoing at the RCMP laboratory. Persons with information were asked to call the hotline.

The car, a vintage model two-tone blue Dodge Polara, had no plates, but it had been traced to an elderly widow in British Columbia. She was quoted as saying it had been taken early in April. At the time, she said, she had suspected her former foster son, Paul Boudreau. She claimed that she hadn't reported the theft because she was very frightened of Boudreau, whom she described as "pure trouble." He was an evil man. He had been in jail for thieving many times before this, she was quoted as saying. She was pleased to know the car had been found since it belonged to her beloved late husband, who'd passed away right before the car went missing.

With the article was a photo of Paul Boudreau that appeared to have been taken by the police or in a jail. His face displayed the raw anger of someone who believed he had been cheated. Sources at the local RCMP station in Richer indicated that it was known he was wanted on a parole violation in British Columbia.

Mark quickly turned the page. He was sick of reading about wild teenagers who were getting away with it. Good thing he'd never had children. *Kleyne kinder – kopveytik, grosyse kinder – hartsveytik.* Little children bring headaches, big children bring heartaches. His direct phone line rang, interrupting his train of thought. It was Beryl. She was so concerned about Rona that she had gotten up at 6:00 a.m. Vancouver time to call Mark at the office.

"Rona says she doesn't want to be alive. Doesn't see the point anymore. I am worried about her."

Mark fought a crazy impulse to set the receiver down and bang his head against his mahogany desk. He was tired of hearing about Rona's moods.

"Guess what else?" Beryl continued. "She said, 'I want to feel something, even if it's pain.' That's what she said to me last night. Can you believe it? Talk to Ben, will you? I wonder if he can get her to go for counselling. I couldn't get anywhere with her. Mother's Day wasn't mentioned. She didn't say anything, so I didn't say anything. I think we were right that it was better not to acknowledge it this year."

"I don't believe she'd do anything to harm herself," answered Mark. Some days he thought Rona was taking a pleasure that seemed almost perverse in mourning Georgia Lee. She refused to speak to him, so since the funeral, they had only talked through Ben or Beryl. That was bothering him. He'd lost 12 pounds, and his fridge was stuffed with half-eaten cartons of takeout food. None of it tasted good to him. He'd told his cleaner to throw everything out every Friday.

Yeah, yeah. Rona again. Well, she was always a little on the edge. A passionate nature, that's what she had.

"Beryl," he said, "I'll talk to Ben. Remember we all contributed to this situation when we agreed that the McKay family would bury Georgia Lee at Footprint Lake. Rona was a zombie. Ben and I talked her into that plan. Well, it was Ben, but I agreed with him and so did Zach. You said you did, too. There was a risk of a blow-up from her later, and she's having it now. She needs to do her grieving. We chose not to sit *shiva* and that left her, left us, with no order to our days. All of us have to find our own way through this time. Let her be. You know our sister," he said. "You know what she's like. She's a highly emotional person."

Beryl did not respond to this. Both of them knew that Rona would forgive Mark. It was a simple problem of time. He must wait, frozen out, until the moment arrived – when Rona decided he'd suffered enough.

Beryl talked on and on about Ben and Rona as parents. How, she contended, they had been inclined to indulge and neglect their only child. "So, in a way, and I know this sounds harsh, I am relieved that this chapter is finished. Relieved," she repeated. "They had such a hard time trying to be a family."

She continued to *kvetch* about how everyone spoiled Rona after their mother died, especially their father. He'd always said how much she looked like their mother, so Rona got away with everything. When she was 5, she had cut off the long, golden hair on Beryl's favourite doll, but it was Beryl who had been scolded for leaving her school scissors out on the dresser in their bedroom. "I felt sorry for Poppa," she said. "He tried so hard for us, tried to build us a good life."

Mark let her talk. No point telling her what he thought, that the story of Pa's life was the story of a man who had built up a business to give to a son who didn't want it. Nor did Beryl or Rona, so they had agreed to sell the deli right after the *shiva* for him was over, and soon it was a done deal, and Beryl left with Zach and made it abundantly clear that she wouldn't return to Winnipeg unless it was for a wedding or a funeral. She was liberating herself, was Liberation itself, and they should move on, too.

He and Rona had pooled their money and bought a solid brick up-and-down duplex on Dorchester near Lilac in the south end, where they set up their separate lives layered one top of the other. He had finished his first year at university and was already thinking about a career in Law, and Rona was, well, being Rona. She was doing a little of this, a little of that. She had taken a few courses in fine arts and design but hadn't settled into anything. Then she and Ruthie Hirsch had started a catering business, strictly for small affairs, in private homes or businesses. They had made a specialty of parties and events with themes, and they were (who would have believed it?) ultimately very successful. She had met Ben at a fundraising dinner that they had catered for the *Shalom Achshavniks,* and from that moment on those two had eyes only for each other.

Mark did not believe that Georgie's story would ever be over for any of them. He kept reading the newspaper, quietly turning the pages over on the bare surface of his desk while Beryl talked. He saw a report that a city works crew investigating a water main break in the North End at Redwood and Charles Streets had found the remains of three individuals, two adults and a child, which appeared to comprise a family of aboriginal origin. They had been buried along with some tools, crockery, and fragments of animal skin clothing. Commuters were advised to use an alternative route, as a team from the university's Anthropology department and Native elders would be on the scene for the next two days.

There it was. In that brief article was the proof of his argument. Every time he read the paper, there would be a reference to Native people or something else that would remind him of Georgia Lee. He'd never be finished with it. His head felt heavy, as if filled with wet mud or turned to stone. He could hear her voice like a faint rumour from a lost world.

Winnipeg   May 24, 1997

Life in the city returned to normal quickly. To its usual pace and patterns. The crest of the river and that danger were past. There were dozens of calls to the hotline at CJOB Radio for the annual biggest pothole contest. City Hall gave homeowners permission to put their unneeded sandbags out at the curb. And, boy oh boy, they disappeared fast, didn't they! Winnipeggers did love a bargain.

Delia Fallon had the broadloom on the first floor of her house shampooed and then arranged to have her furniture and appliances brought back from storage. On reflection, she decided it was not necessary to return the boxes of books and papers to the cellar. Liam's old bedroom would be converted into a library, and she happily went around town collecting fabric and paint samples in woodsy masculine tones that she knew her late husband would have approved. This all seemed right to her, as did her feeling that now it was time to go home to Dublin. "Let grief be a fallen leaf /At the dawning of the day." The old poet Patrick Kavanagh's words sounded in her ears as first they had in – what was it? 1946 or 7? Surely no later. Yes. She knew she'd like to take a look at Merrion Square again. Stroll along Grafton Street and angle over to meet old friends for a glass downstairs at McDaid's.

Maud might be persuaded to go along. She'd not been to Ireland since she was 16 or so. Would do her the world of good, it would, to get away from the job and that man of hers for a while.

Jake took some time off. He didn't go on the vacation everyone suggested he take. He retreated to his condo, wanting nothing more than a few quiet days. He lived alone on Armstrong Point, almost in the West End, fewer than a dozen city blocks from the Kay-Sterns's home on Canora. His condo was on the top two floors of an enormous old cream-coloured brick house with a mansard roof of slate that had been renovated into four suites during the boom times of the mid-1980s. He had a living room, eat-in kitchen, spacious bedroom, and bath, plus an upstairs loft that was the attic of the old house. It had been converted into a 20- by 20-foot square room with large new windows that looked out over the back garden and the Assiniboine River. He'd bought the place because of this room, which he had furnished as his study.

He'd installed track lighting and set up a reading room within it, bounded by the old gold-toned Turkish carpet he'd bought at auction. He had his easy chair with a good light and an old farmhouse-kitchen flop couch covered in black leather that he often dozed on. He had installed banks of drawers to hold his growing collection of maps and charts. This was the room he withdrew to and from which he went on expeditions, journeys of exploration. Models of ships, of the solar system, artefacts numerous and diverse, and a library of books and journals and chronicles of the great explorers covered other shelves and tables. All the adventure he needed was here in his wide range of maps and charts, from the planets and stars to polar wasteland. He travelled with Cook, with Lewis and Clark, with Shackleton. He enjoyed their successes and sympathized with their failed attempts. A map was a fine thing to study when you were disinclined to think of other things. It was covered with names that chimed and enchanted, rolled on the tongue, hinting of exotic adventures. His miniature empire was off-limits to all save himself.

There was a framed print of Thaddeus Fowler's bird's-eye map of Winnipeg, dated 1880, hanging on the wall above his couch. Back then the city had been incorporated for only seven years, and its population was about ten thousand souls. On this map, Jake could see the confluence of the Red and the Assiniboine and upper Fort Gary nearby. He preferred this map to others he had that were dated in the 1870s. Here Fowler depicted the sinuous course of the rivers more elegantly than on his earlier maps, and Lot 82, the prominent point of land originally owned by Moses F. E. Cornish, where Jake's neighbourhood and this house had been built a further twenty years afterward, was on the horizon. This map showed the struggling city prior to the land boom of 1881, which had followed the news that the national railway would cross the Red River at Winnipeg. A time when the city's horizons had appeared limitless.

He thought about calling Maud but stopped himself. He knew she was going to break up with him soon. He didn't want it to happen tonight. He wanted to go to her. He wanted to take her without speaking. He wished he had the ability to forget how sweetly he was eased by her touch.

The case of the frozen girl troubled him still. He had worked flat out for seventy-two hours. Interviewing, checking, and scouring hard. Nothing. Then a week passed. The funeral. Still nothing. Another week passed and he knew, knew with absolute certainty that he couldn't, he wouldn't break the case. It had gone stone cold. He found himself whistling *Georgia*, the old Ray Charles version. The facts of the case were carefully filed in his memory, but disorder ruled his dreams. It overtook him, deep and swift as a winter twilight advancing with such weight it might not lift.

Although it was a few minutes past 9:00 p.m., there was still a faint band of dulled golden peach light showing at the horizon when Maud dropped over. Jake had stepped out of the shower only a minute earlier and only by chance had heard the doorbell.

She said she wanted to take a drive out to City Park to see the 24th of May, the Queen's birthday fireworks. She was wearing a red scoop-necked t-shirt tucked into a narrow, blue denim skirt that stopped short of her knees. She'd knotted the sleeves of her navy cardigan around her neck like a scarf and tied her dark hair back with a red-and-white farmer's hankie. He could see the faint beat of her pulse thrumming at her temple. And he thought, *fresh and pretty as always. She's the kind of woman who wants to get married and have a family. She should.* She deserved that chance. A chance he did not want to take. He dreaded the normal chaos family life brought. There would be toys underfoot and no room for him to think. Yeah, toys everywhere, like that spooky little grinning monkey he had seen at the last hanging he'd attended. What the fuck did the guy mean by doing that?

"Come on out with me," Maud coaxed. Tried for a laugh. "I know you do enjoy a brood, but do you think you'll need ten days' worth? I'll treat you to an ice cream sundae afterward. The Bridge Drive-In opened today. How can you turn that down?" She had a low voice, soft as a touch that asked, that whispered.

"No," Jake said with a smile. "But thanks. It's a tempting offer, but I'm in for the night." He ranked the pleasure of denial over all others. He softened enough to offer to make her a cappuccino. While he prepared the coffee, Maud used the bathroom. When she noticed the prints of his bare wet feet on the dark brown bathroom mat, she sighed. That plaintive, almost inaudible sound escaped into the damp air. She slipped off her right sandal and stepped into his footprint. Her foot was two-thirds his size. Not as wide. She knelt down and traced the damp outline of his right foot. She knew that for sanity's sake, she needed to find a new job and a new love. She was weary of arguing with her desires. Jake wanted to be done. Not tonight. She would pack his things up over the weekend. It's not as if they had any plans.

"There's a goddam bug in here." Maud swatted at the air ineffectually with her spoon. "It must be the first mosquito of the season. The little monster's buzzing in my ear." They sat on opposite sides of a round glass-topped table in an alcove beside the fridge.

"What do you want me to do?" asked Jake. "Should I get out my gun?"

She didn't return his smile. He reached over and opened the small mullioned window in the wall of the alcove, letting in the fresh, sweet air. "There, now he's got an escape route. Satisfied?"

They sipped their coffee, and though they didn't speak of it, both knew that they had come to a flat place in their life together where they had lost that urgent interest in each other's views and delights, and they'd begun to realize that they didn't have enough in the way of love or even fond affection to carry them forward.

He wished he had known her father; that might have told him something about the kind of man she might love.

"Are you still thinking about that sweet little Georgia Lee?" Maud asked. "Such a sad story." She was pleased he wasn't drinking too much. It was a relief that he was brooding and working on his map collection.

"She was not. Not completely sweet or innocent. The lab found Rohypnol in her system. You gotta admit that at some point she stepped over the bright red stupid line."

"He must have given it to her. You know, she was very young for an 18-year-old." Maud reached out and pushed the sugar bowl across the table. "She died because a man got angry." She watched as Jake lifted the lid as if to check the contents, then pushed the bowl back to the exact centre of the table. She looked away.

That elusive line – *You can sing of a king's death, not a child's* – continued to haunt her. It was not one of W.B.'s, was it? Daddy would be disappointed to know she'd forgotten her Yeats. The girl under the ice was no longer a child. It was her innocence and inexperience that had made Maud think of her as one. Like many before her, the girl had made a mistake in judging a man's intentions. How was she to know that it would mean the end of her wild and precious life? Maud wanted to talk about it, but she knew Jake did not want to get caught up in a discussion of male violence again. There was no point in hashing over their old arguments.

"You are thinking about her. Admit it," Maud said. "Are you ever going off-duty?"

Jake didn't answer her. He was thinking about all the pages of notes they'd made on the case, the interviews that led nowhere, the boot print in the snow, the bite marks. All the exhibits they had collected that grew dustier with each passing day in the evidence locker. Loose ends, no matter how short, how tangled, whatever the case, bothered him. Even routine matters like the running of prints taken at that last suicide. It wasn't likely that the suicidal drifter's prints were in the system, but the check needed to be done. He'd get on Petrie at the Ident unit on Monday. He must be back from his vacation by now. Off duty. What a concept.

Jake had to acknowledge the truth: that they were no closer to solving this case than on day one. He hated the idea that the man responsible was walking free somewhere while the answers Jake needed were lost in the grey secrecy of intervening time.

"Hey, don't mistake me for someone who cares," he said after a while. His words belied his teasing tone. The sight of the girl encased in the ice-rimmed blue tarpaulin remained frozen in his mind. He did care, perhaps not so much about her young life (it was too late for that now) but for her two families.

"That's something I would never do," said Maud. "Cut open an old detective, and what do you find? Crumpled leads, discarded theories, rusty shell casings, stray fingerprints?" Maud felt as if she were running out of breath, rushing to get those thoughts out into the cool air between them. Her eyes were welling up. *Perhaps you'll find the list of those who love you,* she thought while waiting for his reaction to her question. She didn't say it aloud; it wasn't light-hearted, and she was determined to smile and keep it light. He didn't like to see tears.

That's it, she thought. *That's what I can't take any longer: his calm indifference.* When she tried to talk to him about things important to her – poetry or why she didn't read any these days – he'd give her a slightly puzzled look, as if she'd raised the weirdest topic, and change the subject. How could he be the one?

"Stray fingerprints? Discarded leads? Right. In my case, make it all of the above." He smiled. "Guilty as charged. Who is playing the cynic now?"

"And what, my love, is a cynic but a disappointed innocent?" She pushed her chair back from the table but did not stand. "What gets to me is knowing that in the city we live in, the city we love, there are these pathetic losers. They have no education, no work, nothing to offer. Swimming in the shallow end of the gene pool."

"I agree with you on that," Jake said, leaning towards her. "There is evil in the world. You have to believe that, if you believe in good. We live in a black-and-white universe. If you believe in good, know that its opposite is here, too. I don't know why God is so slow to punish the wicked. I've learned to live with uncertainties; that's how the job works. This case is depressing me because it had 'unsolved' written all over it from the very beginning. I can think about it all the time or not at all. There is choice."

"Which do you pick?"

"Today, the answer is not at all." He smiled again and reached for her hand. "I've been thinking about you."

"Don't lie to me."

"Never, my love. Never to you."

"Lying is a way of life for you," she insisted. "Admit it." She dropped his hand and looked away.

"Sometimes I have to lie. Never when I'm off the job. I never lie to you, lover."

She stood up and turned away. He pulled her into his arms, and she laid her head on his chest.

"I keep thinking about her family. Perhaps they were not really happy. And that's what made her change," she murmured. She pulled away from him.

"No, Maud, no. It doesn't matter if the family was happy or not. It was wrong place, wrong time. Fortune and misfortune are unequally distributed. A happy family cannot protect you. Admit it. We all belong to someone, and family is the backstory we don't escape."

"Who do you know who had a happy family life? Can you name a single person?" She shook her head. "We're all marked by family kisses, family scars. And who sees these faint marks? Go look in the mirror. They are blooming all over your body like fingerprints, though no one but you sees them. They are there."

He would not let her see his. Perhaps she loved him more than he loved himself. She knew he loved his work and its heroic nature. *A hero has something at stake,* her father had said. *He stands in for a god.* Jake's number-one allegiance was to the job, and she knew that this soured their love, betrayed it in a way she would not accept. She felt she was missing him already, the way you miss the sound of your name being called by your beloved. Like the feeling of a ring being slipped off your finger.

"I thought I, I mean – my family," he said. "My family was happy. Is happy." Half the time, he didn't want to answer her questions. Didn't want to get caught up in trying to discuss and define the indescribable.

"Being happy? Is that like being loved?"

"You're trying to put words in my mouth and you're probably enjoying that, aren't you?"

"We're always trying to earn love."

"Are we?"

"We all want to be praised. We all want to be loved."

"Then what's going wrong between us?"

"I talked about myself. You talked about yourself. We should have talked about each other. About us."

"I find you very alluring." He reached for the sleeves of the cardigan looped around her neck. He untied them and hesitated, and for a second, it seemed he would pull her close. Then he pulled the sweater up on her shoulders and retied the sleeves, flipped the cuff ends back over her shoulders.

"Alluring." She moved in close and whispered the word into his ear. "Alluring," she repeated, almost breathless, drawing the syllables out. "Well, detective, I wanted to move up to irresistible."

Jake turned his face away. He had no response for her. He'd had a whiff of her scent, didn't want to feel her warm breath flashing through his eardrum and straight on to his cock. He wished she would leave, for even her attempt to comfort him reminded him of his failure and his discontents.

She almost said, "All right, I wouldn't expect that." Irresistible. That was as much as she could hint at without fully feeling the weight of failure. No amount of charm would work now. All you could give your lover was what he would take.

They said good night as formally as strangers, with one brief kiss as hesitantly exchanged as their first.

What do you owe to those you love? Jake wondered. He needed to keep some part of himself private. A place, like his study, that he could retreat to when he felt stymied and powerless. Somewhere. A place in his mind that this soiled world could not touch. She was going to leave him. Soon.

Dr. Charles and Mrs. Caroline Nash left Canada ahead of schedule, and Rona and Ben moved back into their home on Canora Street just before the end of May. Ben had their help, Mary Vachon, come in for five days to give it a complete spring cleaning. She showed Ben the collection of things the English people had left behind: various loose teas, half-finished jars of condiments and jams, tinned kippers, washing soda, and a large box of muesli that looked to be industrial strength. "Odds and sods, she called them," said Mary. "Said I could have them, not that I'm interested, but I thought I should ask you. She gave other things to your neighbour," she added, inclining her head in the direction of Ruth Oddy's house.

Thank heaven for honest souls like Mary, thought Ben – with them for over twenty years and the soul of discretion, though she knew every nook and cranny of their lives. He was content to work along with her and bring their personal linens and their prized belongings out of storage.

The old elms on the front lawn were fully leafed-out now. That's how Georgia Lee had liked to see it, the world as a wall of green outside her window. "It's my window into the forest," she'd said.

They had set a framed copy of her high-school graduation photo on the end table in her old room and put her pine rocking chair under the window overlooking the street, and they'd installed Nikolai Gadol and his shining cage beside the window over Canora Street, but otherwise the room looked the same as during their sabbatical year. Georgia's room's transformation to guest room with pale sage-green walls and an unfamiliar new hideaway bed was disconcerting. They had left Winnipeg without spending any time in this redecorated space, and the new order had the force of an undeserved reproach.

On the fifth day of the clean-up, Ben walked to their neighbourhood's Italian grocery and, as the carefree notes of Rigoletto's *La Donna e mobile* filled his ears, he hummed along softly and selected fresh pasta, tomatoes, peppers, garlic, spicy green olives, Rona's favourite lamb sausages, and crusty bread. Near the Misericordia Hospital, he bought fresh flowers – tulips glowing red – and put them with forsythia and pussy willow branches cut from their garden. Mary Vachon arranged these in a low, white bowl on the bare oval mahogany dining room table. The house – with its gleaming floors, the French ormolu clock ticking life away again on the living room mantle, a lemony hint of furniture polish in the air, and the surround of familiar things – looked like home again. They sat at the breakfast table and had a cup of tea and some of the delicious nutty crescent cookies Mary had baked. Both cried a few tears as they spoke of Georgia Lee, and as they talked, she seemed to become more alive with each of their recollections.

Ben and Rona took their morning coffee on the deck, surrounded by greenery, trading sections of the morning paper wordlessly. Summer skies blued above. Mark had sent a note saying that they could go out to West Hawk and spend as much time as they liked at his under-utilized cottage, but Rona wouldn't go. So they didn't.

Rankling hot anger was gone, turned off as if by a switch. At night, Rona moved quickly, happily in Ben's arms now. She never had been shy in bed. Things weren't back to normal, that wasn't expected, but there was a kind of forgiveness in their loving, a surrender that flooded her senses.

She did try to throw some pots, but each time she started her wheel, the clay, the water, all revolted under her hands. Not even in her novice days when her teacher, Mr. Nakamura, had carefully inspected and then with cool indifference smashed each of her first nine bowls, had Rona known a dispiriting sense of failure this complete. *That's over,* she said as she closed the door to her studio and took up the less-rebellious craft of quilting. Ben encouraged her in this, agreeing that she needed to be doing something creative or expressive, something tangible to keep the nightmares at bay. She bought a large backing of cream-coloured light cotton canvas and a quilting frame that she set up in Georgia Lee's old room.

The canvas was large, a rectangle of fabric 4 feet square. She sketched a scene of deep, thick forest. There was no water in the drawing, no way out. At the base of a tall red cedar off to the left of the canvas's centre, she drew three elfin figures nestled under the tree's wide skirts: two naked baby boys, her stillborn sons, and beside them, watching over them, a dainty girl of about 5 years with dark hair spilling over her shoulders. The children appeared to be sleeping. The girl was lying on her right side, behind the two boys. Her right arm was bent at the elbow, and she was supporting the weight of her head with it. Her body was curved slightly, protectively curled around the boys. She was wearing a long, plain blue gown with a rounded white collar. The trio occupied about 12 square inches of the quilt. One could see the river, only a hint of reeds at the sandy brown shoreline that ran along the right lower edge of the scene.

Rona embroidered this scene, then used another layer of canvas and batting underneath to create a slight trapunto effect. She bought dozens of remnants in all the shades of green she could find – grass, moss, turf, leaf, lime, greengage, jade, aquamarine, celadon, loden, emerald, sage, bottle, willow, pea, apple, chartreuse, avocado, olive, and the sea greens. In the upper right-hand corner of the quilt, she sketched a patch of light above the dark valley. It could be the light of dawn or sunset. The under-branches of the trees that stood in the light's path were to be burnished with its gold.

Rona began at the centre, covering the three little figures with leaf-shaped pieces of her darkest green, covering them with wide skirts of pine, hiding them from all eyes, covering them as if evening were brushing over them like a dark wing. She treated them tenderly, her babes in the woods, all her pretty ones, robbed of their chance for life. And while Nikolai Gadol sang to her, she thought all day about the world of yesterday, of the dreams she had had for her daughter – never of what her own mother's had been for her. Of these, she knew nothing.

Rona decided that she had talked so much about Georgia Lee, there was nothing more to say. So she almost entirely stopped speaking about her. The only person she wanted to answer her questions was gone. *Why did Georgia Lee send us all those e-mails?* They had been a smokescreen, a continuous prattle about the little details that together said that there was no real news. *There's lots of snow and it's getting colder, my classes are interesting and I have lots of reading, yes, I am taking my vitamins, Nikolai Gadol is singing, he likes our new apartment.*

What kept a heart from falseness? Something unknowable, like the dream life of angels. Nikolai Gadol fluttered and preened, grooming his tired blue plumage, safe in his cage in front of Georgia Lee's window into the elm trees. Rona asked him: "You were the last to see her. Did she smile at you? Was she happy, do you think?"

What could Rona do with her unanswered questions? She no longer said "G-d only knows." He was not just. Not loving. No longer in her life. She didn't even say that short prayer: "From your lips to his ears." She had thought of herself as a spiritual person, if not an observant Jew. There were those years in the '70s when she had been a faithful member of the women's *minyan* at the interfaith chapel at the university. Back then they had given every aspect of their rituals careful consideration, from the making of a *mikvah* at Obie's Steam Baths to the selection of poetry read at their services on new moon *Shabbats*. Ben's complete rejection of all organized religious activity made sense to her now as the only possible response to their loss. She gave up on her G-d, who had not watched out for Georgia Lee.

Ben went to the university three mornings each week. He had no formal obligations until the new term began in September. He filled his days with what he called *administrivia*. Officially, he remained on sabbatical. He was two years away from retirement; maybe, he thought, he would go sooner. He felt his winter approaching. He didn't seem to have the strength, the heart, for teaching now. All at once, he felt the thrust of the next generation pushing hard. Those fresh faces, those bright minds – he couldn't face them.

When the police returned Georgia Lee's computer, he had copied the postings from her journal to a diskette and printed three copies. The same 147 double-spaced pages as the police had given him earlier that he had read over and over. The simple record of a young woman's first months of living this life on her own.

When I go to my Anthro class, I take the escalator up to the second floor and walk right past Ben's office. Wish he was there. His story is sort of the same as mine. No family left. He was born in Berlin and when the Nazis were going after the Jews, his papa sent him and his mother Charlotte to New York with a whole boatload of people to get away from the trouble. They did, but Charlotte died of pneumonia there in 1939. The Nazis killed all the rest, his father and his whole family. He was only five then and he had to live with his cousin Moishe but he was really old like a *zaida*. Later when he got divorced from his first wife Rivka, she took their boys, Avi and Lior to Israel. We never see them, so like both of us are alone.

He let me photocopy all the pictures he has of his family and I put them on my family tree. I made it with parents, grandparents, aunts, uncles, and cousins dangling from the branches. Two mothers but neither one is really my mom. No pictures of Ruby or my father so I drew her in and used a picture I cut out of a magazine for him. He's a smudge on the family tree. No real sisters or brothers and Ben for a dad type guy. Should I add his two sons as my stepbrothers? How about Louie, Rona's uncle by marriage? I'm putting in everyone I like. That's the way to get the family you want.

There were no clues, no answers there, but when he read what she had recorded about her love for Granny Spence and their visits, he was thankful that they made Georgia's funeral with the McKays and Spences. He loved, and envied, the sweet and smokily beautiful simplicity of their burnt offering of tobacco, cedar, sweet grass, and sage. Nothing like that was available to him. It was right to honour her dance between her two families. Granny had been right when she'd said, "We are more than our problems. Everyone is."

Ben liked the girl he found in those dear pages. She was bright, working hard at her studies, and interested in life, finding new friends and making plans. Her words were clear, pure notes in the silence generated by all their unanswered questions. He could hear her, hear her whisper in his ear, bringing light to her words. Georgie's words. He wanted to call her that, her new name; he wanted to call out to her. *Georgie, look out,* he said. *Be careful of the dark inside of you, that dark territory.* He paged through the journal daily, reading the entries over and over, and he always finished by reading her last sentence: I am happy.

Helga Neustaedter was a godsend. She screened all of Ben's calls and kept visitors at bay. She figured out how to leave messages for Ben on their home telephone answering service without making the phone ring and disturbing Rona. She took on a few duties that Rona could not manage. She arranged for cards of appreciation to be printed in Winnipeg's daily newspapers and the Jewish weekly. Quite a few friends called the office and left messages for Ben with her.

She put Ben and Rona on her prayer list and worried about the grey tone of his complexion that did not want to lift. His face was sad, always pensive, his expression of that sort of submissiveness she had seen on the faces of old and religious people. She prayed for his strength to return. *How hard it is to be human,* she thought. *You never get a day off, and you must live until you die.*

In the beginning, Ben and Rona's friends had been very concerned, very attentive. They had sent cards, called frequently, and many sent soups or casseroles, kugels or coffee cakes, sent flowers or made donations to the memorial scholarship fund they'd started in Georgia Lee's name. It was hard to know what else to do. There was no Jewish funeral, and the other one had been over before they'd read about it in the newspaper. And no *shiva.*

Rona did not want to see anyone. She had told Ben to send an e-mail to all their friends. *I cannot go out to dinner with people. I cannot listen to anything about their children. Their happy families.* She said she'd heard enough of that bad-things-happen-to-good-people crap.

She did not want to be on anyone's prayer list. She demanded Ben find a nice way to tell Helga Neustaedter to take them *off* her list.

She thought about trying to find that blonde friend – was her name Chick? – the one who had given her the photos she carried in her purse, the one from the video rental place. But she didn't know how except by going down there, and she couldn't do that.

Rona talked to Ruthie Hirsch and Carol Halprin on the phone. She told them, two of her oldest friends, from childhood days really, that she was not ready to go out with people yet. Not even with them. Too depressed, she added. I have to force myself not to care. BURNT OUT – she wanted a lapel button that said that.

After a few more weeks, most people had stopped calling. It was summer, and they were busy – going off to the lake, and usually there were out-of-town guests coming. Ruthie and Carol did not give up, though. They phoned Rona on alternate days. Left messages: *You won't have peace by avoiding life. You must find whatever light you can. I am here if you need me. Give yourself time. Call me when you want company. I love you.*

Ben was grateful to these women for their faith that, one day, life would be easier. (Not normal – no one was talking about normal. That was not possible.) He remembered their warmth, the laughter, the sense of sisterly sharing with Rona on that last happy occasion not twelve months earlier when they'd made a surprise farewell party with their closest friends. Thirty-eight of them had crowded the Canora Street house and deck and garden, eating, drinking, laughing, and singing until long after the moon rose on an August night that was warm and free of mosquitoes. "We'll do this again as soon as you are home," the friends had promised. From the sabbatical, from their year of adventure.

283

Ben hadn't settled back into his ground floor study. The house had a strange ambiance now, somehow unfamiliar, and they felt Georgie's absence sharply. Every room held memories of her. Walking and talking and laughing and playing.

Ben wished they had not dismantled her cosy peach-coloured room so she could use the bedroom furniture in her apartment. *We didn't leave her carelessly,* he reminded himself. He had said this to Rona many times. *We made the mistake of trusting that, like a blessing, her goodness, her innocence would shield her from the more savage possibilities of everyday life.* He tried to believe in these condolences and explanations, these merciful excuses; he could not admit he found their comfort hollow. What else could he offer Rona? He did not know. Nothing had sheltered his first family; nothing had intervened to save this third child. Nothing stopped sorrow falling like black rain.

Ben was determined to wait for Rona. He had to. Loving her was his joy. He was patient, knowing that love did not come all at once. This knowledge shone steadily within him, like a red beacon. It required that he focus on it, never let his attention fade. If he could hold onto this light, he would survive. He did not call it faith, not in any religious sense, but it was a burning core that seemed to mean something grand about the reality of this life. He could stare inwardly at it while all else was pale and empty. It was the only kind of thing that could save you, like love.

Rona had told him she felt a sense of calm and relief now that they'd settled at home again. He heard her humming as she paged through her cookbooks. He knew that she kept her copy of Georgie's journal there, bookmarking the recipe for her favourite lasagne. They had not yet talked about the journal directly, but when he looked at those pages, he saw they were well-thumbed. He was glad that he had given her a copy of the journal when they'd moved back into their house.

Ben knew her grief must run its own slow progress and, only then, he was certain, would he regain her full attention. He reminded himself that they needed to build a world they could survive in. They spent much of their time in their daughter's old room. Her absence was now a presence in their house, in their small private rituals. He bought a comfortable club chair in soft, olive-green leather. This room needed another chair, he'd announced as he set it down opposite the old pine rocking chair that he now thought of as Rona's. He framed and hung Georgie's drawing of her family tree on the wall above the hideaway bed. He often spent his afternoons there, with Rona, looking at his sabbatical notes, and he daydreamed about writing a brief history of the flood. He wondered about the informal groups of flood relief workers. He imagined their new friendships and alliances. He watched his wife's busy fingers stitching.

Rona hung a photo of the three of them on the wall opposite the window. It was the one they had brought back from Georgia Lee's apartment, taken at her debut at a pow wow when she had been 12 years old; in the photo, she stood tall against the blue spruce in the back garden, wearing her jingle dance dress and feathers in her braided hair. She looked so pleased and excited. So happy.

Rona hadn't been happy that day. It showed in her face. A hot, long, and dusty afternoon at the Forks Park. Hours of that monotonous drumming, thundering on and on under the cloudless blue sky. Clouds of prairie dust rising from the steady feet drumming on the earth. She remembered that she'd made a fuss about Georgia Lee's costume for the jingle dance. It had offended her to see that the dancers' costumes, which by tradition would be decorated with rows of bone or shell rattles, now had rattles made from strips of aluminium cans. Rona had made a sarcastic remark about the amount of beer consumed to make these costumes sound authentic. She thought of herself, of Ben, of them as tolerant, but really, she knew she was not.

The dress looked sadly bedraggled hanging in the closet with Georgia Lee's party dresses and Brownie uniform. She couldn't change that. Why hadn't Rona been more reasonable about Georgia's curiosity about her birth family? It was natural, wasn't it? She wished she had been more open, more accepting of Georgia Lee's history. All she had now was a memory album filled with scenes of regret.

She looked at the photo again and at Georgia Lee's beautiful smile. Such a lovely face she had. What a sweet, lovely heart. Rona was smiling back at the photo with tender feelings when she thought she almost heard a bright, metallic clink as a chink opened her armoured heart.

As a mother will sometimes feel the forehead of a child she knows is perfectly well, Rona dusted this framed photo and the room every day, mysteriously transfixed like some kind of zoned out Buddhist monk. In a strange yet comforting way, she felt Georgia Lee was watching over her, and she was peaceful.

On her way back from lunch, Helga Neustaedter saw a young Native man loitering in the hallway of the Anthropology department. He was reading the notices and cartoons Scotch-taped to Ben Kay-Stern's office door. He was standing so close to the door she thought he must be myopic, and he seemed to be studying each page carefully. As she approached the office door, he slipped a worn knapsack of camouflage fabric from his shoulders and set it on the floor with great care, as if the contents were as fragile as a newborn child.

"Do you wish to see Professor Kay-Stern?" she asked. "He's in a meeting now. But I must tell you that he's not officially available to meet with students during summer session. He's on leave from the department until September." She hesitated. "Are you registered in the Aboriginal Access Program?" She was concerned because she thought he looked tired, as if after a long journey, and in need of a welcome. He was something over 6 feet tall with chin-length, straight black hair combed back severely from his broad forehead, and he had a strapping build with enormous shoulders like a football player. He seemed powerful yet had a gentle manner.

"No, I am not a student," he said. "I came here to find Ben because we had trouble and sadness in our family. My cousin Rosie, who is also his daughter that he calls Georgia Lee, got killed. I guess you know about that. I missed her funeral that was back in April, but I was away and didn't get the news in time. Today," he continued quickly, "I want to speak with him about something else. I will go to his house later." He made a slight bow, picked up his knapsack, and turned away, walking briskly and lightly down the hall with a narrow and economical gait.

Now she recognized him, placed who he was, his story cobbled out of many she'd heard from Ben, Rona and Georgia Lee.

"I'll tell Ben that you were here looking for him," she called out. "*Waylon* – isn't that your name?" At that, he looked back at her. "Yes," she added, "he's talked about you. He'll be pleased to know you came by."

Helga returned to her desk and efficiently made note of the date, the time, and the young man's request. He was that favourite cousin Georgia Lee had talked about. Waylon Spence. Yes, that was the name. She really missed that girl's sweet, happy laugh. Professor Kay-Stern would want a full report on Waylon's visit when he returned from his meeting.

Earlier that morning, Waylon had made a promise to Granny that he would go to see how Rosie's white family was doing. Granny had spoken so softly he'd had to lean in close enough to smell her fruity breath. It worried him that she seemed so weak and so tiny, lying there on her right side on the hospital bed with the tubes running from her thin chest to the dialysis machine; he could see her dark blood coursing through the tubes. An urgent had beeping sounded from some part of the mysterious equipment attached to her, and one of the nurses had bustled her fat self over to peep at the little screen with the green line pulsing for Granny's heartbeat.

"Slow down, Granny," the nurse had said, talking loudly through the ballpoint pen she had clenched in her small, even teeth. "You're throwing off extra beats." She'd smiled a gap-toothed smile and patted

Granny's hand, as if these gestures could translate her instructions into Cree.

"Can you tell her that in your language?" the nurse had asked Waylon. "Tell her to take some slow deep breaths, would ya?" She demonstrated the technique loudly for them. The old one had managed to huff and puff louder but not any deeper. The nurse had sighed and shaken her head. "Keep trying, Mrs. Spence," she'd gone on in a weary tone. "All we can do is try."

"That green line tells the story of my heart," Granny had whispered to Waylon. "I like to watch it. My blood is the river that feeds my body."

Waylon had said nothing. He had simply smiled at her and listened to her coarse breathing and patted her small, dry-skinned hand.

"The land is our body, too," she'd said, "and its rivers are its blood. You came home to feel the North wind on your face. The wind answers itself if you listen for it. It turns one way, then another. Trees and grasses bend for it and rise up, and you can hear all the voices you've heard before."

He'd said, yes, he knew. He thought he'd heard Rosie's voice all the way in Japan. She was gone. Ashes to ashes, dust to dust.

He'd told Granny he was planning to see Ben and Rona. He was going to be heading for the university to find Ben first, since he was easier to talk to.

Granny had handed him a small circlet made of braided sweet grass and tied with a red piece of yarn. "Give her this," she'd said with a wheeze. Her eyes brightened with the effort of talking. "We all live in the voice of another. Tell her that. She is the mother."

After leaving the university, Waylon walked down Portage to the main police station down in the Exchange District. The cop on the front desk quizzed him about his interest in Georgia Lee's case, and finally, when he'd heard enough, called upstairs to the detectives, but the ones working her case weren't there right now. Sorry, the cop said, but it didn't sound as if he'd meant it.

A really tall, lanky cop with a handlebar moustache who had been standing nearby came over to the desk. "You're her cousin. Waylon, isn't it?"

"Yes," said Waylon.

"I thought so. I'm Tim Petrie. I'm with the Identification unit. Come on with me," he said. "I've got a few minutes right now, and maybe I can answer your questions." He led Waylon to the elevators, and they went up to the fourth floor, where the elevator doors opened onto a wide linoleum-floored hallway stretching the length of the building with many doors leading off from both sides. He led Waylon into an office and sat down behind a grey metal desk.

"Have a seat, son," he said. "This all must be pretty tough for you to come home to. We know you've been away in Japan. So I wish I had better news for you." He began to speak about the details of the investigation in a slow, steady, deep voice, as if dividing the information into two columns – what we know, what we don't know.

Waylon had already heard much of what the cop told him. He looked hard at the stuffed monkey with the bright yellow noose around its neck that was on a corner of the desk. He waited until the officer had finished speaking and held out his business card.

"How come you've got that little monkey there?" Waylon asked, pointing at the toy. "Where'd you find him?"

The officer looked stunned for a couple of seconds, then gave a nervous, shaky sort of laugh. "I guess that doesn't look too good to visitors. I found it when I was out on a case and just hung onto it for a souvenir. Not a very good joke is it, I don't guess."

"Oh," said Waylon. "May I look at it for a minute?"

The officer handed it to him, and Waylon immediately turned it over and examined the monkey's back, lifting up the edge of its tiny black velvet vest. The uneven red stitching was there. Why did this guy have Rosie's old friend, Mr. Mischief?

"Where'd you say you found this?" He held the toy up by one of its wobbly little arms. "Where?" He dangled the toy in front of the cop's face.

"It was from a strange case of suicide." Petrie seemed embarrassed to be seen at a loss for the details.

"Suicide?" Waylon leaned forward and planted his elbows on the desk. "How do you mean?"

The officer nodded as he reached for the toy. Waylon pulled it back and looked at the red stitching again, running his index finger along the bumpy seam on the monkey's back.

"That's freaky," said Waylon. "I know for sure it used to belong to my cousin, Georgia Lee."

"How's that?" Petrie looked puzzled.

"The first time that Rosie, or Georgie, came to visit us at the rez, well, she was a curious little girl. And she showed me how when she was only 6, she'd cut open her monkey to see what was inside him, 'cause that day I was talking about trapping muskrat and fox and cleaning them. After she saw he was full of cotton, she sewed him back up with the red thread because that's what her mother gave her to use. That's how I know it's hers. He's called Mr. Mischief. She always liked to sleep with him even when she grew up. Ask her parents. They'll tell you." He held Mr. Mischief out to the cop.

Petrie took the toy. He pulled the yellow noose off and chucked it into the waste basket beside his desk. He placed the monkey belly down on the desk, studiously examined the red stitching on the monkey's back, turned it over, and looked at its face, which seemed to be smiling helplessly, like an old man who can't find his glasses.

"Well, it is stitched up just as you claim," he said to Waylon. "I'll need you to give me a statement to that effect. About the monkey and all the rest, I mean." He passed a legal pad and ballpoint pen across the desk to Waylon. "Write down just exactly what you told me and anything else you remember and then sign it. It will take some time to put your information together with what we've got on her case."

Petrie felt a blush crawling up out of his tight collar. He had lucked out. Already he saw himself retelling this story in the squad room. They'd buy him drinks at the club. How could anyone be expected to put those two cases together? The murdered girl and that suicide. That would take a fucking psychic. He might even get a commendation. Mother would be so proud. He'd already run the guy's prints and knew he'd jumped parole on fake ID and stolen a car out in BC. *Boudreau,* yeah, that's the name. He'd never got around to processing the exhibits from the girl's place. There didn't seem to be any need to rush down that cold trail. But now he could hardly wait to get at it. He was certain he'd get a hit. He loved this feeling. He was flying now.

And the family. Yes, her parents would be glad to know, but in the meantime it better be hush-hush until they were sure.

"I'll be right back," said Petrie. He went to find his sergeant and dashed up to Homicide with the news. Only four minutes left in his shift. Unfucking believable. There was going to be some excitement. All kinds of hell was gonna break loose, that's for damn sure.

Petrie returned as Waylon was finishing writing out his statement. This time Petrie had another guy in a suit with him that he introduced as a detective. Rob Dunblane, he said, adding that he and his partner had been on Rosie's case from the beginning. The two men looked over Waylon's statement and turned back to him with matching sober-sides faces.

"Thanks for coming in," said Petrie. "We are really glad for your information. Maybe, maybe, it's going to make a huge difference. We better not say any more until we've reviewed some other evidence from the case, but it looks like you've given us the break we need. We'll get in touch with you and the family as soon as we're sure. Meanwhile, here's a copy of the journal your cousin was keeping. You should have it. You are the one she was writing to.

"Let's keep this quiet for now. We don't want to get the family all worked up until we know for certain."

As soon as the door closed behind Waylon, Petrie's face lit up with a grin from one jug ear to the other.

Waylon took a slow walk toward the West End. He felt he was float-ing along, and by turns he was angry, excited, delighted, and sad, so sad about Rosie and Mr. Mischief. He stopped in at the Salisbury House on Portage for a couple of their famous cheese nips and fries, and a slice of wafer pie. It was cool inside and comfortable in the familiar red vinyl booth, and he was content to think in silence over his lunch. He sat for a while reading over some of the journal pages the cop had given him.

I do love Granny. That's the good part. She knows her medicines, her plants and roots but she can't cure herself from diabetes and she's getting weaker all the time. I think I'll take Rona and Ben to see her when they get home. That'll be interesting; my families meeting face to face. She is so sweet. She tells me stories and talks about how the beavers live and their lodges are built with the dome shaped roof half out of the water. She says that's the same as us, the people, living on top of the earth under the dome of our sky. She's got her stories but she's got her Bible too. I wonder which she likes best. Next time I'll ask her. She says we Indian people have our stories to tell us how to live and that we are more than our problems.

You taught me to make the call like a loon. I do it when I walk alone over the bridge and I think of those dark northern trees. I love you like the brother I never had. You said all they're doing up there on the rez is sitting around waiting for the dog to fart. You said you have to get away from the rez so you can be somebody. And you did. I feel you are watching me from far away, protecting me.

I loved your Big Plan. You did it! Took off to the States & trained to be a pro wrestler. I am so proud of you! Now your studying Sumo wrestling. I wish you were here. If school sucked, I was going to get you to do a road trip. Rona still doesn't know I got Ben to let you store your Harley in our garage. Your Black Beauty is crouched in the rafters. Vroom, vroom. She never goes in there. If you get home soon, maybe we can head out on the highway like we planned. All the way to the coast. Some sweet morning, soon as exams are over. The parents don't need to know. They get back the end of June. I hate to bother them with details. Like they can find out about my beautiful tat in summer.

We are alike in so many ways. Being alone for one thing. Your parents went fishing out on the lake and drowned. Then Hank died in that house fire. No brother, no father, no mother. We have ties between us, ties of open love. It's like we have a secret place in each other's hearts, almost a home where only we can meet. It's the most beautiful thing about my life. We're orphans, both chasing the shadows of our vanished parents. I got that last postcard you sent of Mount Fuji asking me to visit Granny Edna. I am wearing the yin-yang medallion you sent me for luck. It's beautiful.

This is my year. All mine. I turned eighteen and got my own place in August when the parents left on sabbatical. I like university. My grade point average is 4.0. Aren't I a good girl? Only got 2 more weeks of classes, and papers in English and History, then finals. French is way easy. All I have to worry about is the drama audition for fall term.

And I am still a VIRGIN!!! It's OK. There was that time when you touched me and kissed my eyelids. Do you ever think of it? Hot tingling nipples. Lips. Opening wide. Fainting dizzy. Like when you want to do it to see where it will get you. It never happened again and something makes me think that you like men, which is OK. Maybe that was in a dream.

You stopped uncle Archie from getting his grubby broken off fingers on my privates. You took out that filleting knife and said you'd cut the rest of those creeping bits off. I was so scared. That was the last time I was there. You left soon after. Uncle Archie made sure you didn't get any work or money on the rez so you came to the city. Remember? I used to snitch meat out of Rona's freezer for you. I was 14 then and you were 18.

It's good I had a change of heart about Granny Edna. I like going to her place for teatime. We talk and talk. I never looked into my mother's eyes. Granny says my eyes are like Ruby's. Ordinary brown eyes with short dark lashes. So I guess when I look into my own eyes in the bathroom mirror I see something of her. Granny is so wise. I like going to the hospital with her. I can talk to the doctors for her. I want to find her a nicer apartment. In a safer neighbourhood. It's scary walking past those boarded up places all dirty with graffiti and tags from the Indian Posse and the Warriors.

Waylon wasn't in a hurry to get to the Kay-Stern house on Canora Street. Ben would probably be home by four o'clock so that would be a good time to show up there. It was over a year since he'd been there, and now that his little sister, sweet Rosie, was gone, he really did not have the heart for a visit. He had to think hard about how to tell them the news about Rosie's ashes.

His bike was waiting there for him, suspended high in the rafters of their garage. He hoped it would be in okay shape to ride out to the coast after a year of being stored. You never know as you begin a journey how the road will curve and what lies around the next bend or how your dream will end. The trip he and Rosie had planned all the way to Vancouver, riding out on his bike under an open sky, panniers loaded, knapsacks crammed with their on-the-road gear – that trip he could take in his imagination as often as he liked. He wanted to keep it straight in his head: that special time when the moon was full and it all felt right. He vowed he'd make that trip soon, her spirit mounted on the pillion behind him, her long, dark hair blowing free. He'd sail out across the prairie under the wild-throated sky.

Everything he wanted to say to Ben and Rona about his meeting with the police was off-limits now. He had to sit on it. He'd promised those cops that he would wait until they said it was okay, and he didn't want to screw it up for them. He hoped it was true, that Mr. Mischief would tell them who killed Rosie. They'd tried to be cool about it, but he could tell they were busting. He felt like he was busting, too. Waves of it. Over his head. So much grief, so much joy overwhelmed him as he sat letting it all wash down over him.

He didn't see the waitress approach. She silently refilled his coffee and handed him a wad of paper napkins. "You all right?" she asked.

He hadn't even known he was crying.

"Tears are often better than words," she said as she reached for his empty plate. "They can tell of real joy and real sadness." She patted his shoulder. "Just sit a minute now and rest easy. I'll be back with your bill."

The Kay-Stern's house looked the same as when Waylon had brought Rosie back there after she had run away three years ago. Its brown bricks spelled lives lived in a solid and reassuring pattern. He'd liked the way the wall of caragana bushes had made a thick green fort around the borders of the property. A man's home is his castle. That's what it looked like.

Ben had thrown the door wide open then and hugged Waylon and Rosie. He'd fixed them a monster batch of blueberry pancakes. Rona had never really laughed or smiled the whole time he was there. Waylon had told himself (and he'd read the pancakes as a favourable omen), *here goes nothing.* He'd told Rona that he knew that she wasn't crazy about him being the one Rosie had run to, but, he'd said firmly, "I am the one who talked her into coming home." He hadn't stayed much longer than for breakfast that time. It had been easy to see that those three needed to talk.

This time Rona answered the door and, to Waylon's surprise, invited him in with a smile. She never was what you might call friendly to him before. That's why he'd tried to find Ben at the university first.

She made them some Red Rose tea and led him upstairs to Georgia Lee's room, where she was working on her quilted hanging.

"You're making a beautiful picture there," he said as he carefully placed his knapsack on the carpet beside the rocking chair. "It looks something like Footprint Lake. I know that place. All my family, my mom and dad and my brother, Hank, are buried there. It's quiet, peaceful there, under the big pines, like in your picture here." He reached over and traced the outline of a triangular piece of sage-green fabric. "I was there a week or so ago," he said, thinking of the ancient perfume of the cool green cedar leaves he'd crushed in his hands.

"I remember the river, the blue and the green. Sweetgrass burning. A shimmering dream." He drew his index finger across to the centre of the forest she'd made. "Your picture makes me want to go lay down there myself."

Rona noticed that his long and slender fingers that spread out from squared palms were identical to Georgia Lee's. Her eyes shone with unshed tears, and when she returned Waylon's gaze, he took her soft, white hand and held it tenderly as a baby's.

"We all cry for her," he said, "but nothing, not even the tears of an angel could save her."

Without speaking, she looked down at the unfinished quilt draped over her lap; she smoothed it out like a pastry for strudel and folded it up.

"It was her time," he said. "She is gone. We are here."

She sat there holding the square package of fabric as you hold something sacred, the way a mother holds a soldier son's flag after his coffin is undraped.

Waylon continued. "I got a job now. I've been living out on the West Coast at a place they call Haddington Island near Alert Bay. That's where we Turtle Island people have our training camp. Our athletes come there from all over the country. We're getting ready for the Aboriginal Summer Games. It's like the Olympics for us. I got my black belt in karate and I teach kick boxing, too. Right now I'm coaching the wrestling team. You might've heard that I was studying to be a wrestler. And all the great ones, they all got a kind of act, some kind of Hollywood number, so I decided that I was going to be the number one First Nations Sumo wrestler, and so I knew I wanted to go to Japan to study it. Anyways, I guess you heard about that from Rosie. I mean Georgie. I was there in Japan for a long time. They've got Native people there, too. Call 'em the Ainu. They sure look a lot like us. Checked out the Sumo thing, but I couldn't get that fat. Too much noodles to eat. So then I was learning about the martial arts from some samurai guys.

"Later I ran out of money. Japan is so expensive, one of the most high-price places in the world, even if you stay in a hostel. So I heard that you could take this meditation course for free or you could barter some work, and that's how I began living with some Buddhist guys in a monastery there in Kyoto, the old capital. Doing meditation and stuff. I liked it. My face didn't look so different from everybody there except for my fat Cree cheeks. Since I came back I've been teaching the other Warriors some things I learned about how to think like a Buddhist. And I even learned to speak some of the Japanese language. I know we can use these ideas to make us strong and help every Indian find his way. That's my plan. I am going to open a martial arts studio, a *dojo* to teach them how to defend themselves. That's how I kinda hope it works out. We have to be free within ourselves. Our strength is in the love we have for one another. That's what Granny Spence always tells me. We are more than our problems.

"I came back here to get my bike. I guess you know by now that Ben let me store it up in your garage."

Rona smiled, though she had not been smiling on the day she'd discovered his shining bike. That had been a day of madness. An early heat wave had come on the last day of May, and she had been down in the basement looking for an extra fan, for without checking the weather forecast, she'd decided to bake a double batch of her favourite cheese knishes and had the dough all stretched out ready for filling and the oven turned on, so the kitchen was sweltering.

The fan she had been looking for was sitting on the counter of the wet bar in their unused rec room next to an old ping-pong table covered with the boxes and bags of Georgia Lee's things that Ben had brought back after clearing her apartment. The sight of this small collection had set off waves of anger followed by waves of sadness pressing down on her like a dark louring sky. She'd slid to the cool tile floor and simply stared at them. She hadn't bothered opening the lights when she'd come down. Some pale light had come in through the low pebble-glass windows, casting the cool room into an odd sort of midday twilight.

She'd sat perfectly still with her back straight against the wood panelling. She was at once almost wishing she'd never had a daughter and wanting to rid their home of all traces of Georgia Lee and wanting to open the bags and boxes to see again those precious reminders, and Rona had known she should not do that. She'd known she could not bear to see those books and clothes.

For ten minutes or so she had sat there on the cold lino doing yoga breathing – in for four, hold for four, exhale for four – periodically checking her pulse as it dropped to a slow, steady rate. *Steady, stubborn,* she'd thought. *It keeps its rhythm and even as you think you cannot go on, you do, in spite of yourself.* It was the same for Ben, she saw that now, and for the others. *We're all going on, each learning to live without Georgia Lee. Death takes and takes from you, it becomes a blur, and in this way, all that is left of your memories is a faint tracing of spilt ash.*

She had eyed the boxes once more and the word *garage* had dropped into her head like a falling star. Saved. Yes. She'd propped open the back door and carried the bags and boxes out one by one. It had taken eleven trips in all to ferry them out of the house and to hide them. *Out of sight, out of mind,* she'd kept repeating as she stacked them roughly on the shelves at the back of the garage. It was the smell of oil that had caught her attention, and she'd seen the bike when she'd looked up.

Ben had told her last week that Georgia Lee had planned to go off on a road trip across Canada with Waylon. And if she hadn't died, they might be out there cruising now. How she wished that were so.

"It's one more thing that connects them," she'd said to Ben that evening. "One more thing. Him to her, him to us. Please say he is coming back for it. I want to talk to him."

"I better stop talking about myself now," Waylon said. "I wanted to talk to you about Georgie, or Rosie, that's what we like to call her by. You know my mother was her auntie. You and Ben don't call her Rosie, I know. It doesn't matter; she was the same girl if you say it in English or in Cree."

He smiled then: a beatific smile, an impossible-to-resist smile, which employed more than his even, white teeth. It illuminated his face from within, and Rona saw how he was family to Georgia Lee. Saw a sweet echo of her face in his.

How do we choose the people we let into our lives, our hearts? Or do they choose us? We stumble on the ones we love best in the oddest ways. Waylon was now her closest link to the girl they both loved. They were family now. She smiled back at him. Warmly. Sweetly.

"Rosie was good to Granny Spence," said Waylon. "She brought her food and visited with her all last winter. She brought her to the doctor and got her the taxi slip for going to the kidney machine. Nothing can take away her good deeds. Not the fire or the winds, not even her death. I have a feeling that the cops are soon gonna find the guy who did it." He couldn't, he didn't want to say anything more to her, afraid he might blurt the news about finding Mr. Mischief on the cop's desk.

Rona sighed. "The detectives haven't found anyone, and I think they are giving up on her. My brother, Mark, talks to them every week, but it's hopeless. They haven't been able to find a single clue."

"Granny is praying for you. She prays every day for the broken-hearted."

"Oh, she does?" Rona started rocking in her chair as he talked. "She does, I'm sure she does. Yes, she would." Rona was thinking about the way the warmth of Granny's hand had flowed into her cold one as they'd sat side by side at the funeral chapel. She had felt she received an infusion of a calm energy from that soft touch.

Waylon took the sweet grass from the front pocket of his knapsack. "Look, she sent this to you." He held out the circle of braided sweet grass, and Rona took it lightly with both hands. She ran her right index finger over its braided surface and examined the red yarn bow.

He sat back in Ben's chair and watched as her finger stroked the sweet grass braid.

"It's good," he said, "that we can sit together and talk about her. Even if she is gone and we are here, we can still hear the world breathing. Listen quietly – don't even hear your own heartbeat. Listen to this earth breathing. She is still with us. Everybody lives in the voice of another. She will always live in mine."

Yes, we can hear the world breathing, thought Rona. *It is so still and peaceful now in our circle of two that we can hear ourselves in our world breathing. Deeply, softly.*

That's how Ben found them, together in Georgia Lee's old room. Waylon lounging in the new easy chair, opposite Rona in her stilled rocker. The milky dregs of their tea cooling on the pine table between them. There was a feeling of ease in the air, a palpable warmth that was, he thought, attributable, perhaps in part, to the late afternoon sun streaming in through the window, or perhaps this warmth and ease signalled the considerable but unexpected shift that they'd made from a separate to a shared world. Ben felt unexpectedly elated, buoyed up by a feeling of rich, peculiar joy.

"We're catching up on old times," Rona said to him. "We've been talking about how we miss Rosie, I mean Georgia Lee."

For the first time in weeks, Rona's eyes were open to the present. *Yes,* Ben reasoned, *this is what you do when your dreams for your child are gone; you have to find new ones.* It was if she saw that the words *accept* and *forget* could be linked, holding hands like dolls cut out of paper.

"Here, Ben," said Waylon as he leaned forward to stand, "take your chair back."

Ben waved his offer away and perched on the arm of the hideaway bed beside Rona's chair.

"I've got something important to say to you both now," said Waylon. He looked at Rona. "You know how I said I hope that thing with my martial arts training works out but we know that in real life things don't always go the way you want them to? The way it happened is that the family wanted to take Rosie back to Footprint Lake. Your family all did agree we could, and Teddy Boy thought he had it all lined up just right, but in the end the damn Feds, the Indian Affairs wouldn't pay for the airfare because her application for status wasn't granted before she died. I heard about this last week when I went up to the rez."

Ben leaned forward, and his face went slack and white with shock. Rona reached for his arm and pulled herself close.

"Now Granny felt really sad about that we couldn't do what we agreed to, so Teddy Boy got a cremation done and Granny thought that you folks should have half of the ashes. Teddy Boy took the rest to the rez and buried them with Ruby, her other mother. He gave me the rest, and I've got them here in my knapsack. I thought about how I could tell you all this. I thought we could walk down to the river by that little park she liked to go to and put them in the river."

"You mean you've got her ashes here?" Ben jumped to his feet. "With you? Now?"

Waylon reached forward to open his pack. He carefully drew out a baseball-sized pouch of tanned deerskin secured with a thong of the same hide.

Rona reached out a hand and almost touched it before drawing back and holding her hand over her heart. She shook her head back and forth in amazed disbelief. Waylon placed the pouch squarely on her lap, and she surrounded it with both hands and caressed it hesitantly.

Ben threw his arms around Waylon and hugged him fiercely, almost succeeding in lifting him off his feet.

"This is wonderful. A wondrous turn of events. Waylon, you have made my day." He turned and knelt on one knee beside Rona. "Rona, sweetheart, let's take this chance to say farewell to our girl." He stood, took the pouch from her, handed it to Waylon, and pulled her to her feet.

In what seemed like an instant, they were walking three abreast through the lilac-sweet early summer evening toward the river. None of them spoke any prayer or blessing, any word of love aloud as they stood on the grassy, daisy-spotted bank of the still-swollen, muddy Assiniboine.

Waylon cupped Rona's hands and poured some of the ashes into that open, living bowl. She crouched down and put her cupped hands right into the water and let it carry her daughter's ashes away downstream toward the confluence.

Waylon shared out another portion into Ben's waiting hands, and the last into his own. In turn, each knelt and let their small burden float away. The handfuls of ashes cast into the vast waterways of the inexhaustible universe brought a feeling of peace, a feeling of beauty, a feeling of Georgia's presence. By this act of tenderness, they restored something good, and the old world smelled sweet again.

They joined hands and turned to make the short climb up the grassy bank to the little park and continued silently together down the sidewalk to the waiting house.

"What's next?" Rona asked as they stood inside the embrace of the caragana hedge. She felt confused now, unsure about what they had done so quickly. She began trembling and shaking her head from side to side. Ben and Waylon encircled her with their arms, Waylon humming a chant, murmuring *om,* that sacred syllable, and she felt a peaceful release spread outward from her chest like a rose opening. Rona reached an arm around each of their backs and they, three, leaned forward into their circle, touching foreheads, hearts together.

"Come," she said, "I know what we need." She tugged at their hands as she led them into the kitchen. "We need to eat together now. To break bread."

Waylon lounged with his back to the tiled countertop, at his ease like a favoured guest while he and Ben drank a beer and talked about sports while Rona bustled about. She fed them an easy dinner of cold roasted salmon, green beans in vinaigrette with pecans, a crisp baguette with sweet butter, and poached pears with cheeses for dessert. "Eat." she teased Waylon, "Eat or I'll say you did."

By 8:00 p.m., Waylon's motorcycle had been carefully lowered from the garage rafters, and their talk fell to tire pressures and mileages and maps. When the bike roared to life on the first kick-start, Waylon let out a whoop of joy. Ben grabbed him in a bear hug and whispered, "I love you, son," but the words disappeared in to his dark hair. He fished Georgie's yin-yang medallion out of his shirt pocket and put it into Waylon's hand, covering it with his own.

"Thanks, Ben." Waylon grinned. "I'll keep it close."

He wheeled his bike down the driveway. Turning, he waved to them with both hands raised and then joined in a champion's salute.

For a long while after Waylon left, Ben and Rona sat silently, the unread newspaper on the table between them. So deeply by themselves. After perhaps half an hour, Rona reached over and took Ben's right hand in her own. She studied his palm intently and then turned his hand over, softly rubbing the freckled back and each finger in turn, as if much depended on her careful memorization of its every feature.

"We'd better call Mark and tell him what we've done," she said.

Ben pushed a stray curl back from her forehead and cradled her face with his broad shaking hands. Gently he stroked along her cheekbones under each eye with his thick thumbs as though brushing away tears, though the tears were in his own eyes. "Yes, we'll tell him. We'll all go down to the river together. You and I, and Mark. To her watery grave, and we'll sing, we'll say *Kaddish* there for her." He could feel his wife's eyes resting on him, weighing these words. They repeated his words like vows – we'll sing for her and we'll say *Kaddish*.

It seemed to Ben that it must be the very thing they needed to do, the next step in their journey, that making peace with Georgie's death would be their perfect consolation. He longed for peace to flow through him like a mighty river and lift him, and he would take Rona's hand, and it would carry them forward toward the end, as on the long arc of their lives they carried each other. *The dead are always with us in our dreams. We remember them. We must. Memories are the only thing that bind us to our younger, our better selves. We struggle to find what was lost. This is what the living do.*

The sky to the west was light when Waylon headed west on Portage. He knew that the farther he rode, the bigger the sky would appear above the fields of unripe grain that were running to the horizon. He took a long look at that bluest sky and he put it in his pocket. Zoom,

zoom, and he'd be chasing the sunset across the plains to the foothills, over the mountains and down to the sea.

Acknowledgements:

I am grateful to everyone who read this book in manuscript form and offered suggestions and writerly advice, and in particular to Barbara Berson, Joe Fiorito, Zsuzsi Gartner and Michael Redhill. Thanks also to Wanda Wuttunee, and to Jessica Bonney at FriesenPress for her kind advice. I am particularly grateful to my good friend singer/songwriter/actor Ron Nigrini for allowing me to "sample" some of the lyrics from his albums Above the Noise, undisguised hearts, and Songs from Turtle Island.

Finally, thanks to my family and friends for their loyal support.

Excerpts from the novel were published in a/**cross**sections and Exile: The Literary Quarterly.

CPSIA information can be obtained
at www.ICGtesting.com
Printed in the USA
LVHW09s1744121018
593317LV00001B/3/P

9 781525 528699